Aspects of Modern World History

SR

B

ASPECTS OF MODERN WORLD HISTORY

HISTORY

Evan Davies

Hodder & Stoughton

LONDON SYDNEY AUCKLAND TORONTO

Many thanks to Mrs. Cheryl Dunkley, my typist, for her patience
and good humour.

© 1990 Evan Davies

First published in Great Britain 1990

British Library Cataloguing in Publication Data
Davies, Evan, *1931–*
    Aspects of modern world history
    1. World, 1900–
    I. Title
    909.82

ISBN 0 340 48530 2

Typeset in Palatino by Wearside Tradespools,
Fulwell, Sunderland
Printed and bound in Great Britain for the educational division of
Hodder and Stoughton Limited, Mill Road, Dunton Green,
Sevenoaks, Kent by St Edmundsbury Press, Bury St Edmunds

CONTENTS

PREFACE

This book has been written to meet the National Criteria. Historical knowledge and understanding, the use of evidence and empathy and the realistic reconstruction of historical situations are all essential elements.

The main topics that will be encountered at GCSE level are covered in a way that should appeal to a wide range of students. The language level has been pitched at the age group of candidates and each topic is split into convenient units, with clear, manageable sections.

The main components of the book are:

The text. The text presents historical events and issues in a manner suitable for GCSE candidates. It is broken up into sections that enable students to digest information and ideas easily, while still maintaining the flow and pace of history. Information is often presented in the form of charts, diagrams and maps for clearer comprehension.

The text contains extracts from many types of documentary sources. The vocabulary and expression of these have sometimes been adapted to make them more accessible to students, but the sense has never been altered. The sources are always used to develop students' skills and responses.

The illustrations. These have been chosen not merely to illustrate the text but to add substantially to students' understanding. They are made to 'work', either as sources of evidence or to stimulate a response.

The questions and exercises. These arise naturally out of the text. They are mostly open-ended to allow for different levels of response. Towards the end of most chapters, tasks are included to produce an overall assessment of the events, ideas and personalities that have been dealt with.

The case studies. Most of the chapters include case studies, which are integral to the text and focus attention on important issues.

The extension exercises. These also arise naturally during the course of the topics, but they are optional. They occur in a variety of forms and are designed to develop a deeper judgement.

Comparative exercises. These 'Links' exercises are also optional. They develop an assessment of historical situations across normal topic boundaries.

Further work. Suggestions are included at the end of each chapter for essay work and for discussion.

THE GREAT WAR

Off to war

When wars break out, there are always people who say, 'It will all be over by Christmas'. This was certainly said and believed in 1914. Such is optimism. Almost four Christmasses later, the war juddered to a sudden halt. Nothing was ever quite the same again. It was the worst war that Europe had ever known and it was called simply the 'Great War'.

There are millions of facts known about this war, but simply knowing the facts does not help us. In order to understand it we must try to understand the effect the war had on people who actually fought in it or whose lives were changed by it.

People were exhilarated when war broke out in 1914. Men flocked to join the army. Recruiting officers turned a blind eye to under-age youths eager to fight. Cheering crowds saw them off to fight in France and Flanders. These people were like us, but they were living in different times and different circumstances. Their emotions were not simple and we can only guess at them through the evidence of the time.

Wilfred Owen, one of the most famous of the soldier-poets, wrote of a young recruit . . .

It was after football, when he'd drunk a peg,
He thought he'd better join—he wonders why.
Someone had said he'd look a god in kilts,
that's why; and maybe, too, to please his Meg;
Aye, that was it, to please the giddy jilts.
He asked to join. He didn't have to beg;
Smiling they wrote his lie; aged 19 years.
Germans he scarcely thought of; all their guilt,

and Austria's, did not move him. And no fears
of Fear came yet. He thought of jewelled hilts
for daggers in plaid socks, of smart salutes;
And care of arms; and hints for young recruits.
And soon, he was drafted out with drums and cheers.

War time propaganda too, had its effect. Posters like the one on the opposite page encouraged men directly to join up. There was also 'atrocity propaganda' to influence people. Stories of events which simply did not happen were circulated as gospel truth. It was commonly believed that the Germans cut off the hands of women they captured (see the cartoon). Another story printed in a British magazine and claiming to be official, went as follows . . .

SANG WHILE THEY MURDERED

As the German soldiers came along the street I saw a small child, whether boy or girl I could not see, come out of a house. The child was about two years of age. The child came into the middle of the street so as to be in the way of the soldiers. The soldiers were walking in twos. The first line of two passed the child; one of the second line stepped aside and drove his bayonet with both hands into the child's stomach, lifting the child into the air on his bayonet, and carrying it away on his bayonet, he and his comrades still singing. The child screamed when the soldier struck it with his bayonet, but not afterwards.

Enlistment poster

A French view of German atrocities

Popular songs give us some indication of what people thought and felt . . .

Your King and country want you

We've watched you playing cricket
and every kind of game.
At football, golf and polo
you men have made your name.
But now your country calls you
to play your part in war.
And no matter what befalls you
we shall love you all the more.
So come and join the forces
as your father did before.
O we don't want to lose you
But we think you ought to go.
For your King and your country
both need you so.
We shall want you and miss you
but with all our might and main
We shall cheer you
Thank you, kiss you
When you come back again.

Goodbye-ee

Brother Bertie went away
To do his bit the other day
With a smile on his lips,
And his Lieutenant pips
Upon his shoulder bright and gay.
As the train moved out he said,
'Remember me to all the birds.'
Then he wagged his paw
and went away to war,
Shouting out these pathetic words:
Goodbye-ee, goodbye-ee
Wipe the tear, baby dear,
From your eye-ee.
Though its hard to part, I know,
I'll be tickled to death to go.
Don't cry-ee
Don't sigh-ee
There's a silver lining
In the sky-ee
Bonsoir, old thing,
Cheerio, chin chin,
Na poo, toodleloo,
Goodbye-ee.

Vera Brittain, a young student at the time, wrote of her brother's reaction to the declaration of war . . .

Already my brother and his friend were discussing the possibilities of enlisting. When they returned from the theatre, Edward related, with much amusement, how he had seen a German waiter thrown over the wall of the Palace Hotel.

At home the atmosphere was electric with family rows, owing to Edward's expressed wish to 'do something'. My father strongly forbade Edward, who was still under military age, to join anything whatsoever. Our house was quite intolerable. A new row boiled up after each of Edward's efforts at defiance. And these were numerous, because his enforced obedience seemed to him the same as everlasting disgrace.

Vera's fiancé Roland, who was about to go to university, told her . . .

Anyhow, I don't think in the circumstances I could easily bring myself to endure the secluded life of university. It would seem a somewhat cowardly shirking of my obvious duty. I feel that I am meant to take an active part in this war. It is to me a very fascinating thing—something, if often horrible, yet very ennobling and very beautiful. You will call me a warmonger. You may be right.

In September 1914 a new recruit wrote to his rector . . .

Dear Sir, I received your letter at half past nine this morning. I likes Taunton very much, but there's so many down here we don't get nothing to eat hardly. This is now our headquarters and we are going to Devonport or else Aldershot today—and a good job too. I am going to try to keep away from gambling, smoking and cursing and do as I think right. We are having our khaki suits tomorrow. Dear Sir, we are having dinner now. For breakfast we have bread and jam. At dinner we gets potatoes and we goes to the soldiers' home to tea. I wrote to Mother last night. I expects she was upset. She did not want me to go. I wanted to serve my country the same as every young chap ought to do. I am sorry I could not write better. There is so many hitting your arms for jokes. I could not get a pen because we are not allowed outside the barracks before night. I think I must close. I am, yours sincerely Albert Ball.

Q

1 To what emotions is the enlistment poster appealing, in your opinion? Do you think that it would have been effective?

2 What was the purpose of 'atrocity propaganda'? Do you think it was effective?

3 Using all the evidence above, explain why a young man would want to join up in 1914?

Trench warfare

In August and September 1914, the German army moved rapidly into Belgium and Northern France. It almost reached Paris but was stopped by French and British resistance. In October the Germans dug the first trenches. Movement suddenly stopped. It was the same story shortly afterwards on the Eastern front in Russia and, later, on the Italian front. Once the enemy was entrenched, it was impossible to get him out. The only thing to do was to dig another trench within firing distance of the enemy's trench. Then one had to try to capture the enemy trench by charging 'over the top' and across the space between—no-man's-land. When this was done on a large scale it was known as a 'big push'.

The Great War was a series of big pushes. These usually took place over a relatively short section of the front line, only a few miles long. They lasted for some weeks, or even months. They were never really successful in breaking

Trench warfare

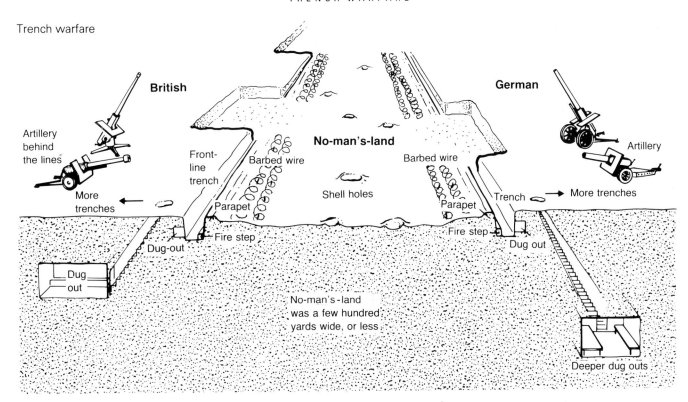

through the enemy positions. Whereas previous wars had been wars of movements, the Great War was a static war and, when it ended, the trench lines were in much the same places as they had been in 1914. The developments that might have brought the war up out of the trenches came too late. These were the invention of the tank and the use of smaller pushes on a much longer front. These new methods were only just beginning to work when the war ended in 1918.

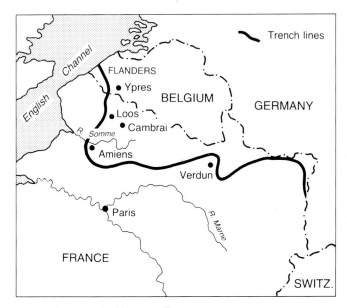

Trench lines on the Western Front

The weapons of the Great War

A typical day for a British soldier during an offensive usually began before dawn, when the British big guns, massed together far behind the lines, would pound the enemy trenches with a massive bombardment. The purpose was to destroy the enemy's barbed wire, dug-outs and machine-gun nests. It rarely succeeded. As soon as the big guns stopped, the British soldiers would charge over the top and the German soldiers would rush up from their deeper dug-outs, set up their machine guns and start firing on the approaching British. The machine-guns did their killing very effectively indeed. There was also poison gas, which killed stealthily and silently by eating away at the lungs and the eyes. Shrapnel shells, too, would burst over the trenches, releasing their packing of jagged metal to kill and wound.

Against all these methods of destruction was the PBI—the 'poor bloody infantryman'. As you can see in the pictures, the PBI has his rifle, with its long bayonet for hand to hand fighting. Steel helmets only became standard issue in 1915. The soldier often went into action with his heavy 66 lb pack on his back. In it he carried hand grenades, a trench-digging spade and, to protect himself from gas, a respirator. Was it any wonder that millions of soldiers died in trench warfare?

The ordinary soldier was certainly the sufferer in the Great War. On the first day of the Battle of Somme, July 1st 1916, 20,000 soldiers were killed and another 40,000 wounded. A five-day bombardment in which millions of shells had been fired on the German lines had failed to destroy the barbed wire. About one hundred German machine-gun teams were able to do most of the killing that day. By November, when the battle ended, the British front line had moved about five miles forward at the most. 400,000 British soldiers had been killed and wounded and this was only one of several similar pushes on both sides.

It is impossible to understand fully the experience of war for those who fought in it, but we must make the effort. Once again, reading the evidence of the time is the best way of improving our understanding.

A British officer wrote of how he collected boxes of ammunition one Sunday afternoon . . .

Going over the top

> The misery of that carrying-party was a typical infantry experience of discomfort without actual danger. What we were doing was quite ordinary; millions of soldiers endured the same sort of thing and got badly shelled into the bargain. We were among the debris [remains] of the intense bombardment of ten days ago, for we were passing along what had been the German front line. Wherever we looked the mangled corpses reminded us of death. Shell-twisted and dismembered, the Germans maintained the violent attitudes [positions] in which they had died. The British had mostly been killed by bullets or bombs, so they looked more resigned. But I can remember a pair of hands (nationality unknown) which protruded from the soil like the roots of a tree turned upside down; one hand seemed to be pointing at the sky with an accusing gesture. Each time I passed that place the protest of those fingers became more like an expression of an appeal to God in defiance of those who made the war. The dead were the dead; this was not time to be pitying them or asking silly questions about their outraged lives. Such sights must be taken for granted, I thought, as I gasped and slithered and stumbled with my miserable crew. Floating on the surface of the flooded trench was the mask of a human face which had detached itself from the skull.

A soldier keeps watch in a trench while his comrades rest

A German soldier wrote of a British attack . . .

> A series of lines of British infantry were seen moving forward from the British trenches. The first line appeared to continue without end to right and left. It was quickly followed by a second line, then a third and fourth. They came on at a steady easy pace as if expecting to find nothing alive in our front trenches. The front line was now half way across no-man's-land. 'Get ready!' was

passed along our front, and heads appeared over the edge as final positions were taken up for the best view, and machine guns were mounted firmly in place. A few minutes later, when the leading British line was within one hundred yards, the rattle of machine guns and rifle fire broke out from along our whole line. Some fired kneeling so as to get a better target above the broken ground, while others in the excitement of the moment stood up, regardless of their own safety, to fire into the crowd of men in front of them. The advance rapidly crumbled under this hail of shells and bullets.

All along the line men could be seen throwing their arms in to the air and collapsing, never to move again. Those badly wounded rolled about in their agony, and others less severely injured crawled to the nearest shell-hole for shelter. The British soldier, however, has no lack of courage, and once he has started is not easily turned from his purpose. Within a few minutes the leading troops had reached within a stone's throw of our front trench. They rushed forward with grenades and with fixed bayonets. The noise of battle became indescribable.

The shrill British cheers as they charged forward could be heard above the violent and intense fusillade of machine guns and the bursting of bombs. With all this were mingled the moans and groans of the wounded, the cries for help and the last screams of death. Again and again the British lines broke against the German defence like waves against a cliff, only to be beaten back. It was an amazing spectacle of unexampled gallantry, courage and bull-dog determination on both sides.

A German writer E. M. Remarque, wrote in his novel *All Quiet on the Western Front* . . .

The new recruits are almost entirely young fellows just called up. They give us more trouble than they are worth. They are helpless in this grim fighting area, they fall like flies. Modern trench warfare demands knowledge and experience. A man must have a feeling for the contours of the ground, an ear for the sound and type of the shells, must be able to decide

beforehand where they will drop, how they will burst, and how to shelter from them.

The young recruits of course know none of these things. They get killed simply because they can hardly tell shrapnel from high explosive. They flock together like sheep instead of scattering, and even the wounded are shot down like hares by the airmen.

Their pale turnip faces, their pitiful clenched hands, the fine courage of these poor devils, who are so terrified that they dare not cry out loudly, but with battered chests, with torn bellies, arms and legs only whimper softly for their mothers and cease as soon as one looks at them. Their sharp, downy, dead faces have the awful expressionlessness of dead children. It brings a lump into the throat to see how they go over and run and fall. A man would like to take them by the arm and lead them away from here where they have no business to be.

Between five and ten recruits fall to every old hand. A surprise gas attack carries off a lot of them. They have not yet learned what to do. We found one dug-out full of them, with blue heads and black lips. Some of them in a shell-hole took off their masks too soon. They did not know that the gas lies longest in the hollows. Their condition is hopeless, they choked to death with haemorrhages and suffocation.

In the few hours of rest we teach them. We sharpen their ears to the malicious, hardly audible buzz of the smaller shells. We show them how to take cover from aircraft, how to pretend to be dead when one is over-run in an attack, to use hand grenades so that they explode half a second before hitting the ground. We teach them to fling themselves into holes as quick as lightning. We show them all the tricks that can save them from death.

They listen, they are quiet—but when it begins again, in their excitement they do everything wrong.

We see men living with their skulls blown open; we see soldiers run with their two feet cut off. They stagger on their splintered stumps into the next shell-hole. We see men without mouths, without jaws, without faces.

Still, the little piece of battered earth in which we lie is held. We have yielded no more than a few hundred yards of it to the enemy. But on every yard there lies a dead man.

Vera Brittain describes her visit to a shell-shocked friend. Shell-shock was the name given to mental disturbance caused by the experience of war . . .

I found him huddled over a gas fire with a rug across his knees. Though the little wound on his left cheek was almost healed, he still shuddered from the deathly cold that comes after shell-shock. His face was grey, from which his haunted eyes glowed like twin points of blue flame in their sunken sockets. He was not, he told me, a successful officer as he knew my brother to be. In the trenches he always felt afraid, not of the danger, but of completely losing his nerve with a suddenness that he had once seen overwhelm another officer.

'It's awful the way the men keep their eyes fixed on you,' he said. 'I never know whether they're afraid of what's going to happen to me, or whether they're just watching to see what I do.'

He still worried perpetually over his decision to retreat, wondering whether they should all have stayed to face certain death. As he talked he clasped and unclasped his hands; I have never seen any face so overshadowed with sorrow and anxiety as was his when he spoke of his brief but unforgettable weeks in Flanders.

A British soldier on the Somme wrote . . .

That day I saw sights which were passing strange to a man of peace. I saw men in their madness bayonet each other without mercy, without thought. I saw men torn to fragments by the near explosion of bombs, and—worse than any sight—I heard the agonised cries and shrieks of men in mortal pain who were giving up their souls to their Maker.

The mental picture of the eye may fade, but the cries of those poor tortured and torn men I can never forget. They are with me always.

Another British soldier wrote of the Somme . . .

We had to wait an hour before going over the top, and the enemy's bombardment was hitting our trenches with unpleasant frequency. It was a most unnerving experience; officers were wondering if they would be alive to lead their troops and, if so, would there be any troops to lead, and men were wondering if they would be alive to attack and, if so, would there be any officers left to lead them. It was a most interesting thing to note the different reactions of different temperaments—some were laughing and joking in a rather high-pitched voice, others were white and tight-lipped with flashing eyes and jerky movements, but all were keyed-up for the great moment.

Q

1 Why were such large numbers of soldiers killed in the Great War? Bring in to your answers the methods of fighting and the weapons used in the war.

2 Using the above evidence, make a list of the different ways in which the soldiers were affected by trench warfare.

Extension

Two views of the Somme

At the beginning of August two quite different views of the Somme were expressed. One view was expressed by Winston Churchill in an official report . . .

In numbers of casualties the results of the operation have been disastrous; in the gaining of land they have been absolutely barren. And, although our brave troops are at the moment delighted by the small advances made, the final effect will be disappointing. From every point of view, therefore, the British offensive has been a great failure.

In reply to this, the British Commander in Chief, Sir Douglas Haig, wrote . . .

> A. We have relieved the pressure on other parts of the front line.
> B. Our ally Russia's successes last month would certainly have been prevented had the enemy been free to transfer troops from here to Russia.
> C. Proof given to the world that the allies are maintaining a vigorous offensive. Also impressed on the world, England's strength and determination, and the fighting power of the British race.
> D. We have inflicted very heavy losses on the enemy. In another six weeks the enemy should be hard put to it to find men.
> E. Keeping up a steady offensive pressure will result eventually in the enemy's complete over-throw. Principle on which we should act— MAINTAIN OUR OFFENSIVE.

These are two clear views, one in favour and one against, but perhaps the real story of the argument between Churchill and Haig was not quite so straightforward. Another piece of evidence might help us to understand it better. General Rawlinson, one of Haig's Chief Commanders, wrote of a visit to the front in early August 1916 by King George V . . .

> He was very cheery, looked well and was certainly in good form. He told me many things, the chief one being that there was an intrigue in London led by Lord French, Winston and F. E. Smith criticising Haig and saying that the present offensive was a waste of life and energy. It is disgraceful that people should be able to do such unpatriotic deeds, and all through jealousy.

Q

---

1 How useful and reliable are the two views of the Battle of the Somme as expressed by Churchill and Haig? Bring into your answer their reasons for holding such views. Is General Rawlinson's evidence reliable in helping you to come to your conclusions?

One day on the Somme

The battle for High Wood

This is the story of the capture of High Wood on 15 September, 1916. On that day, half way through the Battle of the Somme, a big push took place to move forward the British front line into enemy territory. As you can see from the map, the 47th Division, containing about 20,000 officers and men, was allotted about 1,500 yards of the front line. This short space included High Wood, a German strong-point. Several times already the British had failed to take the wood, which was on high ground opposite the British trenches. You can see from the photograph on the next page, how heavily bombed the wood had been and how close together the British and German trenches were.

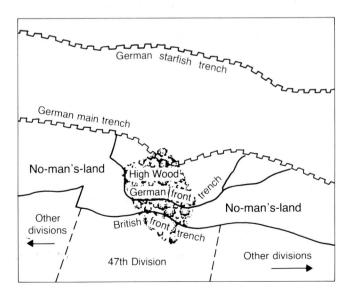

High Wood Battle Front

The day's orders

On 15 September two thirds of the division were to take part in the push forward. The remaining third would be in reserve. There was to be no bombardment of the wood itself before zero hour because the trenches were so close together. The rest of the front, however, was heavily bombarded. Instead of the bombardment, four tanks were allotted to High Wood. This was the first time that tanks had ever been used in warfare. Their role was to surprise the Germans one minute before zero hour, 6.20 a.m., to reach the main German line within half an hour and then to help the infantry to capture German strong points in the wood before going on northwards. The infantry themselves would go over the top at 6.20 and were expected to clear the whole wood of Germans by 7 o'clock, before moving on to the German Starfish line.

The events of the day

Before 6.20 a.m.

During the previous day and evening those who were due to go over the top were crowded into the front line British trenches. As was usual before a battle, rum was issued at dawn. So crowded were the trenches that the first wave of infantry moved out into no-man's-land, where they lay still, waiting for the whistle which would announce their advance. As it was already growing light, the German machine-guns just forty yards away began to shoot them. German artillery also began to bombard the British trenches where the men were waiting to go.

6.20 a.m. Zero hour

The tanks were slightly late, and moved so slowly that the infantry overtook them. They did not surprise the Germans. Within a few minutes one had broken down, a second was stuck in a ditch, the third was caught on a tree stump and the fourth had been shelled.

In High Wood itself the first waves of infantry were mown down and made virtually no progress at all. They had over four fifths casualties. The British trenches became so full of dead and wounded that succeeding waves could not get out over the top. Some tried to climb out further back and were immediately killed. One man remembered . . .

> The yells were soon death screams and man after man went down before that awful machine-gun fire. Our officer led us on. He had a walking stick in one hand, a revolver in the other and his face fixed in a set smile. A big, fine-looking man he was. Men were falling on all sides, some in death agony, and between the groans and cries of men and the eternal awful fumes of cordite, that hundred yards to the German lines is the most fearful memory of France I have.

By 10.30 very little progress had been made in High Wood, although the front line German trench had been taken.

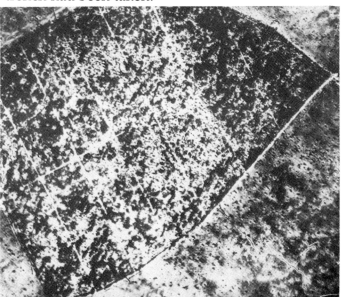

High Wood bombarded. Notice the German and British trenches so close to one another

However, outside the wood to east and west the soldiers of the 47th Division had captured some sections of the main German trench, although they could go no further because of German firing from the wood itself.

10.30 a.m.

The delay in capturing High Wood was holding back the progress of other divisions on either side of the front. Therefore a decision was taken to bombard both sides of the wood for a quarter of an hour or so. After this the waves of attack began again from all sides. The bombardment and the unrelenting attacks by the 47th Division soldiers finally demoralised the German defenders. Those who had not been killed or wounded began to give themselves up. By 1 o'clock the wood was clear of Germans.

1.00 p.m.

Now it was time to move on to the Starfish Line seven hundred yards further north. Already small sections had been captured to the east and west, but not opposite High Wood. German artillery was now bombarding the 47th Division with immense force. Even so the section of the Starfish Line opposite High Wood had to be captured at all costs to enable the whole front to advance at an even rate.

3.30 p.m.

So devastating was the German defence of the Starfish Line that little advance had been made. It was decided to bring in the reserve part of the 47th Division.

5.30 p.m.

Six hundred men of the reserve section, who had not thought that they would be in action that day, moved forward, picking up as they went along soldiers from earlier waves who were still holed up in shell-holes. One man who saw them reported . . .

> They nearly all had their rifles slung over their right shoulder. Shells dropped among them and they must have lost hundreds by the time they reached our position. As they passed, one said, 'Cheer up boys, we'll see you right.' Another beside him had a pipe in his mouth and a bag of bombs or rations on his back. Mostly the faces were set and white, but not a falter as they went to the hell in front.

By dusk very little of the Starfish Line had been captured. The 47th Division's soldiers had to dig in at various points between the main German line and the Starfish Line.

Under cover of night, patrols went forward to collect the wounded and to begin to bury the dead. All night long the Germans bombarded them at their work. One man saw soldiers escaping back to the British trenches from their holes in no-man's-land . . .

> Some returned late that night and went right back as our officer would not take responsibility for them—a mere handful, a few whimpering, a few crying like babies. Poor devils, they had it rough.

Afterwards

High Wood became a symbol of British determination and courage. Press reports were full of praise for the 47th Division. One journalist included in his report the following passage about the use of tanks at High Wood . . .

> Then to their great joy they saw the tanks advancing through High Wood and on each side of it.
>
> 'It was like a fairy tale!' said a cockney soldier. 'I can't help laughing every time I think of it.
>
> 'They broke down trees as if they were matchsticks, and went over barricades like elephants. The Germans were thoroughly scared. They came running out of shell-holes and trenches, shouting like mad things. Some of them attacked the tanks and tried to bomb them, but it was not a bit of good. O Crikey, it was a rare treat to see! The biggest joke that ever was!'

The report of the Commander in Chief, Sir Douglas Haig, went as follows . . .

> The 47th Division failed at High Wood on 15 September and the Commanding Officer was sent home. The new Commanding Officer arrived on Sunday so has not had time to make his personality felt. I told him to teach the Division 'Discipline and Digging'.

Fortunately, Haig's opinion of the battle for High Wood was not known to the men of the 47th Division. That day the 47th Division had 4,500 casualties. It was perhaps the worst day for a single division during the whole war.

1 Draw a map and mark on it the main events of the day's fighting.
2 How do you account for Haig's assessment of the 47th Division's fighting that day?

3 Was the journalist's report of the tanks' part in the day's events an accurate one or not? Give your reasons.
4 Write a short account of the day's events for a war memorial to commemorate the taking of High Wood.

Thoughts on the war

The war had frightening effects not only on those who fought in it but also on the history of the world afterwards. Great nations were defeated and humbled, new nations emerged. No nation was quite the same afterwards, even the most stable and victorious. The men who killed and saw death around them wanted changes when they returned. As the war ended governments began to fall. It is no coincidence that a communist revolution took place in Russia in 1917 and that Fascists came to power in so many places only a few years later. The war had a great deal to do with all of these developments. They took place largely because the experience of war had been so catastrophic. The soldiers who fought and died, the crowds that cheered them on, the families who suffered bereavement on such a vast scale; these were the people whose experience led to such important changes.

Once again, the evidence left by the war should help us to think about what it really meant. The picture is not at all clear. People were affected by it in different ways.

A British soldier wrote afterwards . . .

Now came disillusionment for those of us who had joined up in a fine spirit of adventure. The frenzied butchery of this war was eventually to kill at least ten million young men. After being dressed in uniform, fed and drilled, cheered and cried over, these ten million were then filled with hot lead, ripped apart by shell splinters, blown to bits, suffocated in mud or allowed to die of diseases after rotting too long in trenches. Death, having come into his empire, demanded the best, and got it.

Another British soldier . . .

The terror of the front sinks deep down when we turn our backs on it; we make grim, coarse jests about it when a man dies. That keeps us from going mad; as long as we take it that way we maintain our own resistance.

But we do not forget. It's all rot that they put in the War News about the good humour of the troops, how they are arranging dances almost before they are out of the front line. We don't like that because we are in a good humour. We are in a good humour because otherwise we should go to pieces. Even so we cannot hold out much longer; our humour becomes more bitter every month.

Lawrence Binyon, the poet, wrote . . .

With proud thanksgiving, a mother for her
   children,
England mourns for her dead across the sea.
Flesh of her flesh they were, spirit of her spirit,
Fallen in the cause of the free.

They went with songs to battle, they were young,
Straight of limb, sure of eye, steady and aglow.
They were staunch to the end against odds
   uncounted.
They fell with their faces to the foe.

They shall grow not old, as we that are left grow
   old;
Age shall not weary them, nor the years
   condemn.
At the going down of the sun and in the morning
We will remember them.

They mingle not with their laughing comrades
   again;
They sit no more at familiar tables of home;
They have no lot in our labour of the daytime;
They sleep beyond England's foam.

A British soldier wrote to his rector back home, after the armistice, about the General Election that was being held . . .

Most of the fellows here that are in our constituency have not voted at all. They don't fancy Kendall, and yet will not vote for Pilcher as he is a soldier, and after all they are right, as officers in the war have treated men like dogs. We have put up with it for our country's sake, but there is no getting away from the fact that the majority of the officers that I have come into contact with are a bad lot.

A chum of mine that joined the army in 1914 and had never had a scratch before, had bad luck in losing the use of his leg the day before the armistice. He had a piece of shrapnel through the knee. Downright hard luck I call it to get it so near the end. It is awful when I think of the poor chaps in this company that were killed the same morning as the good news came through. We had sixteen knocked out at nine o'clock, nine of them killed. We are not in a very nice spot but of course Christmas this year is bound to be better than last, it could not be worse.

I must thank you for the newspaper which I have received from time to time. According to the Government's new programme there will be drastic changes in Blighty [Britain] if they get in, and I think it is a foregone conclusion that they will. England should be a better place for the soldier when he gets home, if they do all they promised for him. I don't think the Labour candidates will stand much of a chance after the way that labour unions have acted in this war with so many strikes.

A soldier-poet wrote the following poem to represent the feelings of the British soldier . . .

We march in fours today, mate,
But tomorrow man by man.
For its 'up the line' tonight, mate
And dodge it if you can.
It's a damned infernal pity
You should have to do your whack
But better men than you are

Have trod the self-same track.
You ain't the only pebble
On the beach; there's plenty here
Been out three bastard winters,
And you joined up this year.
You're ruptured and rheumatic
You were never fit for France?
Well, Fritz'll cure your guts ache
If you give him half a chance.
You support a widowed mother
And a sister who has fits?
For sure he'll never kill you,
If you tell that tale to Fritz.
You're a poor faint-hearted soldier
But if you only knew
The whole great British army
Was made from stuff like you.

Wilfred Owen, who wrote the poem that you read on page 8 about the boy who lied to join up, concluded the poem in a different spirit . . .

Some cheered him home, but not as crowds cheer goal.
Only a solemn man who brought him fruits
THANKED him; and then inquired about his soul.

Now, he will spend a few sick years in Institutes,
And do what things the rules consider wise,
And take whatever pity they may dole.
Tonight he noticed how the women's eyes
Passed from him to the strong men that were whole.
How cold and late it is! Why don't they come
And put him to bed? Why don't they come?

---

1 What was it about the Great War that made people think so deeply?
2 People did not always react in the same way to war. Give examples of different reactions.

3 Which of the evidence do you find most valuable in increasing your understanding of what the war was really about? Give your views.

THE TREATIES

11 o'clock, 11 November, 1918 . . .

From war to peace

As you can see from the evidence on this page, the news of the armistice suddenly released everyone's emotions. Most people had expected the war to go on until 1919. They were not ready for peace. How would they react to it?

Harold Owen, the young brother of the famous soldier-poet Wilfred Owen, was serving as a lieutenant on his warship off the coast of Africa . . .

> . . . I realised with a surge of happiness that the war had not broken my family. Wilfred must be alright now. He was safe and so was I. But I could not get him out of my mind.
>
> A few days later, I went inside my cabin and to my amazement I saw Wilfred. I felt shock running through me. His eyes were alive with the familiar look of trying to make me understand. But he did not speak, and smiled only his most gentle smile. Suddenly I fell into a deep oblivious sleep. When I woke up, I knew with certainty that Wilfred was dead.
>
> It was Christmas week before I got my letters from home, but I did not need to be told about Wilfred. I opened my mother's latest letter. They had received the dreaded news by telegram at 12 a.m. on 11 November, Armistice Day. The Church bells were still ringing, the bands were still playing and the jubilant crowds surging together. Later that day I went ashore and cabled my love to them at home.

Cyril Falls, a soldier, was at the front line . . .

> Just before 11 a.m. many British guns fired defiant last salvoes, carefully aimed as ever. Then silence fell. The gunners' gesture was not a sign of excitement. There was little of that. Many thought of lost relations and friends, but the main mood seemed to be a groping realisation that the war was over.

LET THEM HAVE IT.
GERMANY IS ASKING FOR PEACE WITH JUSTICE.

The original drawings of Mr. Staniforth's cartoons may be purchased at two guineas each.

A typical British cartoon of October 1918

An officer, Charles Petrie, was on leave in London . . .

Inside the Savoy Hotel a number of young officers were trying to burn a German flag in spite of the protests of the management. As I was going home a rather drunken workman got into the carriage and kept repeating, 'We've won the bloody war, but we'll lose the bloody peace.'

Why did the war end so suddenly?

In October 1918 every one of Germany's allies suddenly collapsed and surrendered. Germany had very few reinforcements and supplies. Her people were weary of war and were tiring of their government. Already riots were breaking out in German cities. The government knew well enough that Germany was beaten but they were determined to save her from invasion and conquest. An armistice seemed a clever idea.

On the other side, the Allied governments were not so sure about granting an armistice, although they had good reasons for bringing the war to an end . . .

War-weariness

Most people would welcome the end of the war. Their spirit was weakening after four years of hardship, suffering and slaughter.

Fear of revolution

Russia was already in the grip of a violent communist revolution. The Allies were afraid that communism would spread to Germany if they continued the war.

Disagreement among the Allies

The Americans wanted to end the war quickly and go home. The French wanted to invade the Rhineland area of Germany on France's border. The British were not prepared to go on fighting just to help the French. Both Britain and America deeply distrusted France. They thought that she would keep them involved in the slaughter just to serve her own interests.

Britain's Commander-in-Chief, Earl Haig, gave the following advice about granting an armistice.

The French Army is worn out and has not really been fighting lately. The American Army is not yet fully organised. The British Army was never more efficient than today, but it has fought hard and it lacks reinforcements. As it becomes less effective, its morale is bound to suffer. At this moment only the British might bring the enemy to its knees. But why spend more British lives— and for what? I advise that we ask in the armistice for what we want and that we oppose the French entering Germany to pay off old scores. In my opinion, the British Army would not fight keenly for what is not really in our own interest.

The war might go on for much longer, unless the internal state of Germany forces the enemy to accept harsh terms. We don't know very much about what is happening within Germany and so to insist on harsh terms seems to me a gamble.

The situation within Germany did indeed get worse suddenly and the government collapsed. Germany was forced to accept a very harsh armistice indeed. However, she avoided the worst danger of all—invasion. Signing the armistice, as you can see in the painting, was bad enough, but invasion would have been disastrous.

A painting of the signing of the armistice

Peace had arrived, but in a strange, unfinished way. For four years the Allied peoples had dreamed of utterly crushing the enemy. Could they actually do this now that they had agreed not to invade? They had won the war, but they had not marched through Berlin in triumph.

Now the Allies prepared for the peace negotiations, which were going to prove very difficult indeed.

1a How reliable are the four pieces of evidence on pages 20–21 in helping to find out what public opinion was in November 1918 and in what ways?
b What conclusions can you reach from the evidence and from your own knowledge of human nature, about the emotions and views that people held in 1918?
c What sort of peace do you think most people would want with Germany?
d What do you think the drunken workman meant about 'losing the peace' on page 21?

2a In your opinion, are Earl Haig's comments reliable as a source of evidence? Is it biased, or lying, or incorrectly informed? Give your reasons.
b In what ways does Earl Haig's evidence fit in with the three reasons given earlier for ending the war?
3 Do you think the picture of the German surrender was painted by a German or a Frenchman? Give your reasons.
4 In what ways could the Allies not 'crush' Germany, now that they had decided not to invade her?

Extension

Three ways of dealing with Germany

USA
Losses: 150,000 dead; £2 billion, but most of this owed by Britain and France
Economy: The world's richest country
Arms: A large army and navy
Position: Far away from Europe, with the Atlantic as a barrier

Britain
Losses: 1 million dead; £8 billion cost
Economy: The second wealthiest country in Europe, third in the world
Arms: A huge navy
Position: Not a neighbour of Germany; the English Channel a barrier

France
Losses: 1.4 million dead; £5 billion cost; large areas of land and industry destroyed
Economy: The third wealthiest country in Europe, fourth in the world
Arms: A large army, but decreasing because the population was decreasing
Position: A weak land border with Germany

Germany
Losses: 1.8 million dead; £11 billion cost
Economy: The wealthiest country in Europe, second in the world
Arms: Its army defeated, but potentially very strong; its navy given up to Britain

You can see from the information on the table above that the three victorious allies would have quite different hopes and fears about Germany. Now that the war was over, these differences would grow and would cause severe disagreements.

The aims of the Big Three

The leaders of the three Allied nations were known as the Big Three. They were Woodrow Wilson, President of America, David Lloyd George, Prime Minister of Great Britain, and Georges Clemenceau, Prime Minister of France. They did agree on some aims for dealing with Germany, but disagreed deeply on others, as you can see from the chart on the next page . . .

USA	Britain	France

Aim 1: *To punish Germany and to force her to accept total blame for causing the war*
All three nations agreed on this aim. They genuinely believed that Germany had caused the war.

Aim 2: *To cut down Germany's power in the following ways . . .*

a Territory
All three wanted to take away provinces from Germany and hand them over to Germany's neighbours.

	In addition, both Britain and France wanted as many as possible of Germany's colonies for themselves.	
		In addition, France alone wanted to split Germany into two countries, with the weaker part nearest to France.

b Armed forces
All three wanted to cut down Germany's forces so that she could never make war again.

c Reparations (compensation for losses)

America wanted no reparations. Britain and France owed huge sums to America.	Both Britain and France, especially France, wanted vast reparations from Germany for war losses. The French thought that this would help to keep Germany permanently weak.	

Aim 3: *National self-determination*
All three agreed that each race of people, especially in Eastern Europe, should have the right to become a separate nation with its own government. One group of people should not live under the rule of another, except Germans of course.

Aim 4: *To set up a League of Nations. As all nations, except the defeated countries, would be members, they would feel safe enough not to need their own separate alliances for defence. This was known as collective security.*

Wilson was more interested in this than in anything else. He thought that the League would solve all the world's future problems.	Britain was fairly interested in the League, but not as hopeful as Wilson.	France thought that the League would be useless. She wanted separate alliances against Germany, not collective security.

Aim 5: *General disarmament. To reduce all arms to a bare minimum to avoid the danger of war.*

America was very keen on disarmament.	Britain was fairly keen, but not on naval disarmament.	France was not at all interested in disarmament, wanting to keep as large an army as possible.

Q

Comparing the Big Three

1 Under the following headings, write a sentence or two comparing Britain, France and America, saying which country was most affected by Germany . . . Losses   Economic strength   Armed forces   Position in relation to Germany

2 Make a list of the reasons, in order of importance, why the Allies thought that Germany was still a long-term danger.

3 Which country would be most afraid of Germany? Which country would be least afraid of her? Which country would be in the middle? Give your reasons.

4 Which country would, in your opinion, be the most vengeful towards Germany? Give your reasons.

The aims of the Allies

1 List briefly the aims that the Allies agreed on.

2 How do you account for America's idealism and lack of concern about the harshness of the other Allies, even though Wilson disagreed with their aims?

3 How do you account for French self-interest? Give as many reasons as you can.

4 Why do you think that the British always seemed to be in the middle? Give several reasons.

Problems at the Peace conference

> We arrived, determined that a Peace of justice and wisdom should be made: we left, knowing that the treaties were neither just nor wise.

THE WORLD'S DESIRE.

Peace (outside the Allied Conference Chamber). "I KNOW I SHALL HAVE TO WAIT FOR A WHILE; BUT I DO HOPE THEY WON'T TALK TOO MUCH."

The Angel of Peace has to wait. A British cartoon

This was written by one of Britain's representatives at the conference, Harold Nicolson. It is easy to criticise the Big Three, but did they know that the treaties would be so disastrous?

In 1919 there were many problems in the way of a just peace. The war had ended so suddenly that the Allies had too little time to prepare properly for the conference. Germany was not invited to attend the conference. The Big Three made all the decisions on their own. Very often they did not consult even their own allies, the Italians. The biggest problem, however, was disagreement between the Big Three.

Disagreement at the conference

Wilson. Wilson was the most idealistic of the three leaders and he did not like the harsh parts of the Treaty of Versailles. He only agreed to them because he genuinely believed that the League of Nations would solve all problems in the future, even the hostility between France and Germany. Unfortunately the American people did not agree with their President. They were determined not to become involved in Europe's wars again. This feeling was known as isolationism.

Clemenceau. Clemenceau, known as 'The Tiger' because of his strong support of France's interests, hated Germany and wanted to weaken her as much as possible. He knew that the best way to do this would be to split Germany into two. This he sought to achieve with the support of the French people.

Lloyd George. Lloyd George was re-elected as Prime Minister of Great Britain in November 1918. He had to support the British public's demands to 'Squeeze Germany till the pips squeak', 'Hang the Kaiser' and 'Make Germany pay'. However, in reality he did not think like this. He tried to look at the problem from Germany's point of view and knew that harsh terms would only cause trouble in the future.

Behind the scenes Lloyd George tried to patch up the disagreements between the two others. The biggest conflict was about splitting Germany into two, which he and Wilson would not accept. In the end he persuaded Clemenceau to give up the idea, but only when Britain and America signed a special agreement known as the Treaty of Guarantee, promising to help France if she was ever attacked by Germany.

Clemenceau makes a sign. There is an absolute hush. The French ceremonial guards flash the swords back into their scabbards with a loud click. 'Let the Germans enter,' says Clemenceau. Through the door appear six soldiers in single file. And then, isolated and pitiable, come the two German representatives. The silence is terrifying. They keep their eyes away from those two thousand staring eyes, fixed upon the ceiling. They are deathly pale. It is all most painful.

They are conducted to their chairs. Clemenceau at once breaks the silence, 'We are here to sign a Treaty of Peace.' There is tension. The Germans sign. There is relaxation. We kept our seats while the Germans were conducted like prisoners from the dock, their eyes fixed on some distant point of the horizon.

Afterwards I find my colleague standing miserably in the splendid room. We say nothing. It has all been horrible.

The signing of the Treaty

The treaty was signed in great splendour in the Palace of Versailles near Paris. This description was written by a British representative, Harold Nicolson . . .

The treaties

Altogether five treaties were signed. The **Treaty of Versailles** with Germany, the **Treaty of St Germain** with Austria, the **Treaty of Trianon** with Hungary, the **Treaty of Neuilly** with Bulgaria and the **Treaty of Sèvres** with Turkey.

Q

1a According to Nicolson, in what way were the Germans made to feel humiliated? How does this help to explain why the Germans were not invited to the conference?

b What was Nicolson's own view of Germany's treatment according to his two pieces of evidence?

2 How did *each* of the Big Three fail to follow his people's wishes? Being a democratic leader, was each one right or wrong to do as he did?

3 Find out what the word *realistic* means, and explain fully your own views about whether *each* of the Big Three was realistic or not in dealing with Germany. Which of them was the most realistic and which was the least realistic?

4 Explain fully why the hope of 'Peace' in the *Punch* cartoon would not be achieved. Use the information on pages 24–25.

The features of the treaties

Feature 1: The treatment of Germany

The Treaty of Versailles punished Germany in several ways ...

War guilt

Germany had to accept total responsibility for causing the war.

Territorial terms

Study the map opposite, showing the lands lost by Germany. These included four million Germans. In addition, Germany lost all its overseas colonies in Africa and Asia, mostly to Britain. Germany was never to unite with German-speaking Austria.

Military terms

Germany was never again to use armed force.

- The **German Army** was reduced to only 100,000 men. It was not allowed to conscript men nor to possess tanks and artillery.
- The **German Navy** was to have no battleships and U-boats at all and very few other ships.
- The **German Air Force** was abolished altogether.
- The part of Germany between the River Rhine and France, as well as a thirty mile strip on the other bank, was *demilitarised*, that is, no German troops were allowed there and all fortifications

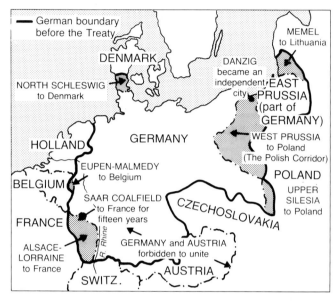

Germany after the Treaty

were destroyed. It was occupied by French and British troops for fifteen years.

Reparations and other economic losses

Germany had to pay reparations (compensation) to the European Allies. This covered not only war damage, but the entire cost of fighting the war. The final bill, not fixed until 1921, totalled £6,600,000,000, payable in gold or in goods such as ships, livestock or timber. The lost territories contained 15% of Germany's agricultural land and 10% of Germany's industry.

Q

---

1 Why do you think the Allies forced Germany to accept war guilt?

2a List the lands lost by Germany and the countries that gained them.

b Draw a map showing Germany's new boundary. Do not forget East Prussia.

c Why was Germany never to be allowed to unite with Austria?

3 Mark on your map the demilitarised area of Germany.

4 Germany estimated that it could afford to pay £2,000,000,000. Was this likely to be a fair estimate? Why did the Allies not take Germany's 'capacity to pay' into account?

5 Which country or countries were responsible for *each* of the terms of the Treaty?

Feature 2: The treatment of Eastern Europe

Eastern Europe was completely changed after the war. Even as Austria–Hungary collapsed in October 1918, its various peoples seized their independence. The cartoon shows these events as British readers viewed them. The Treaties of St Germain, Trianon and Neuilly dealt harshly with Austria, Hungary and Bulgaria. The main terms of the treaties dealt with changes in boundaries, as you can see from the maps opposite.

THE END OF THE JOURNEY.

A British cartoonist's view of the treatment of Austria-Hungary

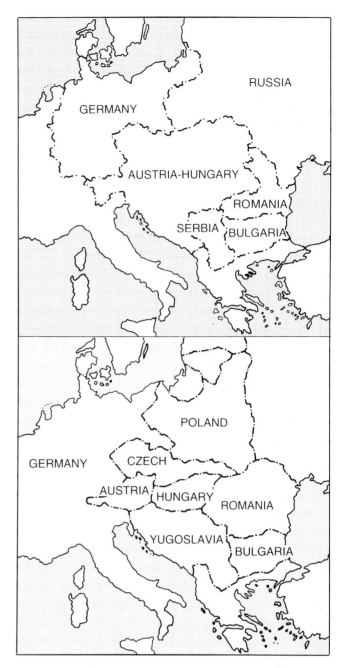

Eastern Europe, 1914 and 1919

―Q―

1 Which of the aims of the Big Three was achieved by redrawing the boundaries?

2a In the cartoon, which countries are shown deciding the fate of Austria–Hungary?

b Which countries, in your opinion, decided the fate of Austria–Hungary—The Big Three or the countries that seized their independence?

3 Name the following countries by comparing the two maps:

● Two new countries, now separated from each other and much reduced in size.

● A new country, splitting away from Austria–Hungary.

● Two already existing countries, now enlarged at the expense of Austria–Hungary. One of these has a new name.

● A new country made up of parts of Austria–Hungary, Germany and Russia.

Feature 3: The treatment of Turkey

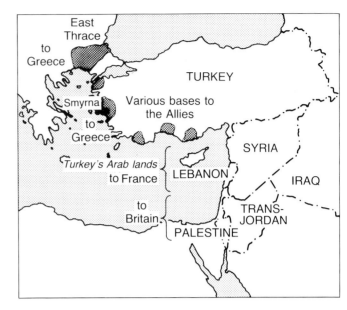

The harsh treatment of Turkey

At the end of the Great War the Allies occupied the Turkish capital, Constantinople. They were convinced that Turkey was finished as a nation. In May 1919 they allowed Greece to invade Turkey and to seize a vast area, with terrible violence. On the quayside at Smyrna, Greek soldiers tortured and killed thousands of Turkish men and boys. The Big Three were shocked, but did nothing. Shortly afterwards the Treaty of Sèvres imposed very harsh terms indeed upon Turkey, as you can see from the map.

Deep inside the country, however, a rebel army of Turkish Nationalists (under the leadership of Kemal Ataturk) rose up in a spirit of outrage. Within two years they had driven out not only the Greeks but the Allies as well. On the quayside at Smyrna the Greeks suffered the same fate that they had earlier imposed on the Turks. The Allies had no choice but to make the new Treaty of Lausanne in 1923, which cancelled almost all the terms of the Treaty of Sèvres.

Turkey, however, was glad to let Britain and France keep her troublesome Arab lands. Even though these lands were rich in oil, they were not an easy prize. The main problem was Palestine. During the war Britain had promised both the Palestinian Arabs and the Jews that they could have Palestine as their homeland. Trouble was brewing.

Q

1 What basic mistakes did the Allies make in dealing with Turkey?
2 Which of the following statements most accurately describes why the Allies made a new treaty with Turkey? Give reasons for your views.

● The Allies realised that the Treaty of Sèvres was unfair and decided to change their minds.
● The Allies had no choice but to change the Treaty of Sèvres.
3 Which present-day problem in this area was caused by the decisions of the peacemakers?

Feature 4: The League of Nations

Vera Brittain was a young student who had worked through the Great War as a nurse and whose fiancé Roland and only brother Edward had been killed. She had bitter words to say about the peace treaties . . .

> Meanwhile, in Paris, the Big Three were making a treaty and calling it peace. Although Roland, Edward and the others would no doubt have welcomed the idea of the League of Nations, they certainly had not died so that the Big Three could make the beaten enemy pay the cost of the war. I was beginning already to suspect that my generation had been deceived, its idealism betrayed. Soon afterwards I lectured often about the League, that international experiment in peace which I felt to be the one ray of hope and progress in the peace treaties.

President Wilson would have agreed with Vera, and he insisted that the League should be included in all five treaties. He and many others thought that the war had been caused by the building up of arms and by making strong alliances. These had only encouraged countries to go to war, thinking that they could easily defeat their enemies. For these reasons the Covenant of the League, which all members had to sign, was based on the following points . . .

> **Collective security.** All members promised not to go to war and to protect one another from attack.
> **Disarmament.** Members promised to disarm at a future disarmament conference.
> **Membership.** Germany would only be allowed to join when it was felt that she was no longer aggressive.
> **Disciplinary action.** The League would, it was hoped, take action against agressive members.

HISTORY TO REPEAT ITSELF?
WILSON: I mean to down him before I've finished.

A British view of Wilson's challenge

—Q—

1 What was the main purpose of the League?
2 Use all the evidence and information in this section to show how the League was based on great hope and optimism.

3 Explain why Vera Brittain felt the way she did about the League.

Criticisms of the treaties

Criticism 1: The failure to solve the problem of Germany

Germany's response to the Treaty of Versailles

You can almost feel the tension and hatred in the photograph opposite. The incident which it shows took place in 1923 when France invaded the Ruhr, an industrial area of Germany. The reason given by France was that the reparations instalment was paid late. Before long they were glad to pull out of the Ruhr, especially when the British refused to support them, but the invasion had done its damage in worsening the German sense of resentment and humiliation.

An old German faces a French soldier, 1923

The whole German people detested the Treaty of Versailles, which was known as the *diktat*, or slave treaty. Even small things to do with it infuriated them, such as this regulation imposed in the occupied Rhineland . . .

> **Regulation of Army of Occupation**
> All male German civilians shall take off their hats, in respect to Allied officers.

A British reporter noted a few years later, 'It is true that, in 1919, British troops might knock the hats off civilians for failing to do so, but the French were still knocking hats off five years later.'

Unfortunately, the government that signed the treaty was not that of the Kaiser, but a new, democratic government struggling hard to be successful. Many Germans blamed their new democracy for losing the war and for signing the treaty, calling it 'the stab in the back'.

Q

1a Why do you think the French introduced regulations like the one above?
b How do *individual* acts like having a hat knocked off worsen a sense of *national* resentment?
2a The photograph on the previous page can tell a whole story. Use the look on the old German's face to explain how deeply he resents the Treaty and the effects it has on Germany and on himself. Bring in the following points and the German arguments against them:

- not attending the Treaty negotiations
- being blamed for causing the war
- handing over land and Germans to other countries
- paying vast reparations
- being disarmed
- not being allowed to join the League of Nations.

Put these points in the order in which they would anger Germans.
b The French soldier too has strong emotions about the same matters. Write an account of his feelings from his point of view.

Did the Treaty of Versailles really crush Germany?

Germany was so humiliated by the Treaty that she never actually paused to ask herself whether her power had really been crushed for ever. Had it?

Germany's economy

None of Germany's industry and agriculture had been destroyed by enemy action, and 15% of her total resources were lost in the Treaty. By 1924 the German economy had become once again the richest and most advanced in Europe. As for reparations, Germany estimated that she could pay about £2,000,000,000 but, in the end, actually paid off £1,100,000,000 to the Allies.

Germany's military strength

Germany was determined to overcome the military terms of the Treaty. Her highly efficient vehicle, aircraft, shipbuilding and chemical industries developed new military vehicles, equipment and weapons in secret. The army was kept at 100,000 men, but most of these were of officer standard. By very well-organised training,

a highly motivated recruit could become a trained soldier in only six months instead of the normal two years. In any case, Germany had millions of trained ex-soldiers from the war years.

The German army develops the use of 'tanks', 1928

Germany's position in Europe

A British cabinet minister wrote privately on the day after the Treaty was signed, 'Germany would not, I think, rashly start a new war westwards, but the confusion on their eastern frontier, and their contempt for the Poles, must be a dangerous temptation.' Look at the maps on page 27 to see what he meant. What massive empires have the new, weak, small states replaced?

Q

Look back at the aims of the Big Three and the terms of the treaties and compare them with the relevant sections on this page. Then answer the following questions . . .

1a In what ways was Germany hit economically by the Treaty?

b How fully was Germany, in your opinion, economically crushed by the Treaty?

2a What do you think is going on in the photograph on page 30?

b What is the connection between a rich, advanced, industrial economy and a country's military power?

c Was Germany's military weakness permanent? Explain your answer.

3 Do you agree with the British cabinet minister's evidence? Was Germany in a better position in 1919 than in 1914, especially if she might become aggressive in the future? Explain your answer.

4 Write an essay on: 'How far were the aims of the Big Three achieved in the treaties with regard to Germany?'

Criticism 2: The weaknesses of the League of Nations

Unfortunately the League's future did not depend on the millions of people who expected it to ensure world peace and solve the world's problems. It had too many weaknesses, as the cartoonist could see.

Collective security and disarmament

Both of these depended on the promises that members made and on the belief that countries would prefer them to their own separate alliances and large armed forces.

Membership

Many countries could not or would not join the League. In addition to the defeated countries, America herself refused to join in 1920 because of her people's isolationism.

Disciplinary action

The League could only take action against a member who acted aggressively if the decision was unanimous.

READY TO START.

A British view of the League's task

1 What does the cartoon tell you of the cartoonist's view of the League?

2 Do you think countries would prefer collective security and disarmament to separate alliances and armed forces? Why or why not?

3 Why would the non-membership of Germany and America weaken the League?

4 Why would strong, disciplinary action be unlikely to be taken?

5 Using the information in this chapter, give as many examples as you can of the following:

• a country that would not feel safe enough to disarm

• a member who used force against another country in the years after the setting up of the League

• a country who would not feel safe enough to give up separate alliances

• a non-member who successfully used force against another country.

Criticism 3: Did the Treaty satisfy anyone?

You have seen how the defeated powers, especially Germany and Turkey, were dissatisfied by the treaties, and how unsuccessful the Big Three were in dealing with them. The victorious leaders and nations too had little cause to be pleased . . .

Italy had entered the war in 1915 with a promise from Britain and France to be given some German and Turkish colonies and part of Austria–Hungary. She also wanted to be treated as a first rate power. In 1919 Italy gained

A cartoon of 1919, showing Italy in the middle of the Big Three

The New REPUBLIC

Published Weekly

Saturday May 24th 1919

This Is Not Peace

Americans would be fools if they permitted themselves now to be embroiled in a system of European alliances. America promised to underwrite a stable peace. Mr. Wilson has failed. The peace cannot last. America should withdraw from all commitments which would impair her freedom of action.

Whitman, Emerson and the New Poetry
by EMERSON GRANT SUTCLIFFE

Communist Hungary
by H. N. BRAILSFORD

Harry Hawker
by FRANCIS HACKETT

FIFTEEN CENTS A COPY
FIVE DOLLARS A YEAR
VOL. XIX NO. 238

An American magazine, 1919

virtually no colonies, not enough territory from Austria–Hungary and was hardly ever consulted by the Big Three. She was outraged by the treaties.

The **American** people's view is shown in the magazine. The presidents who came after Wilson after 1920 upheld this view for many years. America never signed the Treaty, and refused to join the League.

In **Britain** the public soon realised that the treaties should have been less vindictive. They realised that reparations were much too high and that, if the German economy was badly hit, other economies would be stricken too.

The **French** were bitterly disappointed when they found that Germany had not been split into two, and that all they had instead was a promise from America and Britain to help them if Germany ever attacked. America and Britain refused to accept even this promise in 1920.

Clemenceau was forced by the French people to resign.

Q

1 In which country do you think the cartoon opposite was published? Is it a reliable piece of evidence about Italy's treatment at the conference? Explain your answer.

2 Say in your own words what views and fears the magazine cover shows about American public opinion.

Discussion topics

1 Do you think that we have any right to blame the peacemakers for failing to make a successful treaty? Would we do any better?

2 Do you think the situation would have been better if the peacemakers had failed to make any treaty at all?

Essays

1 What were the aims of the peacemakers? What were the main features of the treaties?

2 Why were so many countries dissatisfied with the treaties?

3 How successful were the peacemakers in achieving their aims?

RUSSIA

The Tsar and his subjects

Tsar Nicholas II, on one of the gold and jewelled eggs that he gave to his wife every Easter

political parties, unions, strikes and newspapers were banned if the government disapproved of them. Russia was beginning to change from a backward, agricultural country into a modern industrial nation, but the Tsar would not change with it. He ruled his 150 million subjects with a rod of iron.

The upper class

Some of the richest people in the world lived in Russia, like Princess Yusupov, whom you can see in the picture. Such people had great status

Tsar Nicholas II was the absolute ruler of Russia. No-one shared his power. If decisions were not made by the Tsar, they were not made at all. If they were the wrong decisions, there was no-one to question them. Nicholas was a shy and pleasant person, not particularly intelligent; a man of simple pleasures. He was devoted to his country, but believed wholeheartedly that God wanted him to keep Russia as it was. His dominating wife, Alexandra, supported him and together they chose ministers and advisers who agreed with their backward-looking ideas. All

Princess Yusupov, the richest landowner in Russia

in Russia and owned many large estates. There were also very rich capitalists, owners of Russia's new and rapidly developing steel, coal, oil and textile industries. Linked with these people were the leaders of the church, the civil service and the army. Most of them supported the Tsar in keeping Russia as it was, but some wanted change.

The middle class

Only about two million people came into this class, but they were important in the towns and cities. They owned or managed smaller industries and shops, or were professional people like lawyers, doctors and teachers. They were often well educated and critical of the Tsar. They preferred Russia to be a democracy like Britain or America.

The peasants

The vast majority of the Tsar's subjects were peasants. They were mostly very backward indeed, working on the land with primitive equipment. Some owned small farms but most peasants shared land with other peasants or worked on the estates of the Tsar, the nobility and the church. What the peasants badly wanted was their own land, to give them a greater sense of security and a higher standard of living.

A peasant family

The working class

This class was not large, about three million in all, working in Russia's new industries in St Petersburg, the capital, or Moscow. You can see from the photograph that their wages were very low indeed and their conditions at home and at work were degrading. What they wanted was a better standard of living and more control over their wretched lives.

Many workers lived in factory-owned barracks

1 What can you tell from the pictures about the wealth and status of the people concerned?
2 Did all the different classes have the same demands? Write a short paragraph summarising each class's demands, pointing out the differences between them.

3 If the Tsar banned all legal ways of changing Russia, what sorts of actions were available to those who wanted change? List as many as you can.

The revolution approaches

Many people turned to revolution as the only way of changing Russia. This was very difficult to achieve as the Tsar's spies were everywhere and he often turned his troops, especially the feared Cossacks, onto his own subjects. A revolution would only really have a chance of succeeding in certain circumstances . . .
● if revolutionary discontent and opposition became so strong that the people would take action to overthrow the Tsar.
● if the Tsar lost control, especially his control over the army, and his rule collapsed.
Without both these circumstances combined there would be no revolution.

The 1905 revolution

In 1905 a terrible crisis hit Russia. It is usually known as the '1905 Revolution', although it was not a real revolution at all because nothing much changed. Some people call it a 'dress rehearsal'

A poster from the 1905 Revolution

for the revolution that came in 1917. Why did it not succeed? Try to work out whether the two essential circumstances mentioned above were present in Russia in 1905.

In 1904 Russia went to war with Japan and was badly defeated. Discontent against the Tsar grew to fever pitch and many of the Tsar's subjects rose up against him. The first to protest openly were the educated middle classes who demanded a democracy. They were soon joined by the St Petersburg workers who wanted better wages and conditions. On Bloody Sunday, 22 January 1905, troops shot hundreds of unarmed workers outside the Tsar's Winter Palace. The Tsar was out of the city that day at his country palace, but he was informed of the events in St Petersburg. He wrote in his diary that evening . . .

January 22, Sunday. A painful day! There have been serious disorders in St Petersburg because workmen wanted to come up to the Winter Palace. Troops had to open fire in several places in the city; there were many killed and wounded. God, how painful and sad! Mama arrived from town, straight to Church. I lunched with all the others. Went for a walk with Misha. Mama stayed overnight.

A rather different view of 'Bloody Sunday' may be seen in the poster. Waves of strikes brought the country to a standstill. In the countryside the peasants rose up against their landowners and seized the land for themselves. After months of uproar the Tsar at last agreed to grant a Parliament, known as the Duma. Still the troubles, strikes and riots continued but, by the autumn of 1905, with troops returning from the war, the Tsar regained his nerve and acted with terrible force, especially against the workers and peasants. Bloody reprisals went on for months, and thousands were killed and imprisoned. The 'revolution' was over.

Q

1 Using the evidence of the Tsar's diary, write down two different views of his reaction to Bloody Sunday, one favourable to him and the other unfavourable.
2 What was the view of the poster painter of Bloody Sunday? How has he attempted to get across his

feelings? Do you think he was successful?
3 How fully did the two circumstances, mentioned at the top of the page, which were necessary for a revolution to take place, come into being in the '1905 Revolution'?

Real revolution at last

The Tsar learned no lessons from the 1905 revolution. He became even more hostile to change and dealt with opposition even more ruthlessly than before. He and his ministers ignored the new Duma. 'I have a constitution in my head but, in my heart, I spit on it,' said one of Nicholas' ministers. Russia would never change peacefully. The only opportunity for change lay in revolution, but would the circumstances arise again? Remind yourself of the necessary circumstances on the previous page.

The Great War

If the war had not taken place, would the Revolution have happened at all? How did the war help to create the right circumstances for the Revolution?

The Tsar went to war in 1914 on a wave of patriotic enthusiasm, but Russia was in no state to wage such a war. Its industry could not possibly cope with the vast amount of equipment and weapons needed, nor was the government capable of organising the war effectively. There were not always enough uniforms for the troops, let alone rifles and ammunition. Men and horses were called to war without a thought for who would plough the fields. The production of food fell by half. The railway system was so involved in transporting men and equipment to the front that food was not getting to the cities. Prices rose by 500% in

three years. The government made little attempt to win over its own people. The Duma was dismissed, and the Tsar continued to appoint weak, backward-looking ministers.

Tsarina Alexandra, a German by birth, became extremely unpopular, especially as she came under the influence of Rasputin, a peasant holy-man who seemed to have the power to heal her son of his terrible blood disease. Even though Rasputin was murdered, the Tsar and Tsarina became increasingly hated. Worst of all, Russia lost the war. Victory might have been worth the sacrifice of three million soldiers and untold suffering, but defeat was not. German armies held vast areas of Russia. The Tsar commanded the armies personally. Who else was there to blame?

1917 began badly. Winter was always a hard and hungry time. Now the transport system was clogged up, preventing food from getting to the cities and even to the army at the Front. Desertions began on a large scale. In St Petersburg, now renamed Petrograd, strikes increased and even the middle classes were protesting in the streets. Riots broke out, mostly for food. The Tsarina ordered the Petrograd troops to fire on the rioters. This was not unusual but now many soldiers mutinied, shooting their officers and disappearing into the crowd. The Tsar tried to return to Petrograd from the Front but his train was deliberately diverted. In a railway siding he abdicated, amid immense popular jubilation. No-one was left to stand up for the Tsar.

Two views of Revolution: one artist ridicules the work of another

Q

1 What opposing views of revolution are expressed in the two pictures?

2 Make a list of points to show how the Great War helped to create:

a Widespread revolutionary discontent and opposition.

b A situation of declining power and control, ending in the collapse of the Tsar's rule.

Who's who in the Russian revolution

When the Tsar abdicated so suddenly on 12 March, 1917, there was no proper government to take over from him. Everything that the Tsar stood for had collapsed and it was up to the Russian people to recreate something—or, more accurately, it was up to the various revolutionary groups to see who could win power and keep it. Throughout the year these groups marched and demonstrated their different demands, as you can see in the photograph. It was not at all clear which group would succeed.

Demonstrators in 1917, 'Down with the capitalist ministers'

The Liberals

When the Tsar abdicated, the Liberals in the Duma declared themselves the Provisional (temporary) Government of Russia. Most of their support came from the educated middle classes, therefore they lacked a wide popular following. They believed in democracy and called a General Election to be held to decide who should govern Russia. During 1917 Alexander Kerensky emerged as their leader, a strong-minded, inspiring man. The Liberals, as patriotic Russians, were determined to continue the war and to drive the Germans from Russia. As Russia was in such uproar the Liberal government did not control most of the country and even in Petrograd it shared power with others.

The Social Revolutionaries (SRs)

These were by far the largest revolutionary group, their support coming mainly from the peasants. Their programme was to distribute all Russia's land to the peasants, but on other matters it was not clear. The SRs were very badly organised and badly led, and lacked support among the workers.

The Mensheviks

These were Marxists who believed in the overthrow of all classes except the working class. Most of the workers supported them and in Petrograd they had a majority in the Petrograd Workers' Council (the Soviet), an organisation that was formed when the Tsar abdicated and which shared power with the Provisional Government. They were not interested in the peasants and they did not think that the time was ripe to seize power immediately.

The Bolsheviks (communists)

The Bolsheviks, also Marxists, were the smallest group. They were very ably led and organised by Lenin, who disagreed strongly with the Mensheviks. He thought that the Bolsheviks should seize power at the first opportunity and gain support from anyone, particularly from the peasants and workers, in order to get power.

Q

1 Make a list in two columns of the strengths and weaknesses of each party.

2 Identify the party which the people shown in the photograph supported. The slogan on their banner should help you. Give the reasons for your views.

The aims and beliefs of communism

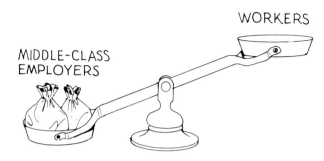

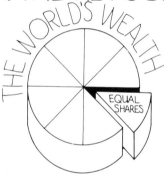

Understanding communist ideas is essential to an understanding of Russian history. These ideas were put forward mainly by Karl Marx, but Vladimir Ilych Lenin added to them. He stressed that the Communist Party would be the organisation that would bring about perfect communism.

Basic beliefs

People are born without any particular characteristics such as greed, kindness, aggression, co-operativeness. It is the society which people live in that causes them to develop their characteristics. A bad society produces bad characteristics. All existing societies are bad, unequal, unfair and ugly. Their worst feature is social class, which divides people from one another and makes them selfish and competitive.

The main social classes are the landowners, the rich industrialists (*capitalists*), the peasants who work on the land, and the workers

(*proletariat*) who work in factories. Only the working class is capable of producing a good society. The workers are so badly treated that in their suffering they help one another. Because they do not possess property and have no desire to own anything personally, they are co-operative and unselfish.

The whole of society could become like the working class—equal, peaceful and co-operative. This would be perfect communism, but how could it be achieved? Marx and Lenin identified three stages...

The three stages towards communism

Stage 1. The revolution

The Communist Party would seize power from the existing government.

Stage 2. The interval (known as the Dictatorship of the Proletariat)

No-one knew how long this stage would last, but during it the Communist Party would have to do several things . . .

● They would ensure that revolutions would break out all over the world. Unless this happened non-communist countries would turn on Russia to stamp out communism.
● They would win permanent power by wiping out the supporters of the former government such as the landowners, the capitalists and the Church, and by setting up a one-party state with complete authority.
● They would nationalise all property—land, factories, shops—by removing it from its former owners into the hands of the government.
● They would start to create equality by abolishing privileges, old customs, old beliefs and ideas. Everyone would become like the working class.

Stage 3. Perfect communism

No-one would own any private property. Everything would be owned in common. Each person would work hard for the community's sake rather than for private gain. People would become co-operative instead of competitive and aggressive. The government would fade away as there would be no need for it. There would be a completely equal, classless society all over the world for ever.

Q

1 Do you agree or disagree with the basic beliefs of communism? Give your reasons.

2 Which of the things that had to be done during Stage 2 (The interval) would be the most difficult to achieve? Why?

The revolution—1917

In 1917 there were two revolutions, one in March and the other in November. During the eight months of confusion in between, the Russian people at last could make their views heard. The revolutionary groups tried hard to gain the support of the people. Who would win? We shall follow some of these exciting events through the writings of those who took part.

The March revolution

N. Sukhanov, a Liberal, wrote . . .

On 9 March the squares were crowded with workers, dispersed by Cossacks but without energy. It was said that elections were being held for the new Soviet (Council) of Workers. The unforgettable 12 March came. The troops sided with the working-class crowd, giving up their rifles. In the Taurida Palace (where the Soviet met), one after another the regiments told of their support for the Revolution and were met with a storm of applause.

Alexander Kerensky, the democratic leader, wrote on 12 March . . .

It was an extraordinary time. We had one inspiration—Russia! In the Duma (the Parliament, which also met in the Taurida Palace), the decision was made to form a Provisional Government with complete power. Room 13 was given over to the Soviet and they had their first meeting there. By sunset on 13 March all Petrograd was in the hands of revolutionary troops.

The return of the Bolsheviks, April 1917

The Germans helped Lenin to return to Petrograd from his exile in Switzerland, hoping to worsen the revolution and weaken Russia. On his arrival, Lenin spoke to large crowds . . .

> I greet you, not knowing whether you believe the promises of the Provisional Government. But they are deceiving you. The people need peace; the people need bread, the people need land . . . we don't need any government except the Soviet.

The peasants join in the revolution, summer 1917

While the various groups in Petrograd struggled for power, the peasants all over Russia began to seize the land that they so badly wanted. A British journalist, M. P. Price, reported from Moscow . . .

> Some 300–400 soldiers gathered round. A burly soldier began to speak about his demands as a peasant. 'What we want is our land. We took up our rifles for mother earth, and we will not put them down until we get it.' Thunderous applause greeted these words. This Soldiers' Soviet was getting on its legs, going on to discuss war and peace and to demand land . . . I went to see a man who had been the local landowner. He said 'Everything used to be quiet and orderly here but trouble makers came from the towns and stirred the peasants up.'

Kerensky wanted to give land to the peasants, but would only do so when the war was over.

The July days

In July there was an uprising in Petrograd, but Kerensky firmly crushed it. The Bolsheviks were outlawed, and Lenin fled to Finland. The Bolsheviks took part in the rising, but was this part of a deliberate *plan* to seize power?

Stalin, the Bolshevik leader, recorded shortly afterwards . . .

> I proposed to prevent the demonstration. The SRs and the Mensheviks, who are now saying that we planned the uprising, seem to have forgotten this fact. Soon it became obvious that it was impossible to stop the demonstration and we decided to take part.

Sukhanov, the liberal, wrote years later in his memoirs . . .

> Lenin was definitely planning an uprising to seize power. This was what Lunacharsky (a leading Bolshevik) told me—that is, this is how I remember it. I may have forgotten, confused or distorted the story. But the precise finding out of an historical fact is the business of historians, and I'm writing my personal memoirs.

Lunacharsky wrote later . . .

> An attempt to seize power by the Bolsheviks was extremely risky. The time was not yet ripe. I clearly realised that no-one could predict how the day would end.

The Kerensky offensive, summer 1917

Kerensky ordered a large, last offensive to defeat the Germans. It failed. An official army report stated . . .

> There is a complete lack of confidence in the officers. The influence of Bolshevik ideas is spreading. To this must be added a general weariness and a desire for peace at any price.

Soldiers began to desert in increasing numbers. You can see this happening in the photograph.

A soldier attempts to prevent his comrades from deserting

The deteriorating situation in Petrograd, October 1917

The Minister of Supplies reported . . .

> Bread supplies are provided for the next 7 or 8 days and rations will continue. Telegrams state that the plundering of food trains is very common. In Saratov the number of starving grows every day, becoming more menacing.

The Provisional Government was failing to provide the basic needs of the people.

The November revolution

By October the Bolsheviks had built up more support than their rivals, but Kerensky's Provisional Government stood in their way. Lenin persuaded his Bolshevik colleagues that the time had come to act. Kerensky, feeling that he had lost the revolution, fled. The cruiser Aurora fired the signal to take the Winter Palace, where the government still lingered on. John Reed, an American supporter of Lenin, wrote . . .

> The doors of the Palace stood wide open, light streamed out and from the huge building came not the slightest sound. We were carried along by the eager wave of men into the entrance hall. The looting was just beginning when someone cried 'Stop! Put everything back! Property of the People!'

The Bolsheviks were in power.

Q

1 Did the Bolsheviks deliberately plan the July Days uprising? Assess each piece of evidence for reliability, then come to a conclusion.
2 Kerensky and his Provisional Government made several mistakes and failed to deal with several serious problems. List these.
3 Use the facts on these two pages to show how Lenin's view of the people's demands, made in his 1917 speech, was correct.

The Civil War, 1918–1920
Russia's suffering

Although the Bolsheviks were, in theory, the Government, they only controlled the area between Petrograd and Moscow. Even here they did not have the loyalty of the majority. There were still important groups determined to oppose the communists, including Britain, France and America, and soon a civil war broke out, one of the worst in the world's history. The Mensheviks had dropped out of sight and the SRs were never really capable of organising large armies. The Bolsheviks' main enemies, therefore, were the Whites. Read these three definitions of the Whites.
1 From a speech of Lenin . . .

> Tsarist generals and landlords. Russian and foreign capitalists.

2 From a Soviet text book . . .

> The overthrown classes, directly supported by the imperialist states, unleashed a bloody civil war.

3 From the memoirs of an upper class woman who escaped from Russia at the time . . .

> My brother joined the 'Volunteers', as those resisting the Bolsheviks called themselves at that time. Incidentally, historians are mistaken when they treat the whole of the 'Volunteer' movement as Tsarist and backward-looking. The only thing these groups had in common was their

resistance to Bolshevism. That was why so many university students, who were enthusiastic revolutionaries in March 1917, were joining the volunteers in March 1918.

Steps to civil war

It is not difficult to explain why civil war broke out in 1918. It soon became obvious what the Bolsheviks intended to do and that the only way to remove them was by force. You can see from the following Bolshevik decisions that millions of Russians would oppose them . . .

The abolition of the National Assembly

This was Russia's first and last freely-elected Parliament which met shortly after the November Revolution. One quarter of its members were Bolsheviks. Most of the rest were SRs. Lenin sent it packing after only one day.

The beginnings of a one-party state

Lenin immediately abolished the freedom of the press, began to eliminate other parties and to persecute the Church and priests very harshly. In December 1917 he set up the Cheka, the secret police, to eliminate opposition. Felix Dzerzhinsky soon became hated and feared as its harsh leader.

Economic policy, December 1917

1 In agriculture Lenin issued the Decree on Land, distributing all confiscated land among the peasants.
2 In industry Lenin issued the Decree on Workers' Control, which gave the factories to the workers.

Peace with Germany

Lenin had to overrule even his own colleagues to make the Treaty of Brest-Litovsk in March 1918, because it was so harsh. It gave huge amounts of land, people and wealth to Germany, but Lenin realised he could not fight the Germans as well as the Whites.

The war

You can see from the map that the Whites

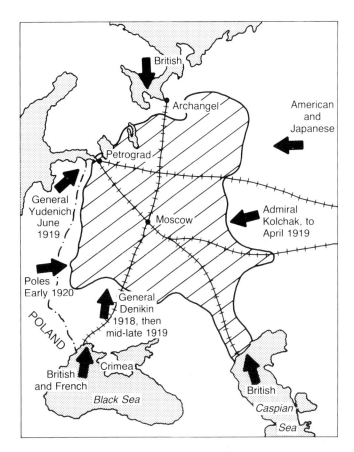

The Civil War

attacked the Reds—the Bolsheviks—in waves, from different directions. Lenin left the running of the Civil War to Leon Trotsky, who built up the Red Army from virtually nothing. In 1919 the Reds were pushed further and further towards Petrograd and Moscow. However, Trotsky was defending a single area and had the use of the rail network to transport Red troops from one front to another. The Whites had no such advantages and, by 1921, the last Whites were being hounded down. Their supporters, the British and French and the Poles were forced to leave Russia.

How well did the Bolsheviks succeed in the Civil War?

Remember that the Bolsheviks had very clear ideas, laid down by Marx and Lenin, of what they were doing. Russia was in the interval between the revolution and perfect communism and the communists had several aims to achieve . . .

A propaganda poster from the Civil War showing troops seizing grain

A poster showing foreign powers with Russian generals as their dogs

Aim 1. World revolution

The Bolsheviks, expecting revolutions to break out everywhere, set up the Communist International or Comintern, whose agents fostered revolution throughout the world. The cover of one of their British magazines is illustrated on this page. In fact no other revolutions occurred and Russia remained the only communist state.

Aim 2. To eliminate opposition and set up a one-party state

The communists had certainly wiped out other parties during the Civil War. All decisions were taken by the Communist Party's ruling body, the Politburo, and the Party was beginning to dominate every part of Russian life. Dzerzhinsky and his Cheka eliminated rivals very effectively.

The Red Terror, begun in 1918 when the SRs revolted in Moscow, removed opposition by mass executions and imprisonment. Often whole groups of people, such as priests, landowners or intellectuals were killed. The Tsar and his family were murdered.

Aim 3. To nationalise all property

In the summer of 1918 Lenin introduced 'War Communism'. In agriculture he needed more control in order to get food to the starving cities and to the army. However, he did not dare take back the land from the peasants in case they rose up in rebellion. Instead the Cheka and the Red Army brutally seized all crops, leaving the peasants with only enough to feed themselves. In retaliation the peasants refused to plant crops in 1919 and 1920. This, together with a terrible drought, caused a famine.

In industry the workers had failed to run the factories properly. Now the factories were taken from the workers and nationalised but even so, industry simply collapsed.

The first issue in English of *Communist International*

Aim 4. To start to create genuine equality and to destroy old ideas

Laws were passed abolishing ranks and titles, and banning non-communist ideas like democracy and religion. The Church was persecuted to remove its influence over the people. The government tried to impose strict and equal rationing of food but this proved impossible. Two categories of people gained extra rations, pay and privileges. These were party members and 'specialists' such as managers, doctors and army officers.

Q

1 Which of the three extracts on page 42, in your opinion, best describes the Whites? Give your reasons.
2 Which groups and types of people would be opposed to Lenin's actions leading to the Civil War (Steps to Civil War)?
3 Why was it better for the Reds to have the White attacks coming from different directions? Use the map to help you.

4 Which of the four aims would the Bolsheviks regard as the most important to achieve? Why?
5 Take each aim in turn and say whether the Bolsheviks had achieved it fully, partly or not at all.
6 Which of the propaganda posters is Red and which one is White? Give your reasons.
7 What do you think would be the attitude of most British people to the Communist International magazine cover?

The end of the Civil War and the coming of NEP

The results of the Civil War

1 General exhaustion

On top of the three million soldiers lost in the Great War, over ten million people had died, mostly through malnutrition. There was a general feeling that people had had enough and that a period of rest and recovery was needed.

2 Political results

The communists had won the war, but in March 1921 came a shattering blow to Lenin. The Red sailors of the Kronstadt naval base near Petrograd, who had always loyally supported communism, now revolted against Lenin. They demanded an end to 'War Communism', especially the seizing of grain from the peasants, and more democracy for Russia. They declared that they had not fought for a dictatorship. Lenin did not wait to consider their case. He sent the Red Army across the frozen sea to storm the base and slaughter the mutineers. However, he was greatly disturbed by the revolt. He called it 'a

A government poster showing a starving peasant, 'Help'

flash of lightning that lit up the real situation'. There was a danger of peasant risings all over Russia.

3 Foreign results

The communists had chased away foreign invading troops, but Lenin was certain that the non-communist powers would try to destroy communism in Russia if they had the opportunity. Any further turmoil in the country would weaken Russia and might give the foreigners their opportunity.

4 Economic results

In agriculture 'War Communism' had succeeded in getting food to the cities, but in the long term it failed. The production of food was down to half its normal levels and the peasants were refusing to plant crops for the year's harvest.

In industry, 'War Communism' had failed to prevent an almost total collapse. Only one fifth of normal industrial levels were being reached, the railway network was breaking down and the cities were emptying of people.

The time for decisions

A furious argument raged in the Politburo. Trotsky wanted to ignore the results of the civil war and go ahead with the nationalisation of land. 'Permanent revolution' he called it. Lenin overruled Trotsky. Only a few days after the Kronstadt Rising, Lenin announced that 'War Communism' would end and that the peasants could keep their crops. He called this NEP—New Economic Policy.

Elizabeth Fen, an upper class woman who left Russia soon afterwards, wrote . . .

> Lenin cared not at all for the people, but only for his theories and the power to try them out—I am sure that he permitted NEP only because War Communism had brought Russia to the edge of complete economic collapse, not because men, women and children were dying of disease and starvation in their millions. In my view the man was a monster.

Q

1 Why did Lenin call the Kronstadt Rising 'a flash of lightning that lit up the real situation'?
2 What, in your opinion, is the purpose of the government poster on page 45?

3 Do you agree fully, completely or not at all with Elizabeth Fen's version of the reasons for NEP? Use the section headed **The results of the Civil War** to help you in this. Explain the reasons in order of their importance.

New Economic Policy, 1921–1928 Success or failure?

NEP is very important in the history of Soviet Russia. Lenin did not like NEP, but at the time Russia seemed to have no alternative. From the brief description below of the aims and achievements of NEP, you can work out why Lenin did not like it and whether it succeeded or not.

The economy

Aims

1 To cause the economy—industry and agriculture, to recover to its former levels.
2 Then to develop industry rapidly to make Russia an advanced, industrial country.

Achievements

1 **Agriculture.** The richer peasants, known as Kulaks—about one million in all—benefitted

most from NEP, keeping their profits, buying up smaller farms and employing poorer peasants as labourers. They became quite well off. By 1928 agriculture had recovered its former levels, but it did not develop any further. It remained very backward indeed.

2 **Industry.** Lenin allowed small businessmen, known as NEPmen, to set up small shops, stalls and factories and to keep the profits. Shortages of goods began to disappear and the former levels were achieved, but there was little growth after that. In large-scale industry the companies remained nationalised. Again, they recovered their previous levels but failed to grow further.

Politics

Aims

To keep complete power in the hands of the Communist Party and to keep a watchful eye on the Kulaks and NEPmen in case they gained too much influence and wealth.

Achievements

Russia remained a one-party state and the communists severely persecuted any remaining SRs, Mensheviks and Liberals. However, many communists became more and more suspicious that the Kulaks and NEPmen would turn into a capitalist class.

Social Affairs

Aims

To prepare the way for communism by stamping out older beliefs and values and to encourage equality.

Achievements

There was a very successful literacy drive, so that most people could read by 1928. Religion was severely attacked and many of its leaders killed or imprisoned. There was very strict censorship of the media and the arts, but new classless attitudes were very slow to grow. Communist Party members, now one million

A street market in Moscow, 1920

strong, and 'specialists' like professional people, officers and managers continued to get much higher salaries and privileges.

Foreign affairs

Aims

To build Russia into a stronger country to cope with the expected attacks from capitalist countries. To prevent the capitalist countries, especially Britain, Germany and France from joining together to attack Russia.

Achievements

Russia did not develop the industry to make her a strong military power. At first Russia managed to keep the British, French and Germans apart from one another, but, in the later 1920s, they began to become more friendly. There was no immediate danger of an attack, but the communists feared that this would happen before very long.

The theory of NEP

Lenin hated NEP because it went against communist ideas. However, when it had achieved its aims, it would be stopped and then the state could move towards true communism. Lenin called this 'one step backwards, two steps forward'.

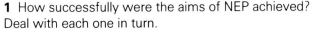

1 How successfully were the aims of NEP achieved? Deal with each one in turn.

2 Explain briefly what Lenin meant by the slogan 'one step backwards, two steps forward'.

3 What is there about the activities in the market, pictured above, which many firm communists would find wrong and offensive?

Extension

An assessment of Lenin

In 1924 Lenin died at the age of 55 after a series of strokes which left him increasingly paralysed. During his illness we know that he thought a great deal about his life and achievements. Lenin was certainly a man who had been inspired and guided by the ideals of perfect communism when making his decisions.

What do you think that Lenin's thoughts would have been on the following statements? With some he would have been satisfied, with others not. Some he regarded as necessary and unavoidable, others were beyond his control.

Lenin seized power in November 1917.

Lenin nationalised industry but did not succeed in reviving it.

Lenin allowed party members and specialists to have extra privileges, rations and wages.

Lenin introduced NEP, which went against the ideas of communism.

Lenin failed to achieve world revolution.

Lenin failed to achieve perfect communism.

Lenin's policy of War Communism resulted in famine.

Lenin introduced the Cheka and the Red Terror, causing terrible suffering and death.

Lenin won the Civil War.

Lenin failed to nationalise the farms and instead gave the land to the peasants.

Lenin made Marxism work—so far—by always putting the power of the Communist Party before anything else.

After Lenin, who next?

Stalin

Stalin or Trotsky?

In 1922 Lenin suffered the first of his several strokes. Lenin himself wrote a letter advising the Communist Party to choose a group of leaders rather than a single individual to succeed him. He warned of the danger of the Party splitting into two and losing its power. Of the two potential leaders, Trotsky and Stalin, Lenin considered Trotsky to be the most capable and inspiring but feared that he was too arrogant and impatient. Instead Lenin built up Stalin, appointing him to the vital position of Party Secretary-General. However, he then quarrelled with Stalin and, in his letter, wrote a PS, advising the Party to replace Stalin with someone 'more patient, more loyal, more prepared to listen to his comrades and less inclined to do as he pleases'.

In fact the Party did not choose the next leader by a simple vote. In the years following Lenin's death in 1924, Stalin gradually emerged as sole leader, and Trotsky was demoted and finally exiled in 1928. The reasons were as follows . . .

1 Stalin's position as General Secretary gave him the right to appoint high officials who were his own loyal followers.

2 Trotsky was not very good at scheming and did not find supporters at the top of the Party.

7 Stalin supported NEP, which most communist leaders supported, whereas Trotsky hated NEP and wanted 'permanent revolution'.

3 Stalin cleverly linked up with other leaders, who were also afraid of Trotsky. Then he got rid of them too.

4 Lenin died too soon. If he had lived, he would certainly have removed Stalin.

The words of an ordinary Russian who worked in Moscow at the time are very revealing . . .

5 Trotsky was very unpopular because he was so brilliant and arrogant. He had only joined the Party in 1917.

6 Stalin persuaded the Party not to publish Lenin's letter for fear of causing a split in the Party. Trotsky agreed with this.

I do not think that ordinary men and women at that time understood the government set-up at all well; I certainly did not. The dreaded name of Dzerzhinsky was much more on people's lips than that of any other high official. Trotsky was well-known as the man who had created the well-disciplined Red Army. Stalin's name was rarely mentioned.

— Q —

1 Why did the ordinary people know so little about the quarrels about Lenin's successor?

2 Write a short explanation of why you think Stalin succeeded in becoming leader. Re-arrange the reasons given above in the most sensible order.

Stalin and the end of NEP

Stalin

A historian of Stalin's rule has written of him . . .

It is my belief that Stalin was a very gifted politician, and one of the great figures of the twentieth century. This does not mean that he was a good man. He had a dark, even evil side to his nature. His suspiciousness resulted in paranoia at the end of his life. He had a first class memory which did not permit him to forget old grudges. Lenin, like Stalin, had little time for opponents and was capable of dealing ruthlessly with them, although the blood that Lenin shed was a drop in the ocean compared with Stalin.

Many historians have a similar viewpoint. At the end of this chapter you will be able to make your own assessment of Stalin. He was a very difficult man to understand. At school he bullied others and came to hate the authorities, not only of the school but of Russia itself. After joining the Bolshevik Party he became active in spreading propaganda and in raising money, even by robbing banks. He was imprisoned and exiled several times before 1917. Then he took a minor part in the Revolution and rose high in the Communist Party as an efficient and ruthless organiser in charge of Russia's minority races. His frightening combination of qualities helped to make his rule one of the most brutal in the world:

He was a ruthless, cruel man, capable of terrible brutality.

He was a cunning, clever politician, especially when pursuing his own career.

He was an ambitious man, more interested in

his own power than in any grand theories. He was an insecure, suspicious man, never trusting anyone and always feeling that others wanted to do him—and Russia—down.

The ending of NEP, 1928

Stalin was the man who suddenly ended NEP in 1928 and changed Russia's direction. We do not know for sure why he did this but have to look at the situation in 1928 through his eyes. There are several possible reasons.

—NEP did not make Russia strong enough in industrial and military might to withstand the capitalist attack that Stalin expected in the future.

—NEP allowed opposition to grow in Russia, especially from the Kulaks who threatened communism.

—NEP was not truly communist because it allowed private ownership and profit.

—NEP, with its inefficient peasant farms, could not produce enough food or modernise agriculture.

Q

1 Do you think that it is possible to see a man's character from his photograph, such as the one of Stalin? Explain your answer.

2 Write a paragraph on the reasons for Stalin's decision to end NEP, in order of importance. Try to look at it from the point of view of Stalin's character.

Stalinism: Socialism in one country

Stalinism is the name we give to the type of communism that grew up in Russia after 1928. Stalin's own favourite term for his system was 'Socialism in one country'. He expressed his views about this in a speech in 1931 . . .

> All countries beat Russia for her backwardness: her military backwardness, her cultural backwardness, her political backwardness, her industrial backwardness, her agricultural backwardness. That is why we must no longer lag behind. In the past we Communists had no fatherland, but now we have a fatherland and we will defend it. Do you want our socialist fatherland to be beaten? If you do not want this you must put an end to its backwardness. There is no other way. We are fifty or a hundred years behind the advanced countries. We must make good this distance in ten years. Either we do it, or they crush us.

Stalinism was what we call a *totalitarian* system of running a country. TOTAL power was in the hands of the government, which interfered in every single aspect of the country's life. Stalin was determined to use his power to change Russia completely by making it a modern, industrialised nation.

The economy: The Five Year Plans

In 1928 Stalin gave to Gosplan, the government's planning body, the task of supervising the whole economy. This it did, and still does, with Five-Year Plans. Targets were set for all products from steel works to radishes. Everything was decided

Stalin's enemies rage against the first Five Year Plan

by Gosplan—prices, quantities, wages, design, the method of production and so on. The first plan was very optimistic indeed, hoping to double or even treble the output of most products.

The plans linked industry and agriculture. Agriculture could be nationalised and the land seized from the peasants, which would provide the money needed to invest in industry. However, the main emphasis would always be on industry, especially on heavy industry—coal,

oil, steel, engineering and chemicals. Every factory, every team, every worker had a plan.

Government and power

Stalin was determined to make Russia a more totalitarian state than it already was. He was carrying out such huge changes so quickly that he needed more power and control to make sure his plans worked. Russia was in for a hard time.

Q

1 Write one sentence explaining the meaning of 'Socialism in one country'.
2 What was the link between industrial and military power?

3 Who, in your opinion, would oppose Stalin's plans for the nationalisation of agriculture?
4 Why would a totalitarian system of power suit Stalin *personally*?
5 How does the poster illustrate Stalin's plans?

The Economy: The Five Year Plans

The collectivisation of agriculture

In 1928 Stalin began to collectivise Russia's 25 million privately-owned farms. This meant combining approximately seventy farms into a vast collective farm, known as a *Kolkhoz*. In this way the land was no longer owned privately by the peasants but was run by party officials and managers. Peasants became labourers on what had been their own land. There were three possible reasons for this:
—Larger farms, run on modern lines, would produce more food and more profit for Russia.
—Collective farms were more in line with communist theory because they ended private ownership and profit.
—Collectivisation would break the power of the peasants, especially that of the Kulaks, once and for all.

Two views of collectivisation

Version 1. The Soviet version

Read this account from a Soviet textbook printed in English in 1982 for foreign readers . . .

The setting up of collective farms is an important result of the first Five Year Plan. Immediately after the end of the Civil War poor peasants showed a desire to work collectively (together). In the late 1920s, when the first tractor factories were started, it became possible to give more money and machinery to agriculture. After that not only poor but middle peasants joined collective farms. Full collectivisation was introduced in whole regions. By the middle of 1930 six million peasant farms were linked in collective farms, and in the summer of 1931 over 60% of peasant families joined collective farms. An end was put to exploitation in the countryside; thanks to collectivisation the last exploiting class in the country—the kulaks—was eliminated.

Sydney and Beatrice Webb, British Labour politicians, who visited Russia twice in the 1930s at the invitation of the Soviet Government, wrote . . .

Strong must have been the faith of the men who, in the interests of what they considered to be the good of the country, could take such an important decision as the rejection of one million Kulaks from their farms. The Kulaks were the oppressors of their poorer neighbours.

Without expecting to convince those who are prejudiced, we give the conclusion of our two visits and of our study of all the available evidence. There was undoubtedly a partial failure of crops. There is always a failure of crops somewhere.

What the government was faced with was a widespread refusal by the peasants to the policy of collectivisation, encouraged by the disloyal sections of the population. Drastic measures were taken against those in the villages who were interfering with the setting up of the collectives, often by personal violence and wilful damage.

Later the government also forcibly removed the peasants who were without food to where they could be put to work. It could hardly have done otherwise. It is not denied that in the cases of whole villages being removed, as in the case of individual Kulaks, great hardship was inflicted. Without such suffering, it is argued, the rapid collectivisation of farms, which seemed to be the only way to increase the food supply, could not have been achieved.

The painting of the peasants at the harvest festival shows the official impression of life on a collective farm.

Version 2. A Western version

An account below contains the facts found in most Western history books about Stalin's collectivisation . . .

The first Five Year Plan stated that 20% of the land should be collectivised voluntarily. The peasants, however, showed no desire to give up their land and resisted by keeping the grain they had grown. Stalin, therefore, in 1929, ordered full-scale collectivisation to be forced on the peasants. Severe laws were passed against kulaks but in fact anyone who resisted was ordered to be treated as a kulak. Most kulak families were not allowed to join collectives. The lucky kulaks were uprooted and deported to barren parts of Russia. Even non-kulak families were put into labour camps. If a village resisted its leaders were often hanged. In some cases whole villages were machine-gunned. Kulak children were sometimes left to die. Estimates of peasant families destroyed in this way vary from one to five million.

The peasants resisted violently. As well as rising up all over Russia they burned their crops, refused to plant seed, destroyed their equipment and slaughtered about half of Russia's livestock. In the Spring of 1930, Stalin called off collectivisation and the peasants poured out of the Kolkhozes. But he only wanted them to plant the crops and soon the whole process began

Official view of a collective farm celebrating harvest

again. Stalin planned a terrible blow against the peasants but he did not have to use it. Famine did the work for him. Millions more were added to the total of dead. The government made no attempt to stop the famine or soften the suffering, though it made sure that food got through to the cities.

By 1933 all of Russia's farms were collectivised, the kulaks were literally eliminated and the rest of the peasants subdued.

One British MP visiting Russia wrote in 1932 . . .

In a train a communist denied to me that there was a famine. I threw orange peel into the spittoon. A peasant devoured it. The communist grew quiet. The government's policy of collectivisation and the peasants' resistance to it have brought Russia to the worst catastrophe since the famine of 1921.

Another British visitor, *The Guardian* reporter Malcolm Muggeridge, wrote in 1933 . . .

I heard again and again and again, 'We have nothing. They have taken everything away.' It was true that the famine is an organised one. It is literally true that whole villages have been exiled. I saw myself a group of twenty peasants being marched off under escort. This is so common a sight that it no longer arouses even curiosity.

The photograph of starving children creates a different impression of collectivisation from the official painting.

Starving, homeless children, 1932

Facts about collectivisation

	1928	1933	1940
Grain production in million tons	73	68	95
Cattle in millions	70	38	60

—Q—

1 In which order of importance do you think that the reasons for collectivisation appeared to Stalin? Give the reasons for your first choice.
2a Pick out the main differences between the two versions of collectivisation.

b The Western version is much closer to the truth than the Soviet version. Give reasons for this, after weighing up the reliability and usefulness of the various pieces of evidence, including the pictures.
3 Did collectivisation work economically? See the figures. What was the 'cost' of collectivisation?

Industrialisation

Facts and figures about industrialisation

An American's description of Stalingrad . . .

The Soviets launched one of their most ambitious projects—the erection of a monumental tractor plant, one of the largest in the world. On 17 June, 1930, in the midst of the first Five Year Plan, the first tractor rolled off the assembly belt of the Stalingrad factory. By the end of 1932 the population of Stalingrad leaped to 400,000. The Second Plan came and passed. The population rose to half a million. The Third Plan arrived. Stalingrad had changed its very appearance. It became, as the Russians came to express themselves, 'an industrial giant', one of the mightiest in the country. Shipbuilding, machine-building, the manufacture of high-grade steel and, of course, an arms factory.

	1928 (end of NEP)	1932 (end of First Plan)	1937 (end of Second Plan)	1940 (last full year of Third Plan)
Coal (tons)	36	64	129	166
Steel (tons)	7	12	31	33
Oil (barrels)	12	21	29	31
Electricity (kw)	5	17	36	48

By 1940, Russia had overtaken Britain and France in industrial production. Only America and Germany were greater and Russia was almost as productive as Germany. Russia's growth rate was the highest of all, 9% a year.

Spectacular projects

Stalin and his planners were fond of immense enterprises like the Stalingrad Tractor Works. Others were the Dneiper Dam, the White Sea Canal, the huge new coal and steel towns of Magnitogorsk and Novosibirsk and the vast oil complex of the Don Basin.

How was industrialisation achieved?

Russia's working class increased from about 18% of the population to 35% in the 1930s. Their hard work was vital to the success of the Plans. Why did they work so hard?

1 Propaganda

The media concentrated on economic growth, especially on Stalin's grand projects. Each workplace held special meetings to work up

Above The Dneiper dam with statues and avenues for sightseers

Below This chemical works was built in six months

enthusiasm among its workers and create a sense of pride. 'Stakhanovism' was a less popular kind of propaganda, designed to spur on workers to exceed their targets. Alexis Stakhanov was a miner who shifted 102 tons of coal in a single day—six times his target. The media dwelt on his exploits and targets were continually raised to keep up the pressure.

2 Rewards

There were several ways of rewarding the workers. One was to award special medals, such as 'Hero of Socialist Labour' to outstanding workers. Another was to give extra privileges. Social reforms too were introduced and living standards and conditions rose rapidly. The government's policy was to make the essentials of life—food, housing and transport—very cheap indeed. Despite this, food was often in short supply and housing was always very overcrowded and poor. Education improved considerably, although secondary education was still not free. The best social reform of all was a free and efficient health service. These reforms were much more commonly provided for industrial workers in the towns than for peasants in the countryside.

The main reward, however, was higher wages, especially for certain categories. 'Specialists' continued to get much higher pay and privileges than anyone else, but workers as a whole got much higher wages than peasants. Workers with greater skills or greater productivity were paid more. Stalin said openly in 1931 . . .

> Wage scales make no difference between skilled and unskilled labour, between heavy work and light work. Thus the unskilled worker lacks the incentive to become skilled worker and is deprived of the prospect of advancement. In order to end this evil we must abolish equality in wages.

A poster for the factory wall with spaces for the names of the worst 'slackers'

3 Discipline

Harsh rules were applied at work. Many workers had their pay cut if they failed to reach their targets. They were ridiculed in public, as in the factory poster, and given harder jobs. Absenteeism, lateness and poor workmanship were made criminal offences. The death penalty was introduced for theft from work. For most workers the 1930s were a period of misery, suffering and hardship.

Q

1 Why does the writer say 'of course' in his last sentence on the growth of Stalingrad?

2 Why do you think that immense projects appealed so much to Stalin?

3 In what ways could pictures of spectacular projects, like those pictured on page 54, be used for propaganda purposes?

4 Assess the economic success of the Five Year Plans by 1940. In what ways would Stalin be pleased? Use the facts and figures to help you.

5 Why do you think Stakhanovism was unpopular?

6 Explain how different types of people would be affected by the three methods of making people work harder. Use the poster in your answer.

Stalin's politicial system—totalitarianism

A totalitarian system, in which the government controls every human activity, suited Stalin perfectly. He used three ways to impose his power – the Communist Party, Terror and Propaganda.

1 The Communist Party

Stalin, like Lenin, believed that only the Party should have power and influence in Russia. He certainly made the Party into a ruling class that dominated Russia very efficiently and deliberately gave better pay, food, housing, medical facilities and other privileges to party members. Lenin had done this reluctantly, but Stalin seems to have approved of it. He discouraged workers and peasants from joining the Party and even at the highest levels would not allow criticism or discussion. The Communist Party increased its strangle-grip on Russia, and membership increased to 3½ million in the 1930s. Even so it was a dangerous ruling class to belong to.

2 Terror and purges

Lenin had used terror ruthlessly during the Civil War. Under Stalin it became a routine part of life. The secret police, known as the NKVD, under Yagoda and Yeshov developed especially brutal methods of terrorising its victims in particular and the entire Russian people in general. A whole network of labour camps grew up in the most inhospitable areas of Russia, where the hardest work was to be found. In 1938 there were approximately eight million inmates and the death rate was 20% a year. Even if a sentence were completed, a new one would be reimposed. Virtually no-one came out of the camps in the 1930s. One lucky woman who was later released wrote about her experiences . . .

We set out every morning in the horror march to the gold mines. The main food was bread, but the quantity was decided by the amount of work a prisoner performed. This was listed by free wardens or by real criminals who are favoured for such posts. It is normal for the wardens to say that part of the work done by the workers has been done by the criminals who 'grease' the wardens in various ways. Even if the work is listed honestly it is impossible for a prisoner to complete his quota. Since he cannot do his full quota, he does not receive the full bread ration; his undernourished body is less able to meet the demands, and so he gets less and less bread, and in the end he is so weakened that only clubbings can force him to drag himself from camp to gold mine.

He is too weak to work, too weak to defend himself when a criminal punches him in the face and takes away his day's ration of bread. He uses his last remaining strength to creep off to a corner where the guards cannot reach him. Only the fearful cold finds him out and mercifully gives him his sole desire: peace, sleep, death.

The purges

Lenin had 'purged' the party—removed 'undesirable' members from it—ever since 1918. Stalin made purges a regular occurrence. The real purges began in 1935, resulting from the murder of Kirov.

Was Stalin involved in Kirov's murder? Background information

In 1934 Kirov, the Communist Party chief in Leningrad and generally regarded as the most suitable alternative to Stalin, was murdered. His killer was Nikolayev, who had been a loyal communist but who had become embittered. Kirov's bodyguard was not present in his office at the time of the murder, but Kirov was known to dislike being closely guarded. Immediately after the murder, Stalin travelled to Leningrad and personally took charge of the murder investigation. Nikolayev was immediately executed and Stalin issued a law making the trial and execution of such 'terrorists' much easier.

Read the following extracts:

1 An extract from speeches made by Khruschev who became the leader of Russia after Stalin's death in the 1950s. He openly attacked Stalin's rule and destroyed his reputation in these speeches . . .

Nikolayev made two attempts before the murder to get into Kirov's office. Arms were found on him but the Secret Police released him on both occasions. After the murder, when Kirov's bodyguard was being taken for questioning, his car was involved in an accident, deliberately arranged. This was no accident but a carefully planned crime. Who would have done this? The driver of the car is still alive. He says the man sitting next to him deliberately steered the car at a house. Later he was told that the bodyguard had been lost in the accident. This means that someone wanted him liquidated and to remove all traces. After the murder, top officials in Leningrad were given light sentences, but in 1937 were shot to cover up the traces of those who organised Kirov's killing.

2 An extract from the autobiography of Stalin's daughter, written in the 1960s. She was a teenager at the time of Kirov's murder . . .

My father was deeply affected by the death of my mother (in 1932) and the murder of Kirov. From this point onwards he trusted no-one.

3 An extract from the biography of Stalin by the historian Isaac Deutscher . . .

It was Kirov's easy-going attitude that enabled Nikolayev to get into his office, for Kirov objected to being guarded by the police. At any rate the police had knowledge of the planned attempt and had done nothing to prevent it.

The assassination alarmed Stalin. Stalin now acted on the idea that it was not enough to hit at his opponents, but to root out the atmosphere that bred them. The purges began.

4 An extract from a history textbook written by the historian Martin McCauley . . .

Some of the details of the assassination are still not known, but it would appear that Stalin was implicated. Kirov was the only likely alternative to Stalin. The murder started off the purges.

The purges at their worst

The first purge was of the Leningrad branch of the Communist Party, which soon spread to the whole Party and to other groups. The purges were at their worst in 1936 and 1937, but lessened in 1938, although they never really ended until the 1950s. Long lists of names were drawn up every day to be signed by Stalin. Victims were shot at once or disappeared for ever into the labour camps. Often their wives and husbands were purged. Special institutions were set up for any small children that they left.

Only a few of the more important victims were tried in staged 'show trials'. Zinoviev, Kamenev and others, old Bolsheviks, confessed to ridiculous crimes like spying for Germany and wrecking trains. Their trials were filmed.

The purges came in waves which removed whole categories of people—about one half of the whole Communist Party, including all its old leaders, over half the officers in the armed forces, including most of the generals and admirals, many scientists, writers, intellectuals, managers and engineers. Estimates of those killed range from one to fifteen million.

It is impossible to assess the results of the terror and the purges. We cannot imagine the suffering, the despair, the hurt or the deaths of such multitudes. The purges weakened the armed forces and caused industrial growth to slow down. They paralysed the whole of society, making Russians terrified to do anything on their own initiative.

— Q —

1 The woman's description of the labour camp on p. 56 is very biased—*and rightly so*. Do you agree?
2 Was Stalin involved in Kirov's murder? In answering this question assess the reliability and usefulness of each of the four pieces of evidence in turn. Take into account the background information too. Then come to your conclusion.

3 Propaganda, indoctrination and censorship

Stalin used every means possible to control the hearts and minds of his subjects, especially the media. Education was used to indoctrinate children in communist ideas. All Soviet children had to join the various youth movements for their age group—the Grandchildren of Lenin (ages 5–11), the Pioneers (age 11–17) and Komsomol (ages 17–25). The arts were strictly controlled and censored. Literature, drama, films, music and painting had to be simple, easily understood by the people and full of heroic stories about the joy of communism. This style was known as 'Socialist Realism' and many untrustworthy artists and writers were purged.

Stalin himself was the subject of much of this propaganda. His part in the Revolution, insignificant in reality, was exaggerated. He was seen as Lenin's right-hand man. Stalin was soon being portrayed as an all-powerful, all-seeing protector of his people. The following speech, by the writer Avdienko, was typical of the time.

> Thank you, Stalin. Thank you because I am joyful. Thank you because I am well. The men of all ages will call on his name, which is strong, beautiful, wise and marvellous. Every time I have found myself in his presence, I have been captivated by his strength, his charm, his grandeur. I have experienced a great desire to sing, to cry out, to shout with joy. I love a young woman with a renewed love, and shall perpetuate myself in my children—all thanks to thee, O great educator, Stalin. Everything belongs to thee, chief of our great country. And when the woman I love presents me with a child, the first word it shall utter will be: Stalin.

On the other hand, the poem by Osip Mandelstam, which contained the section below, received no publicity at all.

> All we hear is the Kremlin mountaineer,
> the murderer and peasant slayer.
> His fingers are fat as grubs,
> And the words, final as lead weights, fall from his lips.
> Around him a rabble of thin-necked leaders—
> fawning half-men for him to play with.
> And every killing is a treat
> for the broad-chested Southerner.

Peasants queuing eagerly to join a collective farm

Lenin and Stalin planning the Revolution. Such a scene had never really taken place

A meeting of the Politburo. In reality, Stalin made all decisions alone

1 All the pictures in this section were used for propaganda. To what use do you think they were put?
2 The writer Avdienko was certainly not lying when he made his speech. What was your initial reaction to the speech? Explain why it was taken seriously at the time.

3 Why did Mandelstam's poem receive no publicity? What do you think happened to Mandelstam?
4 Which of the three methods of controlling Russia was most effective in your view: The Communist Party's dominance; Terror; Propaganda? How are the three linked together?

Extension: Assessment of Stalin

Two views of Stalin

The poet Yevtushenko wrote about Stalin's death . . .

The whole of Russia wept. So did I. I'll never forget going to see Stalin's coffin. The crowd turned into a monstrous whirlpool. Suddenly I saw that a young girl was being pushed by the crowd against a post. I did not hear, but I felt with my body the cracking of her brittle bones as they were broken on the post. I felt I was treading on something soft. It was a human body. I was carried along by the crowd. I was saved by my height. Short people were smothered alive. We were caught between some houses and trucks. 'Get the trucks out of the way!' people howled. 'I can't. I've got my instructions,' a very young, bewildered police officer shouted back. And people were being hurtled against the trucks by the crowd, and their heads smashed. The sides of the trucks were running with blood. All at once I felt a savage hatred for everything that had caused that 'No instructions' shouted when people were dying of someone's stupidity. For the first time in my life I thought with hatred of the man we were burying. He could not be innocent of the disaster. 'Did you see Stalin', my mother asked me. 'Yes', I said discouragingly. I hadn't lied to my mother. Stalin was really what I had seen.

A different view . . .

I remember one of my neighbours, a house painter and former resistance fighter from during the war, who is still a die-hard Stalinist. Every day he came home swearing and shouting how good things had been under Stalin. Then his wife would drag him off to the room where they lived with their two children but we could still hear his drunken praise of Stalin: 'He gave me an apartment, he gave me a medal, he gave me my self-respect . . . You know who I mean . . . He lowered the prices.'

1 What did Yevtushenko mean in his last sentence?
2 Explain why the house-painter had such a high regard for Stalin, despite what Stalin did to Russia.

Comparing Lenin and Stalin

Under the headings below there are some statements about Lenin. Using similar headings write a statement about Stalin, making clear the similarities and differences between the two men.

Aims. Lenin was guided by a genuine desire for communism rather than power for its own sake.

Terror. Lenin was ruthless in dealing with opposition inside and outside the Communist Party.

Propaganda. Lenin used propaganda effectively to make people believe in communism. He did not like propaganda about his own personality.

Agriculture. Lenin wished to collectivise farms but could not do so.

Industry. Lenin wanted to modernise and increase Russian industry but could not do so.

The Party. Lenin built up the power and privileges of the Party in the belief that they were the means of reaching true communism in the future.

Discussion topics

1 What would Lenin have thought of the state of communism in Russia if he had returned in the late 1930s?

2 What is your opinion of communism as shown by Russian history? Is it worth trying?

3 What are the present Soviet leaders doing that reminds you of events or phases in previous Russian history?

Essay titles

1 Outline the main features of Russian history from 1917 to the death of Lenin.

2 What were Lenin's/Stalin's aims and achievements?

THE USA 1918–1941

The political and social structure of America

After the First World War America was the world's greatest, richest and most advanced country. It had a large population of 120 million, and was a confident and thriving democracy.

The very rich. There was a small minority of extremely rich people, whose income came mainly from huge industrial and banking corporations. These people, such as the Fords, the Rockerfellers, the Morgans and the Vanderbilts, were among the richest people in the world.

The middle class. This was a very large class made up of very well-off owners of businesses, and also including professional people like doctors and lawyers.

The lower middle class. This was an even larger class, often known in America as white-collar

workers, who worked as clerks, secretaries, teachers, nurses and so on.

The working class. This was the largest class of all, working in the factories and mines of America. Some of these workers were very well paid, but most were below the subsistence level of $2,000 a year. Lowest of all were servants, blacks and recent foreign immigrants.

The farmers. This was another very large class in American society. Most farmers earned below the necessary $2,000 level. Most of them owned or rented small farms. At the bottom were black labourers, or share-croppers renting tiny farms.

Politics

America was a democracy. The Constitution of America stated that all Americans had equal freedoms. It also described the way that America should be run . . .

The president was elected by the people to run the country and to make policies. However, he could not make laws. This was the right of **Congress**, which contained two houses—the **House of Representatives** and the **Senate**, both elected by the people. There was also the **Supreme Court**, containing nine judges, who had the power to make sure that the Constitution was working properly and was protecting the freedoms of the people. These organisations made up the Federal or National Government in Washington. In addition, in each of America's forty-eight states there was also a state government which had power over state matters such as police, education and health.

The American government did not interfere very much in the lives and business affairs of American citizens. Most Americans believed that the government should not have very much power and that the people should have the right to think, to believe, to act and to behave as they pleased. There were very few laws in America to control or provide things like working conditions, hospitals, the dole, sick pay or housing. People thought that leaving everything up to individuals rather than the government would make America more prosperous and dynamic. This idea is known as 'laissez-faire'. It is shown in the three following quotations . . .

> I didn't realise the competitiveness of workers. I was conditioned to think that joining a Trade Union would take away your ability to stand on your own two feet. It would mean surrendering yourself.
>
> The business of America is business.

> In those days everyone accepted his role, responsibility for his own fate. Everybody, more or less, blamed himself for his delinquency or lack of talent or bad luck. There was an acceptance that it was your own fault, your own indolence, your lack of ability.

This idea of laissez-faire was particularly strong in the 1920s. The two Presidents of the 1920–1928 era were Harding and Coolidge, both Republicans and both elected by huge majorities. They were not great statesmen nor idealists. Neither of them did very much, so strongly did they and Americans believe in laissez-faire. A woman who knew Harding said of him, 'He was not a bad man, he was simply a slob'. When Coolidge was reported dead, one journalist answered, 'How can you tell?' These were the Presidents whom the people of America wanted in the 1920s.

Q

1 Explain briefly how the three quotations fit into the idea of laissez-faire.

2 What does the joke about Calvin Coolidge mean?

America in the 1920s

America was a very confusing place in the 1920s. It was a mixture of good and bad things, success and failure, improvement and backwardness. The outside world was envious of many of America's achievements in the 1920s, yet horrified by others.

'The boom'

America had the first boom in history in the 1920s. A boom is an improvement in the economy that brings prosperity not only to the better-off, but to more and more of the ordinary people too. In the 1920s American industry developed very fast, bringing great prosperity to the economy.

There were several reasons for this dramatic increase. One was that *demand* was growing, as more and more people had the money to buy

goods. The population as a whole was growing quite fast in the 1920s. The rich and the middle classes became larger in number and were spending more. So too were many working class people, especially those in the booming industries, such as car manufacturing, who were paid higher wages than average. Many workers had more than the $2,000 necessary for basic survival.

Another reason was *mass production*. This means that goods were made on assembly lines in greater and greater quantities instead of being made separately by individual craftsmen. Henry Ford was the real inventor of mass production, with the development of the Ford Model Ten car, the 'Tin Lizzie'. Other car manufacturers followed him and by 1929 there were 23 million cars in America, three times the 1919 level and one for every five people. Americans wanted other consumer goods too, like fridges, radios, electric cleaners, cameras, better clothing, furniture and gadgets. As these consumer goods increased so did the basic industries that made them possible. Mass-produced goods were much cheaper than other goods and so more people could afford them, therefore more were made, and so on. The building industry boomed too, as people and companies wanted houses, flats, offices, skyscrapers and factories.

Demand was artificially increased in several ways. Advertising was used on a larger scale, not only in newspapers but on the radio and in cinemas, making people want more and more goods. Mail order catalogues enabled anyone in America to buy goods as long as they could afford them. To make all of this easier, credit (hire purchase) became much more available as banks and manufacturers lent money to people to buy more consumer goods.

The symbol of the boom was the New York Stock Exchange on Wall Street. There people bought and sold shares in companies. Shares started and continued to rise. Normally people bought shares to get the dividend that the company paid to shareholders out of its profits. Now even ordinary people speculated in shares and not just stockbrokers and the rich. This meant that they bought shares not for the dividend but in order to sell them shortly afterwards at a handsome profit. Credit was even available to buy shares on the Stock Exchange.

Everywhere business seemed to be booming,

A mail-order catalogue appealing to its readers

but it could not last. The pace grew hotter and hotter, but by 1929 it was over-heated. The boom was coming to an end.

Q

1 What does the mail-order catalogue have to do with rising demand?
2 'You can have any colour of car you like as long as it's black,' said Henry Ford. What did he mean?

3 Rising demand is the most important cause of the boom. How does it link in with the other causes such as mass-production, credit, advertising, growing population, rising wages?

Prohibition and gangsterism

In 1919 many Americans would have regarded the right to drink alcohol as one of their basic freedoms in the Constitution. However, in 1920 the Constitution was altered and the right to make and drink alcohol was abolished. This was the work of Protestant churches, especially of the Women's Christian Temperance Union, which had been campaigning for prohibition for years. The aims of the Temperance movement were to

Ladies of the WCTU

remove the dreadful and undoubted evils of drink—drunkenness itself, disease, poverty and child-battering. Opponents of the movement saw the Temperance Campaigners as narrowminded, self-righteous, interfering people who felt that they had the right to impose their beliefs on everyone else.

For 12 years, until it was lifted by President Roosevelt, prohibition had several serious consequences. The average citizen was not put off drink and was therefore forced to break the law. The consumption of alcohol certainly increased during the period of prohibition, and along with it the associated problems of drunkenness and disease. New York's 15,000 legal bars increased after 1919 to 32,000 illegal

St Valentines Day Massacre, 1929

'speakeasies'. Another consequence was that all liquor—'bootleg liquor' and 'moonshine'—was now made illegally, with no regard for health, and often with added chemicals to speed up the process of fermentation. Thousands died through poisoned or adulterated drink and there was no legal action to be taken against the criminals.

Gangsters had always been powerful in America. Now they became almost respectable as well. Prohibition was a heaven-sent opportunity for them. The provision of illegal drink and the organisation of the speakeasies fell completely into the hands of rival gangs throughout America. The headquarters of the gangs' activities was Chicago, where rival Irish, Jewish, American and Italian Mafia gangs fought for dominance over one another's territories with deliberate brutality. The slaughtering of gangsters and leaders became very common indeed. It was in Chicago that the notorious St Valentine's Massacre, shown in the photograph, took place in 1929. The public became intensely interested in gang leaders like Johnny Torrio, Big Jim Colismo, Bugs Moran and the king of them all, Al Capone. They flocked to see him driving by in his armour-plated Cadillac with its back opening for the rear gunner. When prohibition ended gangsterism continued to increase.

Prohibition and gangsterism produced corruption in government and politics. The gang bosses soon 'bought off' the police forces of many cities, and controlled many politicians as well, such as Mayor Bill Taylor of Chicago. Even judges were on their payroll.

Q

1 How do you think the painter of the prohibitionist women regards his subjects?
2a List the consequences of prohibition in order of their seriousness.

b Should any of these consequences have been foreseen?
3 Why were pictures like that of the gangster massacre of interest to the public? Are such pictures of interest now?

Prejudice and discrimination

Prejudice is a deep feeling against something. People are, of course, entitled to have prejudices. **All** people have them, but are they entitled to put them into practice when they hurt others? There is no doubt that in the 1920s in America there were many widely held prejudices that did hurt other people on a large scale.

Political prejudices. Most Americans with their strong beliefs in democracy and laissez-faire were opposed to any left wing beliefs, even to Socialism which was acceptable in the European democracies. They were particularly prejudiced against communists and against anarchists, who believed in tearing down all authority by force. Sacco and Venzetti, Italian immigrants and anarchists, were accused of armed robbery and murder. A fair trial was impossible as both judge and jury were prejudiced against them from the start. Sacco and Venzetti were both executed by electrocution in 1927.

Religious prejudice. The Protestant churches were increasing in membership and in the strength of their beliefs in the 1920s. Many of them were fundamentalists, who believed that everything in the Bible was absolutely true. In the 1920s they persuaded several states, including Tennessee, to pass laws stating that Darwin's Theory of Evolution should not be taught in schools because it went against the Bible's account of the creation of the world taking place in seven days. In 1925 Johnny Scopes, a biology teacher in Dayton, Tennessee, was tried in the famous 'monkey trial' for teaching Darwin's Theory. Modern ideas themselves were on trial. Of course Johnny Scopes had broken the law and was found guilty. Nevertheless he went back to teaching evolution, although many teachers were still afraid to do so.

Racial prejudice. In 1919 a black boy swimming towards a 'white only' beach, was stoned by white youths and drowned. His death caused race riots in which many blacks and whites died. Although blacks were 15% of the American population, they were its poorest 15%, mostly share-croppers, servants and labourers. They were legally free and equal, but hardly any of

A lynching

them dared to vote in elections. There were strict laws keeping them apart from whites in transport, restaurants and schools. Intimidation and even lynchings of blacks just for their colour was common, especially in the southern states. The Ku Klux Klan, which was dedicated to taking action against Jews, Catholics, foreigners and especially against blacks, was at its height in the 1920s. With its special costumes, fiery crosses and titles such as Grand Dragon, it appealed to many whites, especially to those in the South who were poor and closest to the blacks.

Q

1 List examples of prejudice in our own day. Do you have any prejudices?

2 Why did the KKK appeal to the poorest whites most of all?
3 Describe the attitude of those watching the lynching.

Poverty

The boom did not reach everyone in the 1920s. Throughout this period 60% of American families had an income of below $2,000 a year. For them there were few consumer goods, poor homes to live in and not enough food. There were no laws at that time to provide the dole, health care, or pensions, to improve working conditions nor to provide housing. Many of the poorer working classes came into this category, as did most farmers, whose farms were so small they could not make a proper living or afford farm machinery. Poorest of all were the blacks.

Laissez-faire did little for these people. Some of them tried to better themselves, and succeeded in escaping from their poverty, but most of them, like the children in the photograph, could not help themselves.

Children picking tobacco

Q

1 Why were many employers able and willing to employ child labourers, as shown above?

Entertainment and social change

A flapper—our image of the 1920s

The picture of the 'flapper' doing the Charleston, is our image of the 'Roaring Twenties' in America. Everything seemed to move faster and faster. There was more money to spend, and a lot of it was spent on entertainment. Hollywood movies boomed, featuring stars like Rudolf Valentino, Clara Bow, Mary Pickford, Frank Lloyd and Charlie Chaplin. They were idolised by the crowds who attended their films frequently. Jazz was all the rage, with its wailing saxophones, its 'blues' and its new, shocking dances like the Charleston and the Black Bottom. Sports stars too had huge followings, such as the boxer Jack Dempsey and the baseball star 'Babe' Ruth. Newspapers became more and more sensational, led by the Hearst Press, emphasising sex, gangsterism, and scandal.

Social manners became freer and morals became looser. Fashion seemed to illustrate this change. For the first time in history women's hair was cut short—'bobbed'—and corsets were discarded. Dresses ceased to reach the ground and bathing suits followed the figure. Much of this was scandalous to the more old fashioned, staid and religious Americans, but it seemed to represent the spirit of the times.

A Bathing Belle being arrested for indecency

Q

1 What do you think were the views of some of the different types of people in the photograph of the arrest?

2 Who was most typical of America in the 1920s? The flapper, the poor, the religious campaigner?

Isolationism

After 1919 America was by far the richest and most powerful country in the world, victorious in war. It could be expected to take a leading part in world affairs. President Wilson, with his high ideals and his attempts to solve world problems in the Paris Peace Conference, would certainly have done this. America's allies also wanted and expected America to lead them. Most Americans, however, did not want this. They were afraid of becoming involved in world affairs and were determined never to enter another war in Europe. They felt satisfied with their own achievements and had no desire to help others, as they had just done in the Great War. This mood was called *isolationism*.

America never finally signed the Treaty of

Magazine cover, 1926

Versailles, and ditched the League of Nations, of which it would have been the leader.

It refused to help Britain and France in dealing with the problem of Germany. Americans wanted their huge war loans back from Britain and France, their former allies, even though Britain offered to cancel its own greater loans to its own allies. 'They borrowed the money, didn't they?' was President Coolidge's curt comment. The Government tried to keep foreign goods out of America by imposing heavy import duties on them and they set up strict laws against immigration. America seemed to be turning in on itself and shutting out the rest of the world. It was a strange thing for the world's leading power to do.

Q

1 How does Coolidge's comment 'They borrowed the money, didn't they?' sum up American foreign policy in the 1920s?
2 Is the magazine cover biased? Give your reasons.
3 EITHER Make two lists, one of good features of America in the 1920s and one of bad.

OR Write an argument between two people, one of whom feels that America is successful, and the other who does not.
4 Which features of America in the 1920s are still features of America today?

The Great Depression

The causes of the Depression

Herbert Hoover, who became President in 1929, invented the word 'depression'. He thought the word was not as frightening as 'crisis' or 'panic'. No-one can ever completely understand the causes of the Depression, but it is important to understand how its causes link in with one another. Historians have identified the following as causes of the Depression. . .

Over-speculation in shares and the Wall Street Crash. Many people were too confident about the success of the American economy, especially those who speculated in shares on the Stock Exchange. More and more companies were set up for ordinary American speculators to invest in. They were known as holding companies, and did not own factories or banks or shops, but only shares in other companies. In the end they owned very little real wealth at all and became very unstable.

People made profits by buying shares at low

prices and selling at high prices. Prices of shares rose and rose simply because so many people wanted to buy them, not because they were worth so much. Early in 1929 some speculators began to sell shares at high prices, realising that the boom in shares could not go on for ever. Suddenly, in October 1929, the majority of shareholders realised what was going on. Everyone began to sell. The Wall Street Crash hit America. The price of shares tumbled. On Black Tuesday, 29 October, 1929, 16 million shares were sold in a day. Fortunes were lost, companies went bankrupt, but, most importantly, people lost confidence in investing their money in shares. Money for investment in industry therefore began to dry up.

Government policy—laissez-faire. The new Republican President Hoover did exactly as his two Republican predecessors had done with the economy—virtually nothing. The Secretary of the Treasury, Andrew Mellon, was warned several times of the imminent crash in share prices and of the coming of the Depression, but felt that it was not his job to do anything about it. Nothing must come in the way of business. The glaring faults of the boom, such as the holding companies and overspeculation, were realised but the government did not feel that its responsibility was to act.

The fall in demand. Everyone was over-confident that the boom would go on and that demand would continue to rise. It did not. By early 1929, several things began to cut down demand. America's population growth was slowing down and fewer goods were needed. Foreign countries put high tariffs on American imports, responding to the American government's similar policy. The demand of better-off Americans for consumer goods was being satisfied, and the poorer people could simply not afford them. A few companies, like the Ford Motor Company, began to over-produce goods, which they could not sell. They began to sack workers, who then had no demand for other companies' goods. They could not even keep up the credit payments on goods already bought. Demand came falling down. The Depression was on the way.

Cause and consequence checklist

In order to check whether you have understood the causes of the Depression, match up the sentences which begin in column one with the correct endings in column two. Be absolutely accurate.

Cause	Consequence
The refusal of foreign countries to buy American goods caused	over production of goods to take place.
The poverty of the majority of Americans caused	no action to be taken to control the faults of the Stock Exchange.
The over-production of goods caused	demand for goods to fall.
The collapse of share prices caused	investment in industry to dry up.
Over confidence of manufacturers caused	demand to be unable to go on rising.
The government's policy of laissez-faire caused	companies to cut production and lay off workers.

Features of the Depression, 1929–1933

Economic features

A depression is an economic slump, a fall in the production of goods. The economy went from bad to worse in these years. By 1933 industry was producing only 40% of the levels of 1928, and the total value of goods had sunk from $110 billion in 1928 to $50 billion in 1933. As more and more people were hit by the Depression, so they could afford less and less food. Therefore agriculture too was hit, with its production falling by a quarter in these years. Many farmers, already poor, became bankrupt and were forced to sell their farms and move to the towns in search of work. The American government, like all other governments at this time, did all the wrong things to deal with the Depression. President Hoover believed so strongly in laissez-faire that he always said, 'Prosperity is just around the corner'. In fact everything he did reduced the demand for American goods.

He *cut government spending* by not giving out contracts for building roads, bridges and by reducing the salaries of government employees such as the police, the army and civil servants. Secondly, he *raised import duties on foreign goods* in order to protect American industries' goods. This was known as 'protectionism'. Other countries responded in the same way, and by 1932, the trade between the nations of the world was only one quarter of what it had been in 1928. Another policy was to deliberately *keep the value of the dollar at a high level* so that Americans would not lose confidence in their own currency. Unfortunately, this made American goods very expensive for foreigners to buy because they had to change their own currency into dollars to pay for American goods.

The final blow to the economy came in 1931. Already many American banks were in a difficult position as so many Americans could not re-pay the loans they had borrowed. When some European banks, owing money to American banks, went bankrupt in 1931, the bank crisis erupted. It soon spread to America and some American banks became bankrupt. People with money were afraid to invest it in banks, and banks were afraid to lend money to companies. No-one had any confidence in the economy at all.

Social features of the Depression

A depression, as we have seen, is a fall in the production of goods. However, following on from this are the most terrible social consequences. Here the key words are

unemployment   poverty   despair   protest

Unemployment. In 1929 only 1.5 million Americans were unemployed, 3% of the workforce. By 1930 it was 4.5 million (9%), in 1931 8 million (16%) in 1932 12 million (24%). Its highest level was 13 million (27%) in 1933. As factories, banks, offices and farms all over America closed down or cut production, all types

Hoboes

of Americans became unemployed—owners, managers, workers, farmers. Employers also cut wages and hours of work, hitting at the living standards of those who were not actually unemployed. And of course, menacing America as the Depression worsened, was the anxiety and fear of unemployment.

Queuing for free potatoes

Poverty. Unemployment meant poverty, even ruin. In America there was no law to state that the unemployed should receive the dole. Just a few of the 48 states began to introduce a very small dole in the late 1920s, but most never did. There were alternatives to starvation—crime, prostitution, begging, sponging off relatives, all of which became common in these years. For most of the unemployed, private charities saved them from starvation. Soup kitchens and bread lines became a regular feature of American towns. There were 82 in New York city alone. Unable to pay the rent, respectable people lost their homes. Youngsters were forced out to fend for themselves. There were probably 2 million hoboes during the Depression, mostly homeless young men travelling illegally on the railroads and searching for work. In every town there sprang up 'Hoovervilles', shanty towns of unhygienic hovels made of cardboard or tin. Here the malnutrition and disease were at their worst. By 1933 the system of private charity was beginning to break down.

Read the following evidence and study the photographs to get an idea of what it was like to be poor in the Depression . . .

A destitute farmer leaves his homestead, 1935

I can't go home to eat anything. This is my sister's day to eat. (New York schoolgirl.)

Hoboes were honest, decent, middle-aged men with faces seared by toil and want, and young men, many of them boys in their teens with thick, unkempt hair. These were the uprooted, unwanted male population of America. They gathered in big cities when winter came, hungry, defeated, empty, hopeless, restless, looking everywhere for work and for crumbs and finding neither. The sight of them was revolting, disgusting, enough to render a man speechless with pity. (A social worker.)

Why, it's the best education in the world for those boys travelling around. They get more experience in a few months than they would in years at school. (Henry Ford.)

Nobody is actually starving. The hoboes, for example, are better fed than they have ever been. One hobo in New York gets 10 meals in one day. (President Hoover.)

Everybody was a criminal. You stole, you cheated through, stole clothes off lines, stole milk off back porches, you stole bread. We made a brief stop at one town. There was a grocery store. I beat it off the train and came back with rolls and this guy standing in the window shaking his fist at you.

It wasn't a big thing, but it made you into a coyote [prairie wolf]. You were a hunter. You had to be. A coyote is crafty. He can be fantastic and coward at the same time. He'll run, but when he's cornered he'll fight. They are mean, but how else does a coyote stay alive? A coyote is nature's victim as well as man's. We were coyotes in the thirties. (A hobo.)

My neighbours were angry with my Mother because she fed hungry men at the back door. They said it would bring others and then what would she do? She said, 'I'll feed them until the food runs out.' It wasn't until years later, I realised the fear people had of these men. We didn't have it in our house. (A middle class girl.)

Despair. Facts and figures do not mean very much when the subject is despair. For instance the suicide rate rose. Mental illness increased. But these facts only *mean* something if we understand what was behind them, as you can read in the following evidence . . .

What the lack of a job did to miners' families and to them. They hung around in corners and in groups. They were loathe to go home because they were blamed there, as if it was their fault for being unemployed. A jobless man was a lazy good-for-nothing. The women punished the men by belittling them, undermining their authority, turning to the eldest son. Making the eldest son the man of the family. These men suffered from depression. They felt depressed, they were ashamed of themselves. They cringed, they comforted one another. They avoided home. (A psychologist.)

The majority of people were hit and hit hard. They were mentally disturbed, because they did not know when the end of all this was coming. There was a lot of suicides that I knew of. From nothing else but just because they could not see any hope for a better tomorrow. Part of them were farmers and part of them were businessmen even. They went flat broke and they committed suicide on the strength of it, nothing else. My husband was very bitter. That's just putting it

mild. He was an intelligent man. He could not see why, in such a wealthy country as this is, that there was any sense in so many people starving to death. (An Oklahoma woman.)

Protest. Many Americans protested against the Depression. They protested by calling their shanty towns 'Hoovervilles', their belongings tied in newspaper 'Hooverbags'. They made bitter jokes and sang bitter songs like 'Brother, can you spare a dime?'. However, very few of them protested *actively* against the government about the Depression. Those that did usually marched about and carried placards, but were usually broken up by the police. The most important protest came in 1932 when 25,000 ex-soldiers marched on the White House claiming their war-bonus which was due in 1945. The government, fearing a rebellion, acted at once. Police and regular troops under General MacArthur cleared them off the streets and broke up the bonus marchers camp outside the capital. Several people, including two babies, were killed.

Q

Economic features

1 Write a paragraph about the causes of the Depression, making clear the relative importance of the various causes and linking them together.
2 Draw a chart to show the decline in production during the Depression.
3 What was wrong about each of Hoover's policies to combat the Depression?

Social features

1 Draw a graph to show the increase in unemployment between 1929 and 1933.

2 Arrange the following key words in the most logical order . . . despair; unemployment; poverty; fall in production; protest.
3 Using the evidence, including the pictures, make a list of the human feelings, attitudes and actions which were the result of the Depression.
4 What different views of hoboes were there in the evidence on page 70? Why were they different?
5 What would you think would be the reaction to the action against the bonus marchers' camp of a) a government supporter, b) an ex-serviceman who was not unemployed, c) an unemployed worker?

Roosevelt and the New Deal

Franklin Delano Roosevelt, commonly known as FDR, came from a rich family in New York State. His education was the best that money could buy; Groton School and Harvard University. Roosevelt was always politically ambitious and very well informed about political matters. In

1910 he became Senator for New York State, and in 1912 Assistant Secretary of the US Navy. Unfortunately, in 1921 he was struck by polio and unable to walk again unaided, but with his wife Eleanor's encouragement, he decided to re-enter politics. He made his name as a positive and popular leader when he was elected as Governor of New York State from 1928 to 1932. There he had to deal not only with the Depression but also with the opposition of those who believed completely in laissez-faire. As Governor he started to increase state government spending on public works, such as roads, bridges and slum clearance. This provided more jobs. Roosevelt also increased the dole. This was just what people wanted.

When Roosevelt put his name forward as Democratic Party candidate for the Presidency in 1932, a group of Democrats started a 'Stop Roosevelt' campaign, fearing that he would act against laissez-faire and increase government spending too much. They said he was too ill and had no real talent. FDR, however, seemed to have the qualities needed to win.

Roosevelt seeks the farmers' vote, 1932

The election, November 1932

Roosevelt campaigned tirelessly and powerfully against President Hoover, making countless speeches and public appearances in his 'whistle-stop' rail tour of America. He was a very good speaker and inspired ordinary Americans with his friendly and sincere manner. He appealed to the 'forgotten man', the unemployed and people like those in the photograph, who wanted the government to do something more positive against the depression. He won over many supporters and opponents alike with his promise: 'I pledge you, I pledge myself, to a new deal for the American people. Give me your help, not to win votes alone, but to win in this crusade to restore America to its own people.'

One of Roosevelt's policies was to end prohibition. This was easily done. Another policy, less easily achieved, was to put into practice the ideas of the British economist J. M. Keynes, who had written a book about demand in the economy. Keynes' idea was that the government should increase demand by

spending more money on public works. This would give people a job and a wage, and would allow them to buy more goods from manufacturers. Thus the economy would begin to grow again. Roosevelt also promised to give more help to the unemployed. Like many Americans, FDR was a firm believer in laissez-faire, despite what his opponents said, and did not like the government to interfere too much in economic matters. He said that government interference would last for only a short time, until the economy was back on its feet again.

Against such promising policies, Hoover's refusal to alter laissez-faire had very little appeal. Roosevelt won the election by a landslide of 23 million votes to 16 million. At his inauguration he made his famous address to the American people to restore their confidence in themselves — 'The only thing we have to fear is fear itself — nameless, unreasoning, unjustified terror which paralyses needed efforts to convert retreat into advance.' Roosevelt had certainly won most people's confidence.

—Q—

1 Identify three different types or classes of people and how FDR appealed to them. Use the photograph to identify one of the groups.

2 Write a paragraph explaining why Roosevelt won the election. Bring in the following points in what you consider to be their order of importance . . . Roosevelt's past experience; his personal appeal; his policies; Hoover's unpopularity and failure.

The New Deal

Immediately, Roosevelt got to work at the White House. He gathered round him a 'brains trust' of advisers headed by Harry Hopkins. He also kept in touch with the American public by beginning his famous 'fireside chats' on the radio. The first three months of Roosevelt's presidency were known as the 'hundred days', when the President did as he had promised and got to grips with the most urgent problems, working far into the night. He made Congress and the Civil Service do the same, passing new laws and putting them into practice. He persuaded Congress to grant him special powers so he could act immediately and powerfully.

At first FDR concentrated on the most urgent problems. These he considered to be unemployment and economic recovery. He started spending money on large scale public works. One of his supporters, the manager of an office, explained FDR's policy for the benefit of his employees by posting up the following notice . . .

FDR has done his part; now you do something. Buy something, anything, paint your kitchen, give a party, pay a bill, fix your roof, get a hair cut, get married. It does not matter what you do but get going and keep going. This old world is starting to move.

For several years Roosevelt provided strong government action to deal with America's problems. Like all believers in laissez-faire, he felt that if the government helped people too much they would not help themselves. This was the reason why he tried to cut the dole in 1936,

although he was forced to increase it soon afterwards. Yet he came to realise that some groups in society would always suffer, even if prosperity returned — the old, the sick, children and exploited workers. This was why, after 1935, he passed more laws to improve their lives through government action.

The aims and measures of the New Deal

During the next few years many measures were introduced by President Roosevelt. Some were laws, others were special policies or government actions, yet others were organisations or agencies known as the 'alphabet agencies' after their initials. Some of them dealt with single, specific problems, others were more complicated. To make them easier to understand they can be divided up into five types, according to their main aims.

- Measures to deal with immediate unemployment.
- Measures to help industry.
- Measures to help agriculture.
- Measures to build up confidence in the economy and to ensure that it worked more smoothly.
- Measures to bring about more basic social reforms to improve people's lives.

One of the most important successes of the New Deal was the Tennessee Valley Authority. Understanding how it helped to achieve several aims will also help you to understand how the New Deal itself worked.

Case study

The Tennessee Valley Authority

The Tennessee Valley had many problems. It was a vast area through which several rivers rushed, all flowing into the mighty Tennessee. Generations of farmers had cleared away the natural forests and grown crops in their place, causing the soil to be washed down into the river

by the rains. They had exhausted the soil by overplanting with crops. The river often overflowed, causing terrible flood damage. The farmers were too poor to modernise their farms with new equipment or to buy industrial goods. There was little industry to provide employment for the growing population.

As the Valley covered seven states only the

Federal Government could solve such a vast and complicated problem. Roosevelt could see that the Tennessee Valley was ideal for the large-scale government help that he had promised the people. During the first 'hundred days', FDR introduced an ambitious scheme to solve all the Valley's problems at once. Immediately he gave huge contracts to construction firms to build many large dams in order to control the ferocious Tennessee and its tributaries. Thousands of new workers were taken on to build not only the dams but also hydro-electric power stations at the foot of each dam, power pylons, canals, locks, docks, flood controls and factories. Using the cheap electricity from the new power stations, new industries sprang up along the river bank—aluminium, fertilisers and paper-making. These industries made use of the new river transport, made possible by making the river navigable for 630 miles. In all these new enterprises thousands of jobs were provided for local people. At the same time farmers were retrained by TVA experts in better ploughing methods and the better use of crops to prevent erosion and soil exhaustion. With their increased income the farmers could buy fertilisers to replenish the soil and electricity to work their modern machinery.

Soon the TVA was being called the 'greatest US invention this century'.

A TVA dam under construction

― Q ―

1 Write down, in order of importance, how the TVA helped to achieve the aims of the New Deal. Use the picture of the dam in explaining your answer.

The measures of the New Deal

Just as the Tennessee Valley Authority helped to achieve several aims, so did many of the measures listed below.

Loans to industry

FDR made available $16 billion to companies if they promised to take on new workers.

Stock Exchange reforms

FDR improved the workings of the Stock Market to try to avoid another Wall Street Crash.

The Social Security Act 1935

A national insurance scheme, with contributions from employers and employees, began to provide pensions for some of the retired and benefits for some of the unemployed. Unfortunately it did not decide how much should be given. This was left to state governments.

The Glass Stegall Emergency Bank Act, 1933

One of FDR's first measures was to close all banks and to pass this Act, which only allowed them to re-open if they were financially sound. This strengthened the banking system and helped to prevent another crisis.

The Federal Emergency Relief Administration (FERA)

Under its leader Harry Hopkins, this organisation provided $5 billion worth of emergency help in the form of food, clothing and other necessities for the unemployed and the poor.

The Civil Works Administration (CWA)

This organisation employed 4 million formerly unemployed people in building roads, schools and airfields. It lasted for only 1 year and was replaced by . . .

The Works Progress Administration (WPA)

This was the largest of the alphabet agencies, led by Harry Hopkins. It employed 3 million people and ran many projects. By 1941 it had spent $11 billion on 2,500 hospitals, 1,000 airport runways and so on.

The National Recovery Administration (NRA)

This was set up by the *National Industrial Recovery Act 1933*, (NIRA). There were two main sections in this Act. One introduced codes of practice dealing with minimum wages, maximum hours of work, union rights and the abolition of child labour in various industries. The other section set up price codes, making sure that price wars did not start between companies, thus causing bankruptcy.

Unfortunately this Act lasted only until 1935 as it was declared unconstitutional.

Agricultural Adjustments Administration (AAA)

This administration allowed the farmers to set quotas for each of 7 products, such as cereals and cotton, in return for government subsidies. Because the amount of produce was deliberately *reduced* in this way, prices rose. The incomes of farmers, therefore, increased and they could afford better machinery and to improve their farms.

This administration was also declared unconstitutional in 1936.

The Home Owners Loan Corporation (HOLC)

The government provided loans to home owners to enable them to keep up mortgage repayments if they were unemployed.

The Wagner Act 1935

This gave workers the right to form and to join trade unions, and prevented them from dismissal by hostile employers.

It also set up the *National Labour Relations Boards* (NLRB) to enforce this law.

Many employers such as the Ford Motor Company worked against this law, viciously breaking strikes and sit-ins with armed guards. However, FDR helped the Unions to develop so that membership increased from 3 million to 9 million between 1933 and 1939. Even so, only a quarter of American workers were in unions in 1939.

The Farm Credit Administration (FCA)

The government loaned money at low rates of interest to tenant-farmers to buy their small farms. This scheme attracted 6 million farmers. It also arranged for farmers to be insured against natural disasters, and it helped farmers to keep their farms in good condition.

The Fair Labour Standards Act 1938

This Act laid down a 40 hour week and prohibited child employment under 16 years and set up minimum wages in certain industries.

The Civilian Conservation Corps (CCC)

This agency provided 3 million young unemployed with food, lodgings and a dollar a day, building canals, stocking rivers with fish and doing other useful things.

Public Works Administration (PWA)

Led by Harold Icks, a close adviser of the President, this agency employed millions on very large scale projects such as slum clearance schemes and the building of the Hoover Dam. You can see one of their many schemes illustrated in the photograph.

Government poster, 1936

Devaluation of the dollar

In 1933 Roosevelt deliberately devalued the dollar. This meant that foreign countries buying American goods could buy them more cheaply, thus raising the demand for American goods abroad.

Q

1 Separate the various measures of the New Deal according to the main aim they helped to achieve. Indicate also which other aims they helped. This should make the list easier to handle and to revise.
2 The large poster was for propaganda purposes. What do you think these purposes were?

3 Looking back at the manager's notice on page 73, how well do you think he explained the New Deal to his employees?

Opposition to the New Deal

Roosevelt always had the support of most Americans, but he did face intense opposition from some groups. You can see one opinion of him in the cartoon opposite.

1 Big businessmen, the rich, Republicans

You can read from these extracts what some of these people thought about Roosevelt . . .

When you say FDR, my blood begins to boil. Roosevelt attacked people—with some reason. But without justice. All people on Wall Street are not crooks. My friend and I often spoke about it. Especially after his hammy fireside chats. Here we were paying taxes and not asking for anything. Everybody else was asking for relief, for our money to help them out. A certain amount of that is OK, but when they strip you clean and still don't accomplish much it's unfair. (Martin DeVries, a well-off Republican interviewed in 1970.)

Roosevelt's name came up with some of the people I photographed, but always with rather a hatred. I don't think we ever mentioned those on the dole. I never saw one bread-line in my part of New York. If they were, they were in Harlem. They were never in this section of town. There was never any sign of poverty. The New Deal meant absolutely nothing except higher taxation. The Thirties was a glamorous, glittering moment. (Gerome Zerbe, a successful high-society photographer interviewed in 1970.)

FDR's grandchildren object to him running over into their favourite programme

To-day, with few exceptions, members of the upper class frankly hate Franklyn Roosevelt. (*Time Magazine*, one of America's leading political journals, 1938.)

2 Extremist political groups

Several extreme political groups developed during the 1930s in opposition to Roosevelt and the New Deal. The most important of them was the Share Our Wealth movement, which collapsed when its leader, Senator Huey 'Kingfish' Long, was assassinated in 1935. Several other similar movements arose at the time, such as Father Coughlin's National Union for Social Justice, a partly fascist organisation, and Doctor Townsend's Old People's Movement, which wanted pensions for *all* old people instead of the minority who gained a pension from the Social Security Act. All of these groups claimed some support, mainly from the poor, but they never really dented Roosevelt's following. These groups opposed him because they thought that the New Deal did not help the poor enough. There were also the German American Bund, a Nazi organisation, and the Communist Party, both of which wanted to overthrow both Roosevelt and Democracy. Their support was always limited. Most ordinary Americans always gave their support to FDR.

3 The Supreme Court

In America every individual has the right to complain to the Supreme Court about any law. The Supreme Court then considers whether this law interferes with the rights and freedoms of the people, listed in the Constitution. If it does, the Supreme Court declares the law to be unconstitutional. This means that the law is cancelled because it should never have been passed in the first place. The Court contains nine judges who are appointed for life. In the early years of Roosevelt's presidency five judges opposed Roosevelt's ideas and felt that the government was interfering too much in economic and social matters. Four judges supported Roosevelt. The Supreme Court, therefore, opposed him by declaring several of the New Deal Laws unconstitutional. Roosevelt threatened to create new Supreme Court judges who would support his views, but in 1936 one of them came over to his way of thinking, giving him a majority of five to four.

1 What view of the fireside chats is revealed by the cartoon?
2 Does the evidence convince you that the rich in general opposed Roosevelt intensely?
3 How effective were the three main types of opposition? Deal with them in order of importance.

An assessment

How successful was the New Deal?

There are differing views of the New Deal's success.

David Kennedy was a government official in the 1930s, dealing with financial matters. He was a strong supporter of Roosevelt in the early years of the New Deal, but in the later 1930s turned against him because of the President's threat to interfere with the Supreme Court and because he thought that Roosevelt was going too much against laissez-faire. In 1970 he gave his opinion about the New Deal . . .

> There was a very, very serious down-turn in 1937. We really had not made a substantial recovery from the deep Depression in the early 1930s. Unemployment was still very high. The New Deal programmes were not stimulating in the way people thought. There was a sort of defeatist attitude—that the government just had to do all this for the people. It was not until the war, with its economic thrust, that we pulled out of it. The war got us out of it, not the New Deal policies.
>
> At the time I felt we were relying too much on the government to save us. I felt people were losing their initiative.
>
> I don't want to be too critical of Mr Roosevelt, because he did, in our period of history, do something. To-day there'd be some rebellion that you did not have then. It was peaceful then. It was law abiding, there was more respect for the law.

A historian who researched into American history wrote in a school text book recently . . .

> True, there had been a frightening rise in unemployment in the later part of 1937, but this had been checked by another massive dose of government spending.

Although few people realised it at the time, the main part of the New Deal was practically completed by 1938. Its most obvious achievement was that it had begun to bring the United States out of the Depression. People from almost every section of the community in fact were better off in 1938 than they had been in the dark days of 1932. But the New Deal's achievement went further than this. By using the power of the government to ensure fairer treatment for the ordinary citizen, Roosevelt had given the American people renewed faith in their country and its way of life.

In contrast to the United States, in many countries, the problems of the time had caused Democracy to be trampled under foot by all-powerful dictators. Roosevelt had shown what 'Democracy at Work' could do.

Changes in agriculture

A majority of farmers, mostly tenants or 'share-croppers', who could not make ends meet, were turned off their farms and forced to emigrate to the cities. There were millions of people like this. In the mid-western states, particularly in 1933, there was a long natural drought, followed by freak high winds. These disasters turned thousands of square miles of farmland into deserts, 'dust bowls'. Again, millions of farmers were forced to move to other states, particularly to California. Known as 'Okies'—people from Oklahoma—they came in their tin-lizzies, piled high with possessions and people. They were disliked and feared, and only during the Second World War, when industry really boomed again, did their conditions improve.

By the end of the 1930s American agriculture was efficient at last. Millions of farmers doubled their income, especially those who actually owned rather than rented their own land and managed to stay in business. They became much more successful and secure as a direct result of the New Deal measures. The size of the average farm increased greatly and schemes like the TVA ensured success for many farmers, but all this economic success was at the cost of those farmers who had been dispossessed of their land, and after great human suffering.

Economic facts and figures

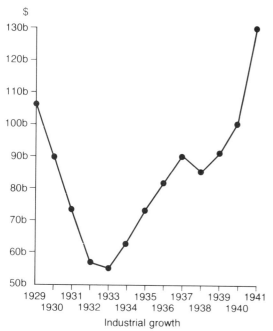

Industrial growth

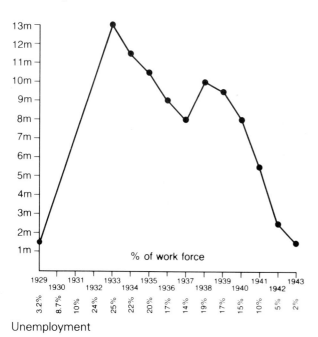

Unemployment

Finance and the smooth working of the economy

Even President Roosevelt's enemies admit that in this area he was very successful. There is no doubt that many of his reforms gave confidence to the economy and prevented many problems, particularly his laws against monopolies, the Stock Exchange reforms and, above all, the Glass-Stegall Emergency Bank Act of 1933, which kept banks under strict control.

Social changes

It is important to remember that in the 1930s most people were never unemployed. For them the average income was much greater in 1939 than it had been in 1933. Even so, throughout the 1930s over 20% of the population was always unemployed. It was for these people, as well as for other groups such as children, the old, the sick and the deprived that Roosevelt introduced the social reforms. Millions of Americans benefitted permanently from the social measures of the New Deal, or were carried through a temporary crisis. The Social Security Act was the most important measure in preventing the worst suffering of the Depression and it gave new hope to many of the poor. Roosevelt himself gained more satisfaction from this law than from any other in the 1930s.

Yet not everyone's lot was improved. The amount of payment was decided not by the Federal Government but by the individual states, some of which gave very little indeed. Many old, sick and unemployed people still received no help at all. Poor farmers, dispossessed by drought and bankruptcy and unable to find jobs in the states to which they migrated, had little to thank Roosevelt for.

At work Roosevelt's measures brought permanent improvements for many, especially child workers, the lowest paid and the most exploited. Many workers took advantage of the laws which gave them the right to form and join trade unions.

Q

---

1 Use the charts to decide which of the two views of the New Deal's success you agree with. Write your own summary.

2 Draw up a balance sheet listing on one side FDR's successes and on the other side his failures, under the following headings:
Agriculture   Finance   Social changes

3 How, in your opinion, would the following respond to the New Deal?
a A rich Republican.

b A dispossessed and unemployed farmer.
c A worker no longer employed.
d An old person.

Extension

How successful a President was FDR?

How should we judge Roosevelt during the 1930s? By his achievements? By his methods of ruling America? By his popularity? All three must be taken into account.

1 Roosevelt's achievements

The New Deal was largely Roosevelt's achievement. Clearly he did not achieve it single-handedly but many advisers and politicians were associated with him in bringing it about. Was it a great achievement? We have already assessed the New Deal on the previous pages.

2 Roosevelt's methods of ruling America

Some American Presidents, like Harding and Coolidge in the 1920s, do very little, hardly using the great powers available to them as President. Others do much more, taking a positive line and intervening a great deal in American life. They use their presidential powers very extensively, and are known as 'Imperial Presidents'. Roosevelt was the most 'Imperial' President that America has ever had.

As President, he could not make laws, but he could influence the making of laws by Congress in several ways. One of these was to use his right to speak to Congress personally, encouraging them to pass laws which he wanted. Another was to use his supporters in Congress to push through his policies. He also had the right to call members of Congress before him and to 'influence' them. Roosevelt was very effective in this way, pressurising and persuading many opponents into his own way of thinking.

One organisation that Roosevelt could not influence was the Supreme Court, which often opposed his policies for being too interfering. His threat to create more Supreme Court judges favourable to his own ideas was so unpopular, and lost him so much support, that he never carried it through. Roosevelt was not personally liked by many politicians and officials because of his rather over-bearing personality and his tendency to use people for his own advantage. He certainly enjoyed power immensely and liked to have his own way.

Yet Roosevelt did believe strongly in democracy. He said, 'Poor men are not free men. People who are hungry and out of a job are the stuff of which dictatorships are made.' He really did want to make life fairer for the poor and deprived millions who seemed ignored and shut out by their more successful fellow-Americans.

After Roosevelt's death in 1945, Congress passed a law stating that a President may only be elected twice. This law had the broad support of all parties in Congress and was based on the fact that Roosevelt had been elected four times. He was admired and respected, but there was a feeling that he had used his powers much too strongly.

3 Roosevelt's popularity and appeal

No leader in a democracy can have 100% support. That would be impossible and wrong. But there is no doubt that FDR always had the firm support of the majority of the population. In his four successful presidential elections, he always had land-slide victories.

Roosevelt was a brilliant propagandist. He made people feel that he was interested in their own problems and he had the 'common touch'. He used all the media cleverly and successfully, getting his personality and his message across to the people. You can see him giving an informal press conference in the photograph. His 'fireside chats' over the radio were immensely popular, particularly in the earliest years of his presidency when America was so troubled by the Depression. He had the ability to stimulate hope and confidence in the American people. Even

One of FDR's informal press conferences

He was God in this country. (A New York taxi driver, speaking in 1965.)

You know it's tough when one of your buddies has to go, and President Roosevelt was our buddy. (A soldier on hearing of Roosevelt's death in 1945.)

Dear Mr President. This is just to tell you that everything is alright now. The mortgage can go on for a while longer. I never heard of a President like you Mr Roosevelt. My wife and I are old folks, and don't amount to much, but we are joined with those millions of others in praying for you every night. God bless you, Mr Roosevelt. (A typical letter. FDR received 5,000–8,000 letters a day similar to this.)

now he is one of the best known American Presidents and his personality still finds a sympathetic response in most Americans. The following pieces of evidence tell us something of his popularity and appeal . . .

Extension questions

1 Did America need an 'Imperial' president in the 1930s? Explain your answer.
2 What does the photograph show you about Roosevelt's dealings with the press?

3 How should we mainly judge Roosevelt—by his achievements, his methods of ruling or his appeal?
4 Write two or three sentences summing up your own assessment of FDR.

Discussion topics

1 Do you agree with 'laissez-faire', OR with the government interfering in economic and social problems—then and now?
2 We get a lot of our impressions and knowledge of America from TV programmes. Are these a good source of evidence?

Essays

1 Outline the main features of American history between 1918 and 1933.
2 What were the main causes and features of the Depression?
3 How did Roosevelt deal with the problems of the Depression? How successful was he?

GERMANY 1918-1939

Germany after the Great War

Could democracy succeed?

When Russia lost the war in 1917 the Tsar and the whole of Russian society came crashing down. When Germany was defeated only one year later, would the same thing happen? There was no question of the Kaiser staying in power. Many Germans no longer wanted him and in any case, the Allies refused to grant an armistice unless Germany became a democracy without a Kaiser. However, as you have seen in Chapter 2, the Allies did not want a communist revolution to occur in Germany and preferred to see Germany stay much as it was. This was one of the reasons why they agreed to an armistice rather than to invade Germany.

In 1918 Germany was a much more modern, industrialised country than Russia, more like the kind of society we would recognise today . . .

The establishment

This is the name we give to the various upper class groups who possessed great power, wealth and influence in Germany. They were the top army leaders, the landowning nobility and the very rich owners of 'big business', Germany's huge industrial and financial companies. These people were monarchists, preferring the rule of the Kaiser, and they wanted no change in Germany.

The upper middle class

This was quite a large class in Germany, consisting of the owners of medium-size businesses and professional people like doctors and lawyers.

The lower middle class

This large group contained white-collar workers like clerks and salesmen, small shopkeepers and self-employed craftsmen.

The peasants

A very large group. The peasants often rented, but did not usually own, small farms.

The working class

Another very large group. They worked in the factories and mines of Germany's industrial areas, mainly in the north.

Politics in Germany

When the Kaiser was forced to flee in November 1918, Germany became a democracy. It was known as the Weimar Republic and its main body was the Reichstag or Parliament. This contained the following range of political parties:

The undemocratic left-wing parties, mainly the Communist Party, which many workers supported. They wanted to bring about a Russian-style revolution, and eliminate class differences.

The democratic parties, mainly Socialists, which most workers supported, and the Liberals with their middle-class followers. These parties wanted to make the Weimar Republic succeed.

The undemocratic right-wing parties, usually known as Nationalists. They had much support from the establishment and the peasants and mostly wanted to bring back the Kaiser.

Democracy needs success

In a democracy, people vote for whichever party they like. The more Germans voted for the democratic parties, the more successful the Weimer Republic would be. Success was what the Weimar Republic needed, but what kind of success did people want?

Economic success, as much prosperity for as many people as possible.

Foreign success, especially self-defence and respect among nations.

Political success, particularly strong, stable government.

We shall follow democracy through its various stages between 1919 and 1933 to assess its successes and its failures. It was not a complete failure from the start.

Poster showing left-wing, democratic and right-wing parties. Underneath are the ruins of the old Germany. 'Help us rebuild' is the slogan

---

Q

1 Which political parties is the poster calling on Germans to support, and why?

2 Which groups and parties were unfriendly to democracy from the very beginning?

3 Democracy needed success in economics, foreign affairs and politics. Do you think that any one of these is more important than the others in making people support democracy? Explain your answer, in the order which you think is most convincing.

1918–1919 The German revolution

Foreign affairs

The first act of the new government was to sign the armistice on 11 November, 1918. The picture on page 84 of the 'Stab in the back', which you read about in Chapter 2, sums up the feeling of most Germans, as does the following extract. In it a historian, who was eighteen at the end of the war, later recalls his feelings . . .

In our high school, as in most of the secondary schools of Germany after 1918, there was a noticeable right-wing trend, which most of our teachers followed, at least those who spoke to us about politics. We believed that it was the stab in the back alone that had prevented a German victory. We had one nationalist history teacher who defended this worst form of the legend. We were convinced that we could only be patriotic on the right-wing side. We were not meant to think that the upper classes of the Kaiser's Germany had made serious mistakes and that these had put our victory in danger (if victory had ever been a possibility) as much as the left-wing had. We took up nationalist slogans, while the Republic of which we were making fun was trying to pull Germany out of the mud.

'The stab in the back'

Economic affairs

The German economy was run down because of the war. Many Germans were starving because the Allied armies prevented food from getting through to Germany.

Politics. The German revolution

At the end of the Great War Germany seemed on the edge of revolution, with widespread riots, strikes and street fighting between different groups. As soon as the Kaiser fled, the Socialists under Frederick Ebert formed a government.

They were worried about whether they would be able to keep Germany safe for democracy and feared a communist takeover.

The communists, known as Spartacists, planned to follow Lenin's example of the previous year by seizing power in Berlin. On the right, the army leaders wanted to keep as much of the old system as possible, although they realised they could not bring back the Kaiser at the moment. They were determined to prevent a communist takeover. One very right-wing group of young soldiers, known as the Freikorps, was active in the streets attacking communists.

Within two months it was all over. In January 1919 the Spartacists seized all the important buildings in Berlin as Lenin had done in Petrograd. They ignored Lenin's advice, which was that Germany was not ready for revolution and that the government and army were still strong enough to crush them. A week later thousands of leading Spartacists had been slaughtered and their uprising crushed. The democratic government, led by Ebert, had accepted the army's offer of help to put down the communists. The Freikorps hunted down and murdered many communists in cold blood, including their leader Rosa Luxemburg.

Immediately after the Spartacist uprising a general election was held which produced the following results:

Undemocratic left-wing	Democratic parties	Undemocratic right-wing
8%	77%	15%

Summary

Democracy had some successes. It had 'won' the German revolution and had gained over three quarters of the vote.

It also had some serious failures. It was held back by the 'stab in the back' legend and had to stand up against quite large undemocratic forces, especially many of the most influential and powerful people in Germany.

Q

1 Read the description of the historian's schooldays. Why do you think he was so right-wing at the time? In what way did he change his mind later?

2 Why did the democratic government co-operate with the undemocratic army leaders and the Freikorps in 1919?

3 Which were democracy's most troublesome problems in this period—economic, foreign, or political? Explain your answer. Use the picture in your answer.

4 What chance of survival did democracy have in 1919?

1919–1924 The early years of the Weimar Republic

Foreign affairs

Germany hardly had a foreign policy at all in these years. In 1919 the Treaty of Versailles was made and Germany's only policy was to accept it—reluctantly and resentfully. Germany was forced to give up its territories to its neighbours, to reduce its armed forces and to start the huge reparations payments. Most Germans detested the treaty and hated their government for having to accept it. They wanted to overthrow it by force but, of course, could not do so. The government, however, could not act so irresponsibly. The foreign minister, Walter Rathenau, realised that a better policy would be to carry out the treaty honourably and responsibly. In this way, he hoped, the British and the French would gradually have to become less harsh with Germany and would improve the terms of the Treaty. They would reduce reparations, allow Germany to join the League of Nations and even, in the end, cancel the treaty altogether. This policy was known as *fulfilment*.

Rathenau failed to convince the German people that it was the right way ahead, and in 1922 he was assassinated for his idea. The French refused to reduce their terms. They showed their contempt and their frustration by invading the Ruhr area in 1923. The German government's only course was one of 'passive resistance'. This meant boycotting French goods, encouraging strikes in the Ruhr and issuing protests, but it was not a success. Only when a new Chancellor, Gustav Stresemann, called off this policy in November 1923 did the French withdraw. German foreign policy was a failure.

Economic affairs

Here there was a mixture of successes and failures:

Successes

By 1923 German industry had fully recovered from the war and had become once again the most productive and competitive in Europe. Businesses were booming, full employment was returning and the wages and conditions of the workers were improving.

Failures

A terrible economic disaster, hyperinflation, struck Germany in 1923. It had never happened before on such a scale. In 1918 a loaf of bread cost half a mark but in January 1923 it cost 250 marks. This was 'ordinary' inflation. Then came *hyperinflation*. By November a loaf cost 200,000,000,000 marks. The value of money became meaningless, changing twice a day. The government had no idea what to do and simply printed more and more bank notes. Soon people were taking basketfuls of paper money to buy a few vegetables. Barter—exchanging goods for other goods—became more usual than paying in money. Some people benefited from hyperinflation; people not on fixed incomes who could charge higher prices daily for their goods and services—farmers with their produce, manufacturers with their goods, professional people who were lucky enough to charge fees for their services.

The vast majority however, suffered greatly. Certain groups of people were the real losers—pensioners on fixed incomes, people on fixed salaries, people living on their savings. These people, often middle class people, were suddenly struck down as their fixed incomes became worthless. The whole world seemed to turn upside down.

Middle-class victims of hyper-inflation: selling valuables in the street . . .

... at a free soup kitchen

The following extract shows how badly people were hit by hyperinflation.

My husband set up his practice as an eye surgeon. My own income was a fixed 30,000 mark loan payable to me. However, 80% of my husband's patients had their fees paid by the government three months after treatment. We were virtually without an income. My brother-in-law had a distillery and, like all businessmen, was well off. His wife and I had our babies within a few days of each other and I remember how I was lying in a borrowed iron bedstead with my baby in a borrowed cradle, while she had everything for herself and her baby in pure silk. And yet we both came from the same sort of family background. When things were at their worst, I had a letter from the woman who was paying off the loan to me. She paid it off in full and the money I got paid for a cheap holiday. I had to put my first child in a borrowed pram, I couldn't pay for a pair of shoes to be heeled, my husband had to get off the train because he hadn't enough money for the ticket—these things I can never forget.

In November 1923, after months of confusion, Chancellor Stresemann managed to control hyperinflation, and the currency returned to normal. But the memory of suffering remained.

Politics

The mixture of failures and successes is difficult to assess.

Failures

Many people did lose faith in democracy at this time because it failed to deal with Germany's problems. A government lasted for only a few months at a time before being replaced by another. Terrible street violence and frequent assassinations by groups like the Freikorps shocked people. There were two serious attempts to overthrow democracy in these years. The first, the Kapp Putsch, was in 1920 when several dissatisfied army regiments tried to seize control of Berlin. The government fled but the attempted *putsch* failed when the people of Berlin came out on strike. The second attempt was led by Adolf Hitler in Munich in November 1923. It was easily defeated by the authorities.

Successes

The main success was that democracy did *not* collapse. Most people were still prepared to give it a try, as you can see from the proportion of people voting in the election of early 1924:

Undemocratic left-wing (communists)	Democratic parties	Undemocratic right-wing
13%	57%	30%

1 Was 'fulfilment' a sensible policy in foreign affairs? If so, why could the German people not accept it?
2 Explain the feelings of the people in the photographs and the woman in the extract.
3 Assess the level of success in economic affairs. Is industrial success more important than hyperinflation in your assessment?

4 In political affairs, which is more important—that there were two attempts to overthrow the Weimar Republic by force, or that they failed?
5 What chance of survival did democracy have in 1924? Were its chances better than in the previous period?

1924–1929 The best years of the Weimar Republic

Foreign affairs

During these years Germany's foreign minister was Gustav Stresemann, the most respected leader of the Weimar Republic. His aim was to restore Germany to its former power and glory by getting rid of the Treaty of Versailles. He thought that the best way to achieve this was to be friendly with Germany's former enemies, Britain and France, and to persuade them to change the treaty gradually in Germany's favour. This had been Walter Rathenau's idea earlier and had failed. Now, because the German people trusted Stresemann, it became more and more successful.

An election poster for Stresemann's party. He is looking over the bridge on the Rhine, towards France

Gradually the treaty was altered. In 1924 the Dawes Plan was made with Germany's former enemies, postponing reparations. In 1925 the Treaty of Locarno was made, dealing with Germany's borders. Germany, Britain and France confirmed the loss of Alsace-Lorraine to France, as laid down in the Treaty of Versailles, but did not confirm the loss of German lands to Poland.

This was seen as a great success for Stresemann. Then, in 1926, Germany was allowed to join the League of Nations, and in 1929 another plan, the Young Plan, reduced reparations, and France agreed to pull her troops out of the Rhineland after ten years instead of fifteen. In these ways the Treaty of Versailles was becoming less harsh and many Germans were even beginning to see that Stresemann's policy was right.

Economic affairs

The Dawes Plan helped to make Germany much more prosperous by making possible a series of huge loans to Germany, mainly from America. Now that hyperinflation had been conquered, the German economy could not be held back and became more successful than it had ever been. Germany's industries became very competitive, new inventions and methods were introduced and German goods were exported all over the world, reaching a peak in 1929. The wages and conditions of the workers improved dramatically.

Political affairs
Failures

Unfortunately for the Weimar Republic, even in these fairly successful years Germany never achieved the sort of strong, firm and settled government that the people wanted. As before, one government replaced another rapidly and was not able to carry out the policies it wished. There continued to be a lot of violence on the streets between extreme political parties, particularly the Nazis and the communists. Law and order seemed difficult to attain.

Successes

Despite these problems, people's faith in democracy was certainly growing again, as you can see from these voting figures from the 1928 election:

Undemocratic left-wing (communists)	Democratic parties	Undemocratic right-wing
11%	65%	24%

Q

1 In foreign affairs, why did the German people increasingly feel that Stresemann's 'fulfilment' policy was right? Give examples in your answer.
2 What does Stresemann's election poster tell you about the German public's view of his foreign policy? Give your reasons for your views.

3 Had the growing support for democracy more to do with foreign or with economic affairs, or both equally? Give the reasons for your view.
4 What chance of survival did democracy have in 1929? Were its chances better than in the previous period?

Nazism up to 1929

The waiting years

Nazism began during the Weimar Republic and found support among some of those who were dissatisfied with democracy. Such people responded eagerly to the ideas of Adolf Hitler, who dominated the Nazi movement from its earliest days. Hitler's ideas were often vague and rambling, very difficult to pin down, not clearly set out like the beliefs of communism. Nevertheless they were very strongly held indeed and appealed to certain sections of the German people.

Case study—The Nazi message

Throughout Nazi writings and speeches several main ideas emerged. These were—racialism; hatred of communism; hatred of democracy; dictatorship; nationalism and hatred of the Treaty of Versailles; hatred of the establishment.

In the following extracts you should get some impression of such powerful ideas, as expressed by the Nazi movement. Most of these extracts are taken from Hitler's own book *Mein Kampf*. Try to identify the main idea, from the list above, expressed in each extract.

1 Parliamentary thickheads are setting themselves up as statesmen. They find thousands of reasons for their lack of success, and there is only one that they will not admit, that they themselves are the cause of all evil. (Hitler.)

We get elected to the Reichstag (Parliament) to use democracy against itself. If democracy is stupid enough to allow that, it is its own affair. We come as enemies. Like the wolf tearing into the sheep, that is how we come. (Göbbels.)

2 Our new movement must not only alter the decline of the German people, but must create the granite foundation upon which some day a state will rest which represents a national body. A Germanic state of the German nation. Once the disgraceful armistice had been signed, disarmament alternated with enslavement, political crippling with economic plunder. We no longer know how to value honour. Since then hardship and care have been the constant companions of our people and our one faithful ally has been misery. (Hitler.)

3 A racial state must set race at the centre of all life. It must take care to keep it pure. Those who are physically and mentally unhealthy must not continue their suffering through their children. Thus the entire nation will share in the blessing of a highly-bred racial stock.

The mightiest enemy of the Aryan is the Jew. Idealism is not present in him. He is always a parasite in the body of other peoples. The Jews are the leaders of the Trade Union movement, of capitalism, of democracy and of Marxism. The ultimate aim of the Jewish struggle is the conquest of the world. (Hitler.)

4 Man can only be controlled by force. In ruling him, everything is allowed. You must lie, betray, even kill when policy demands it.

There must be no majority decisions. The decisions will be made by one man. (Hitler.)

5 The first requirement is the elimination of the Marxist poison from our national body. I have begged for an opportunity for our movement to reach a reckoning with Marxism, but I preached

to deaf ears. On the day when Marxism is smashed, Germany's chains will in truth be broken for ever. (Hitler.)

6 We are enemies of today's capitalistic system with its unfair salaries, its judging of a human being according to wealth and property instead of responsibility and performance, and we are determined to destroy this system. (Hitler.)

Q

1 Which of the powerful Nazi ideas do you detect in the extracts above?

The changing fortunes of Adolf Hitler

Early life up to 1923

Adolf Hitler, born in 1889 into the family of an Austrian customs official, had an unhappy childhood. On leaving home at 16 he failed to get into art college in Vienna and spent five years in poverty and frustration. It was during this part of his youth that he became convinced of the main ideas of his life—his hatred of Jews and communists and his love of Germany. In the Great War he was badly wounded and earned the Iron Cross for bravery. In 1919 he became a right-wing army agent, spying on communists and fostering patriotic ideas among his fellow soldiers. He soon showed his amazing skills as a public speaker, and, on leaving the army, joined an extremely right-wing political party. By 1921 he had become its *Führer* (Leader), renamed it the National Socialist or Nazi Party and adopted an Aryan symbol, the swastika, as its emblem. The party had its own unofficial army, the SA or Brownshirts, under Ernst Röhm, and its efficient propaganda organisation under Josef Göbbels.

The Beercellar Putsch, 1923

While Germany was still suffering from hyperinflation, growing violence and the French invasion of the Ruhr, Hitler sensed that the time was ripe for a *putsch*, a seizure of power. On 8 November 1923, Hitler declared a National Revolution in a Munich beercellar. However,

when the Nazi leaders and the SA attempted to march through the city they were quickly dispersed by the army. Hitler was arrested, found guilty of treason and imprisoned in Lansberg Castle. Here he wrote his famous book *Mein Kampf* (My Struggle) before his release after only nine months' imprisonment.

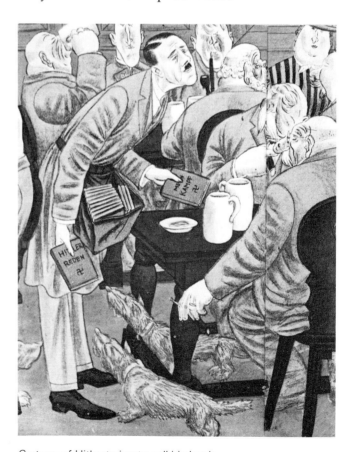

Cartoon of Hitler trying to sell his book

In prison Hitler came to an important decision. He made up his mind not to try to seize power again but to get into power by more legal methods—by winning the support of the establishment, especially the army, and by gaining mass support so that he would be elected into power.

Years of failure, 1924–1929

The Nazis continued to scream out their message to the German people. They gained some fanatical followers but not the mass support that Hitler craved. In fact their support actually declined. In the 1924 general election they had 32 MPs, but this dropped in a later election in the same year to 14 and in the 1928 election to 12. As you saw when reading about the Weimar Republic on page 87 the support for democracy increased during these years. Hitler felt that his opportunity would never come.

Q

1 Why did Hitler, in 1924, discard one method of attaining power, and adopt two others?

2 What does the cartoonist mean in his cartoon? Does it show him to be a clear sighted observer of politics?

The crisis of the Weimar Republic

The Depression 1929–1933

The Depression threw Germany into confusion. The prosperity of the 1920s came to a sudden end as businesses went bankrupt, unemployment rose to six million, and poverty returned on a large scale. The democratic government, led by Chancellor Brüning, failed to solve these problems and power was given to President von Hindenburg, a top army leader, instead of to a normal government, to rule Germany as he thought best. Hitler was delighted. Now was his chance to win mass support and to win over the establishment. Would he succeed?

Winning mass support

Hitler needed over 50% of the vote in order to become Chancellor of Germany. Aided by Göbbels, Hitler was brilliant at using propaganda to increase his popularity. He was a superb public speaker, working up the fears and worries of his audience to a fever pitch and then offering himself as the answer to their problems. His clever use of films, posters, songs, salutes, marches and demonstrations kept him in the public eye at all times. Violence too was deliberately used, especially against communists, to create a sense of tension and hostility and to increase people's fears. Hitler could now add to his long list of grievances, 'I will give you jobs'.

Many people were so shattered and frightened by their problems that they were ready to accept Hitler as their leader. Read the following account by Albrecht Speer, who was a lecturer in 1932, later became a leading Nazi and was imprisoned for war crimes after the war. In 1964 he wrote down his memories of how he became a Nazi on hearing Hitler speak . . .

> Here it seemed to me was hope. The perils of communism, which seemed on the way, could be stopped, and instead of hopeless unemployment, Germany could move towards economic recovery. Hitler mentioned the Jewish problem only in passing. But such remarks did not worry me although I was not anti-Jewish. My mother saw an SA parade in the streets. The sight of so much discipline in a time of disorder, the impression of energy in an atmosphere of total hopelessness, seems to have won her over also.

You can see from the voting figures of July 1932 how successful Hitler was in gaining mass support:

Undemocratic left-wing (communist)	Democratic parties	Undemocratic right-wing
15%	40%	45% mostly Nazis (37%)

Tenants protesting against high rents—Nazis and communists ▲

'Millions stand behind me' ▶

MILLIONEN
stehen hinter mir

DER SINN DES HITLERGRUSSE

After the election President von Hindenberg told Hitler that he had no intention of making him Chancellor and that, if he tried to seize power, the army would crush him. Now Hitler's plan of winning the support of the establishment became supremely important.

Winning over the establishment

Who were the establishment? President von Hindenburg was certainly their chief figure, but he was very old and not a particularly strong personality. He relied heavily for advice on a group of establishment leaders, nobles like Baron von Papen, rich businessmen like von Thyssen and army leaders like General von Schleicher. Such men detested Hitler. He detested them too, but realised that they would make the decision to appoint him Chancellor if only he dropped the anti-establishment parts of his programme. Hitler therefore did this.

Already in 1931, he had come to an agreement with von Thyssen and other industrialists who financed him. The others, however, were afraid to give him power if they could not control him.

In November 1932 there was another general election. The Nazi vote fell from 230 MPs to 196. The communist vote rose to 100 MPs. These figures convinced Hindenburg's advisers that they had no choice but to appoint Hitler Chancellor. They mistakenly thought that now they could control him more easily. It was one of the biggest mistakes in history.

1 What does the photograph tell you about German politics at the time? Use the election figures also.

2 Is the poster favourable to Hitler or critical? What does it mean?

3 How useful is Speer's later evidence (page 90) in assessing Hitler's appeal?

4 Why was the Depression much worse than any of the other problems facing the Weimar Republic?

5 Use the following in your assessment of why Hitler came to power. Make clear which you regard as the most important.

The circumstances of the time

The Weimar Republic's problems, especially the depression.

The individual qualities of Hitler

His ability to lead and to convince others; his decision to get to power by legal instead of forceful methods; his decision to drop the anti-establishment parts of his programme.

The mistakes of the establishment

Their mistaken view that they could control Hitler once he was Chancellor.

The Third Reich

From Chancellor to Führer

In January 1933 Hitler became the last Chancellor of the Weimar Republic. Eighteen months later he was the undisputed Führer of the Third Reich. In these months he took a series of steps to make himself a totalitarian dictator, removing his enemies and strengthening his power.

Step 1 February 1933. The burning of the Reichstag

You can read the following extracts to help you decide who was responsible for burning down the Reichstag building. Van der Lubbe, a communist, who was arrested with other communists after the blaze and later executed, said on oath to the court . . .

> I set fire to the Reichstag all by myself. The others are being tried with me but they were not in the Reichstag.

General Halder, who was not present in 1933 but who later became a top general during the Second World War, was put on trial for war crimes in 1946 along with Göring, another Nazi leader. He swore, on oath . . .

> At Hitler's birthday luncheon in 1942, the conversation turned to the topic of the Reichstag fire. Göring interrupted the conversation and shouted, 'The only person who really knows about the fire is myself, because I had it set on fire.'

Two historians, R. Manvell and H. Fraenkel, who researched thoroughly into the subject in 1974, wrote . . .

> It is beyond any doubt that it would have been utterly impossible for any one man to set the building alight on this scale, let alone a man without knowledge of the building and gravely handicapped, both mentally and physically, as van der Lubbe certainly was.

Whoever was really responsible, Hitler blamed the communists for the fire. The President gave him the power to ban communists from campaigning in the General Election, which was about to be held in March. Despite this and much more intimidation and falsification, the Nazis got only 43% of the vote.

Step 2 March 1933. The Enabling Act

In the Reichstag the moderate parties were so afraid of a communist takeover that they passed the Enabling Act, which gave Hitler dictatorial powers for four years. Using these new powers over the next few months, Hitler abolished all political parties, trade unions and the free press. He set up concentration camps for political prisoners, especially communists and socialists.

Step 3 30 June 1934. The Night of the Long Knives

Hitler still saw two threats to his power. One was the powerful SA with its leader Ernst Röhm, who were much more anti-establishment than

Hitler himself and were planning to act against the establishment. The other threat was from army leaders like General von Scheicher, who really wanted the Kaiser rather than Hitler to rule Germany. Hitler struck at both these threats in the same night, as you can see in the cartoon. Terror squads of the SS, Hitler's own bodyguard, brutally murdered both SA and army leaders. The SA was made smaller and weaker. The army too became subservient to Hitler, when every single soldier had to take a public personal oath of loyalty to him.

Step 4 November 1934. The referendum

A referendum, or special vote, was held, producing 88% support from the German nation for Hitler's rule. There was much intimidation, bribery and falsification of figures.

Step 5 August 1934. Hitler as Führer

On Hindenburg's death Hitler declared himself President as well as Chancellor, not bothering to be elected. However, he styled himself Führer. He was now supreme in power.

No rivals left. A foreign view

---

1 The Reichstag fire.
a Assess each of the pieces of evidence for its reliability.
b Say what each piece of evidence suggests about who was responsible for the burning of the Reichstag.
c Write down your own opinion, taking all the evidence into account.

2 Sum up the point that the cartoon is making about Hitler. Is it effective?
3 Which of the two voting figures more accurately reflects Hitler's genuine support—the 43% in March 1934 or the 88% in November 1934? What is your own realistic assessment?

How Hitler ruled Germany—The Nazi State

Nazi Germany, like Stalin's Russia, was a totalitarian system. It appeared very strong and dynamic, as you can see in the picture of a Nazi rally on the next page. This was the image that Hitler liked to create, but underneath there were weaknesses, as you will see.

Nazi organisation: The one-party state

The Führer

Germany had no Constitution, no rules about how the country should be run, apart from a vague belief that everything was at the will of the Führer. Hitler preferred this unclear state of affairs. He was at the centre of everything. Personally, Hitler was a lazy and disorganised man who was prepared to let others take decisions, although he would overrule them if he wished.

The Nazi leaders

These men were always subservient to Hitler. Hermann Göring saw himself as second to Hitler, being in charge of the *Luftwaffe* (the Air Force) and industrial development. Heinrich Himmler seemed a colourless figure, but, as leader of the SS, grew in importance during the Third Reich. Josef Göbbels, in charge of propaganda and censorship, cleverly controlled the flow of news and views in Germany. Rudolf Hess, the Deputy Führer, was officially in control of the Nazi Party organisation, but in reality he was not very powerful, and the party came more and more under the control of Hitler's secretary, Martin Bormann.

There were no clear divisions of responsibility between these leaders. Hitler encouraged arguments and power struggles among them. He liked to think that only he was solid and stable, while all around him was tension and conflict. The top leaders were certainly not working closely together on a clear, organised programme.

The Nazi Party

This was divided into regions and sub-regions down to groups of houses. There were 42 *gau* (regions), each one under a *gauleiter*. Then came the 760 *kreisleiters*, 21,500 *ortsgruppe führers*, 70,000 *zellenleiters* and, at the bottom, 210,000 *blockleiters*. All of these were new officials who over-ruled Germany's existing government officials. In Berlin the various Nazi Party organisations dealt with things such as foreign affairs and economics, interfering with the civil servants who organised such matters. Increasingly the SS interfered in everything.

Thus was Germany organised in the Nazi way. In practice however, Hitler used the normal methods of a totalitarian state to keep control — propaganda and terror.

A mass rally at Nuremberg

Two Nazi leaders, Göring and Streicher, quarrel in public

Propaganda, indoctrination and censorship

In 1933 most Germans did not have strong Nazi values and beliefs. At the most only 37% had voted for Hitler in a *free* election. Many others had strong democratic, socialist or communist views. Strong religious beliefs too, inspired many Germans. Indeed the majority of Germans were not strongly anti-Jewish. Yet Hitler was determined to make Germans into fervent Nazis, and propaganda was his method of doing it.

Josef Göbbels was in charge of all propaganda and censorship. He controlled Germany's 436 newspapers, daily met the national editors, and even wrote the main headlines. Radios were produced cheaply so that every household could afford one, and were even located in streets, parks and workplaces. Films were cleverly used, especially of the great Nazi rallies at Nüremberg, where the stadium was specially designed for filming. Events like the Berlin Olympics of 1936 were used to impress visitors and were filmed to influence people at home and abroad.

Hitler practising a speech. He had many photographs taken to help him to improve his movements and gestures

Most important was the promotion of Hitler himself. The Führer's speeches were continuously heard; his picture was everywhere. Hitler was portrayed as the almighty leader who would bring power, prosperity and happiness to the fatherland.

Censorship

All newspapers, literature, art, drama, and cinema were severely censored to weed out foreign influences, anti-German and anti-Nazi ideas. Many artists and writers were forced to emigrate. Public book burnings were arranged of unsuitable literature, as you can see in the photograph. Even famous German writings were destroyed if they happened to be written by Jews. Thomas Mann, a famous writer who emigrated from Germany, wrote bitterly as he left, 'Where one begins by burning books, one ends by burning people.'

Burning 'un-German' literature, 1933

The indoctrination of children

It was thought that children were ideal for indoctrination, because before long a new generation would grow up, which had known nothing but Nazism. The school syllabus was very strictly controlled and special lessons were devoted to anti-Semitism. German history lessons and biology lessons were very suitable for nationalist and racialist purposes.

Germany's diet of information and ideas was now confined to what the Nazis wanted it to be. Propaganda was impossible to avoid. The whole of the media was cleverly used to change people's opinions, beliefs and values. For example, people were prepared for the killing of handicapped and mentally ill people by a propaganda campaign designed to ridicule these people by showing deliberately exaggerated pictures. You can see from the following extracts how the Nazis tried to influence people's ideas.

No evil priest can prevent us from thinking that we are the children of Hitler. We follow not Christ but Horst Wessel (a Nazi hero). Away with incense and holy water. The Church can go hang for all we care. The swastika brings salvation on earth. I want to follow it step by step. (Song specially written for the Nüremberg Rally of 1934.)

The evil Treaty of Versailles, imposed by the French and the English, enabled international capitalism to steal Germany's colonies. France herself acquired part of Togoland. If German Togoland, temporarily under the administration of the French imperialists, covers 56 million square kilometres, and contains a population of 800,000 people, estimate the average living space per inhabitant. (A mathematics question from a school text book.)

A man who feels it his duty to become the leader of his people is not responsible to the rules of parliament or to the idea of democracy, but only to the mission placed upon him. And anyone who interferes with this mission is an enemy of the people. (Hitler's speech to the Reichstag in 1938.)

How successful was propaganda?

It is impossible to be accurate about this because the evidence is scarce and often contradictory. For instance, even when Germany was actually being invaded in 1945, a Nazi leader spoke to some farmers. He reported the conversation in a book written in 1964 . . .

Unrecognised in the twilight I stood talking. To my surprise, the faith in Hitler which had been hammered into their minds all these past years was still strong. Hitler could never lose the war, they declared. The Führer is still holding something in reserve that he'll use at the last moment. Then the turning point will come. It's only a trap, his letting the enemy come so far into our country.

On the other hand a secret SS report of 1943 states . . .

The telling of vulgar jokes against the state, even about the Führer himself, has increased considerably recently. In conversations in cafés, factories and other meeting places the people tell each other the latest political jokes, some of which are in opposition to the government.

Terror

Hitler always used violence and quickly made Germany into a police-state. In charge of the whole terror machine was a *Reichsführer*, Himmler. The most important part of his empire was the SS which grew rapidly in power and influence in the later 1930s. It had several sections, but the most important of these were the SD, Security Service, which even spied on the top Nazi leaders, and the SS TV which was in charge of the concentration camps. Himmler was also in charge of the other Secret Police, the Gestapo, as well as the ordinary police.

The first concentration camp was set up in 1933 at Dachau but others soon followed. By 1939 there were 133,000 Germans in concentration camps. At first the camps contained mostly political prisoners, identified by red triangles as socialists and communists, but they were soon expanded to include Jews (yellow star), pacifists (dark blue triangles), Jehovah's Witnesses (purple), homosexuals (pink) and anti-socials (black). Particularly brutal ordinary criminals (greens) were also put into the camps and their purpose was to terrorise the others. Within six years over 100,000 inmates died through cruelty, murder or starvation, and the camps became even more inhuman during the war.

Arrival of prisoners to the first concentration camp 1933

The atmosphere of terror and spying spread rapidly. Children were encouraged to spy on their parents and to report anti-Nazi remarks to the authorities. The following extract shows how careful Germans had to be. . . .

An unknown man knocked at Leidler's and showed him a membership book of an anti-Nazi group. Would Leidler have any weapons? Could he supply the names of any local anti-Nazi? Leidler answered, 'No' to each question and added, 'I'm through, I've had it. All I can do is put you up for the night which I will do for any human being on a night like this.' Just before he left in the morning, the man turned his lapel back and showed Leidler an SS button, then he left wordlessly.

Opposition

Resistance to Hitler was very limited. Terror was his strong point. Even so, some had the courage to resist, although few attempted to overthrow Hitler. At first some political groups opposed Hitler with posters, but were soon suppressed. Underground groups of communists who had escaped from the concentration camps acted as spies or underground opponents. The most famous group of these was known as Red Orchestra. Some socialists too, kept their spirits alive by secret meetings, but could do little else. Religious groups also resisted. The Protestant Church was fairly easy for Hitler to control, because he set up a Reichsbishop, Müller, to dominate it. Even so, many Protestant clergymen, led by Martin Niemoller, refused to accept the new Church and were sent in large numbers to concentration camps.

Catholics were more difficult to control as their leader, the Pope, was not in Germany. Pope Pius XI denounced Nazism in a letter smuggled into Germany and read out in all churches in 1937, but this only resulted in the persecution and internment of thousands of priests. The Catholic opposition was led by Cardinal Galen and Bishop Faulhaber. One great success was to raise public opinion against Hitler's campaign to kill handicapped people in the late 1930s, which led Hitler to call off the campaign. There were also some aristocratic groups who opposed Hitler such as the Kreisiau Circle. In 1944 a group of aristocratic army officers attempted to assassinate Hitler in the famous Bomb Plot, but failed and were brutally treated. Over 5,000 were executed.

Q

The Nazi organisation of Germany

1 How does the photograph of the Nazi rally create the impression that Hitler intended? Does it *still* create this image?

2 List the faults and inefficiencies in the Nazi Party's way of ruling Germany.

3 What do you think would be Hitler's reaction to the photograph of quarrelling leaders?

Propaganda, indoctrination and censorship

4 What does Thomas Mann's statement mean? Do you agree? Use the evidence of the photograph in your answer.

2 Assessing the true effect of Hitler's propaganda is impossible. What sort of evidence would you like to see to give you a more accurate estimate?

3 Do you agree that years of propaganda, censorship and indoctrination would make all children into thoroughly Nazi adults? Explain your answer.

4 Give examples of ways in which history and biology lessons could be used for indoctrination purposes.

5 There were some fanatical Nazis, at one extreme, and a few resisters at the other. What lay in between these two extremes, in your opinion? Use the evidence to help you in your assessment.

6 Why do you think Hitler had many photographs taken of himself practising for a speech?

Terror

1 What sorts of people do you think were put into the anti-social category in concentration camps?

2 Write a Nazi propaganda caption to go with the picture of the concentration camp inmates. Some pictures like this one were published.

3 The resisters did not have much in common with one another, but they were all inspired. By what?

Summing up

What kept Germans most effectively under Hitler's complete control? Arrange the three main methods—Nazi organisation, propaganda and terror—in order of importance. Give your reasons.

Racial policy

Race

There is no doubt that race obsessed Hitler; he was determined to put into practice his ideas about anti-Semitism and about racial purity, and to make all Germans feel as strongly as he did.

Anti-Semitism

There were about 500,000 Jews living in Germany who thought of themselves as Germans. They were not particularly prominent in the political life of Germany and they fitted quite well into German society. There was considerable anti-Semitism in some sections of German society, but it was not at all as strong as in some other parts of Europe.

Göbbels, who was as strongly anti-Semitic as Hitler, immediately got to work to increase the

In a childrens' book illustration, children read the anti-Semitic magazine, *Der Stürmer*

Poster for the Nazi film 'The Eternal Jew'

Published list of women still using Jewish shops

already existing anti-Semitism by clever propaganda, working up and increasing people's fears and converting them into hatred. Hitler could not act as fully and as quickly against the Jews as he wished, for fear of other countries refusing to buy German goods. Even so, between 1933 and 1937 there was an increasing flow of anti-Semitic policies and laws. In April 1933 there was an official boycott of Jewish shops and businesses and Jews were banned from government jobs.

In 1935 the Nüremberg Laws were passed, removing Jews' rights to German citizenship and prohibiting marriage between Jews and non-Jews. In 1936 and 1937 there followed a series of laws banning Jews from the medical and legal professions and ordering Jewish women who had relations with non-Jews to be put into concentration camps. All the time non-Jews were encouraged and pressurised into mistreating Jewish children in schools and boycotting Jewish shops, as you can see in the list of 'offenders' on the opposite page.

Crystal Night—was it planned?

On 7 November 1938 a Polish Jew shot a German diplomat in Paris. On 9 November the diplomat died, and in a storm of rioting, burning and murder, hundreds of Jewish shops, houses and synagogues were burned down or wrecked. Crystal Night took its name from the litter of broken glass strewn in the streets. The following extracts of evidence should help you to decide whether Crystal Night was planned or not.

A Nazi newspaper on 10 November reported . . .

> A spontaneous wave of righteous anger throughout Germany.

The *Times* reporter wrote on 10 November . . .

> In every part of the Reich synagogues and shops were smashed and ransacked and Jews arrested or hounded. Bands of young Nazis and other groups of youths, all in plain clothes, but evidently acting to a systematic plan, smashed the windows of every Jewish shop they encountered. The active participants in this display were youths and boys of the Hitler Youth,

> the only uniformed body which I actually saw taking part in this destruction. In the main street of Berlin, army officers in uniform did try to bring fanatics to reason, but were forced to leave because of threats.

A diplomat, Fritz Hesse, wrote in his memoirs in 1955 . . .

> At a dinner on 9 November Göbbels explained to Hitler a massive blow which he and the SA were going to launch against Jewish shops and synagogues in a few hours. There was no doubting the Führer's approval. Hitler squealed with delight and slapped his thigh in his enthusiasm.

Heydrich, second in command of the SS, telegraphed to all SS and Police Headquarters, soon after midnight on 10 November . . .

> Co-operate with Party and SS Leaders in organising the demonstrations.

Within a month over 30,000 Jews had been sent to concentration camps, Jewish children had been banned from education and all Jewish businesses and shops had been closed down and sold. By 1939 over half of Germany's Jews had fled from Germany. The other half, persecuted and deprived, were unable or unwilling to get out. They were not to outlive the Second World War.

'Racial Hygiene'

This was the name that the Nazis gave to their attempts to bring about the Master Race. In Hitler's view the Master Race could only be 'pure' if Germans were to be physically and mentally perfect. In 1938 Hitler made a frightening decision. Physically and mentally handicapped and mentally ill people were to be murdered by lethal injections given by SS doctors in six official centres. As the public became aware of this, opposition grew, especially from the churches. Eventually the policy was called off, but not before 150,000 had been killed.

Social policy

Hitler's aims

As in his racial policy, Hitler tried to create a new Nazi German nation in which everyone would have Nazi values and beliefs. Propaganda and indoctrination helped to achieve this. Hitler did not really have any clear idea about how to deal with the various groups and classes in Germany, but during the 1930s certain policies did develop.

The peasants

Hitler had always been popular with the peasants whom he regarded as racially suitable and sound. Originally he had promised to give the peasants their own land by confiscating it from the landowners, and some of them still hoped for this. In 1933 he set up the Reich Food Estate to look after the peasants' interests. He did not confiscate the land from the landowners, but instead passed the Reich Farm Law to give those who rented farms the right to keep them perpetually. However, he failed to stop the peasants from moving from the countryside to get jobs with higher wages in the towns.

The workers

The workers had never really supported Hitler, and large numbers of them had always voted for the Communist and Socialist Parties. Hitler hated the working class organisations, the trade unions, and never felt really at home with working class audiences. However, he had promised them jobs.

Soon after coming to power Hitler abolished all trade unions and the workers' right to bargain for higher wages; strikes were made illegal and hours of work increased, often to 60 or 72 hours a week. Hitler set up a sort of Nazi Union called the Labour Front under Dr Robert Ley. Ley introduced two campaigns to encourage workers to work harder for the nation. One, called 'Strength through Joy', organised leisure, sports and artistic activities and arranged cheap holidays for the workers. The other, 'Beauty at Work', provided brighter factories, music at work and efficient canteens. By 1939 unemployment had fallen from 6 million to virtually nil, and the average earnings were ten times higher than unemployment pay had been in 1933.

Women

Hitler and the Nazis were very anti-feminist, and had extremely old-fashioned views about women. Their idea was that women should stay at home and produce more children for the Master Race. Gold Motherhood Crosses were given to women with eight children. Women were made to give up their jobs when they married and they were not encouraged to join the Nazi Party. A separate women's organisation, the German Women's League, was set up. Its motto was 'Children, Church, Kitchen', and it discouraged the wearing of trousers, smoking, bright clothes, makeup and permed hair.

Youth

Hitler once said, 'I say to my opponents, ''Your child belongs to us already, what are you? You will pass on. Your descendants, however, now stand on our side. In a short time they will know

Hitler at a youth camp

A member of the Hitler Youth

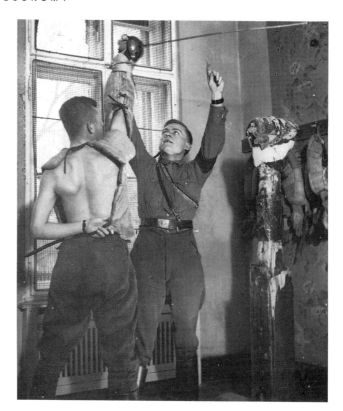

nothing else but this new community." ' Young people were Hitler's great hope for the future. He aimed to make them into a fanatical following, carrying on his ideas into the future. As well as being heavily indoctrinated at school, German youths and children had their spare time organised too. At the age of six, boys joined the 'Little Fellows', at ten the 'Young Folk' and at fourteen the 'Hitler Youth Movement' itself. You can see a youth in his uniform in the photograph. Girls joined a completely separate organisation called the 'League of German Maidens'. In these organisations all young people were taught to be absolutely loyal to Hitler, to the extent of spying on their parents, and to fight and die for Germany.

Q

Racial policy

1 How do the anti-semitic posters on page 98, including the list of non-boycotters, try to get their message across? Do you think that they would be successful?

2 Crystal Night

a Assess each piece of evidence for its reliability.

b Using the evidence, come to your conclusion about whether Crystal Night was planned or not.

3 Do you think that Hitler succeeded in his racial aims?

Social policy

1 Most workers probably had a rather mixed attitude to Hitler. Try to explain what it might have been.

2 Did Hitler deal successfully with the peasants and women?

3 Is the photograph of Hitler and young people a propaganda photograph? Give your views.

4 What do you think the Nazi Youth members thought and felt about the photograph? Use the information about the Youth movement in your answer. What is *your* opinion of the picture?

The Nazi economy

Hitler was not interested in economics and did not really understand economic problems. He was much more interested in getting and keeping power, and did little to develop any economic policies until he had been in power for several months. Historians disagree about Hitler's economic policy, but they have identified four main features in it . . .

1 Reducing unemployment

Hitler realised that unemployment had brought him to power in 1933, therefore he had to cure the problem so that the same conditions would not exist which could enable a rival leader to emerge. You can see from the chart on the next page how this was done. The biggest fall in unemployment was immediately after Hitler

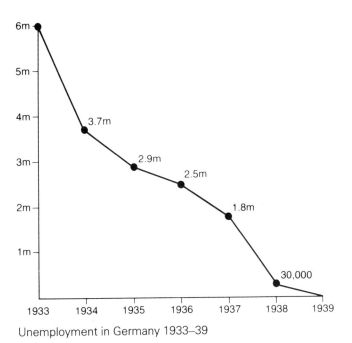

Unemployment in Germany 1933–39

came to power. After this it dwindles to virtually nothing by 1939. The reasons were as follows ...

The up-turn after the depression

This happened naturally. The worst of the depression was already over in 1933 and the economy was recovering anyway, as it was in other countries.

Public works schemes

In America President Roosevelt had started such schemes on a large scale, based on the idea of the economist J. M. Keynes. Hitler began to do very much the same thing. Over one million young unemployed workers were organised on a temporary programme, planting forests, working for farmers, digging ditches and so on. Large amounts of money were also spent on contracts for all sorts of public works. By far the largest was the building of motorways—autobahns—all over Germany. Also there were projects such as the re-building of slums, huge schemes like the Nüremburg Stadium and the digging of canals. In 1935 these schemes were combined to create a National Labour Service. Its members marched to work in military formation.

Loans to industry

Large loans were made to industry on condition that more workers were employed. With these loans, industry expanded and needed more workers.

Altering the unemployment figures

Many Jews, women, and left-wing workers were dismissed from their jobs. They were not counted as unemployed.

Rearmament

Between 1936 and 1939 very large amounts of money were spent on rearmament, which stimulated many German industries, especially steel, coal, chemicals and engineering. The Army also expanded after 1935 to reach about one million men in 1939.

A military parade, 1935

2 Making Germany industrially strong

Germany was already the largest economy in Europe. Hitler realised that a prosperous economy would not only create employment but would make the country militarily powerful as well. By making loans to industry, reducing unemployment and crushing the socialists, the communists and the unions, Hitler and his Economics Minister, Schacht, restored the confidence of big business. Businessmen, encouraged by the government, began to invest more and more money in industry. By 1935 Germany had overcome the slump and was back again to the levels of 1928. The steel, coal, chemical and engineering industries all expanded rapidly. Because so many Germans now had jobs, spending on consumer goods began to rise rapidly between 1936 and 1939. Rearmament played a large part in this expansion after 1936. In 1939 the national wealth of Germany, mostly produced by industry, was up by 75% on 1933's figures.

3 Making Germany self-sufficient

This is closely connected with making German industry strong. Making Germany self-sufficient, and not dependent on other nations for important raw materials like oil and iron ore appealed to Hitler. In 1934 Schacht set up the New Plan which restricted imports of foreign goods into Germany and made special arrangements for oil and raw materials with countries friendly to Germany, such as Romania. This, however, was not enough for Hitler, especially as it did not allow him to spend as much money as he wanted on rearmament. Therefore, in 1936 Hitler introduced the Four Year Plan with Göring in charge.

The purpose of this Plan was to make Germany as self-sufficient as possible in industry and agriculture by using German resources or by inventing substitutes. Secretly Germany was to be ready for war at the end of the Plan. Large factories were built to develop plastics rather than imported rubber, and synthetic oil made from coal and shale instead of imported oil. The huge Hermann Göring steelworks used Germany's low grade ores instead of importing foreign high-grade ores. Research began into all sorts of substitutes or alternatives such as nuclear power and oakleaf coffee. The Plan certainly helped to make Germany more self-sufficient, but was not a great success. Complete self-sufficiency was simply impossible. It became much more tempting to seize other countries' oilwells by war rather than to develop synthetic oil.

4 Nazi control over the economy

Hitler did not believe in nationalising industries. Before coming to power he had made a deal with big business, which had financed him and helped him to attain power. Hitler was not the sort of man who kept promises if he did not want to, but he realised that the economy would develop much more rapidly with big business in charge. He encouraged large companies, like I. G. Farben, to take over smaller companies, thus increasing their size and power. Big business also benefited from the Nazi régime's huge rearmament orders, and, by co-operating fully with the government, helped to prepare for war. Yet there was no doubt about who was dominant in the partnership between Hitler and big business: Hitler was. HE controlled the economy.

Q

1 How did Hitler reduce unemployment? Look carefully at the chart and then arrange the reasons in order of importance. Explain your views.
2 Use the picture in this section to show how public spending on rearmament helped the economy to grow.
3 How did making Germany industrially strong and self-sufficient increase her military power?

4 Why did Hitler not nationalise business as other totalitarian dictators, like the communist leader Stalin, did?
5 What other, non-economic, benefit was there from the Labour Service?

Extension

An assessment. To what extent did Hitler change Germany?

Did Hitler change Germany completely, partly or very little in the following ways?

Politics

—the setting up of a totalitarian state based on one-party organisation
—propaganda, censorship and indoctrination
—terror

Racial policy

—anti-Semitism
—racial hygiene

Social policy

—policies towards the peasants; workers; women; youth

Economic policy

—reducing unemployment
—making Germany industrially strong and self-sufficient
—controlling the economy

Using the above headings assess how fully Hitler changed Germany between 1933 and 1939.

Discussion topics

1 Which parts of the Nazi message still have some appeal today? With what groups or types of people?
2 Which parts of Hitler's policies under the Third Reich do you find most difficult to understand? Why?

Essays

1 What were the main problems facing the Weimar Republic between 1919 and 1933?
2 Why did Hitler come to power in Germany? Describe the steps he took between 1919 and 1934 to become Führer.
3 Outline the main features of the Third Reich between 1933 and 1939.

LINKS

Democracy

Ever since 1918—and, for a few countries, earlier—several nations have had democracy as their form of government. Nowadays we take it for granted. Yet, in between the two World Wars, democracy was not always successful. The Weimar Republic was the most spectacular failure. But, during the very same period, other democracies like America did not collapse—nor even came near to collapse.

Comparing American and German democracy, to find out why one succeeded and the other failed, should help you to understand democracy itself. Think about what you would write in the spaces below.

A How strong and effective was the democratic system of government?

Germany	*America*

Elected government

Germany	America
There were many political parties, none of which ever had a majority. Governments, therefore, were always coalitions of several parties. They usually did not have the confidence to act strongly. There were many governments under the Weimar Republic, mostly lasting only a few months.	

Democratic leadership

Germany	America
	A very effective and dominant democratic leader emerged—Roosevelt. He certainly convinced the vast majority of the people that he was acting in their interests. He provided strong, charismatic leadership.

The establishment

Germany	America
	America's establishment, comprising mainly the rich, and big business interests, was not against democracy. As the democratic system worked well, the American establishment had less influence. Roosevelt usually ignored it.

B How strong was support for democracy?

Germany	*America*

General support and democratic tradition

Most Germans favoured democracy between 1919 and 1929, but after 1929 the number declined to under half.

There was no strong and wide agreement among the people that democracy was the right and most suitable form of government for Germany.

Anti-democratic forces

Some Americans were rather apathetic about democracy, and quite a large proportion never bothered to vote. Only a very tiny minority was opposed to democracy.

Problems causing discontent with democracy

The Weimar Republic faced several problems which it found difficult, or even impossible, to cope with.

The Depression was the worst of these problems. Another was the Treaty of Versailles, which had created the 'stab in the back' legend. Yet another was the instability, tension and violence in German politics.

C Were there any groups willing and able to take over from democracy?

Germany	*America*

Two political parties grew rapidly in the early 1930s as the democratic parties lost support—the Nazis and the Communists. The Nazi's biggest asset was Hitler, whose powerful, charismatic leadership convinced many Germans that he would solve all their problems. The Communists, too, grew rapidly during the Depression.

Both Nazis and Communists offered an alternative to democracy.

Q

1 What would you write in the spaces above? Do not simply write the opposite of what it says in the other column. There will be some similarities and some differences. Write a paragraph under each heading, comparing American and German democracy.

2 Write out, in order of importance, a list of the things that democracy needs to succeed. Give reasons for your views.

3 Apply your list to British democracy now and assess its strength.

Totalitarian government

You have studied two examples of totalitarian government—Nazi Germany and Stalinist Russia. Comparing these two in order to find out which one was the more totalitarian, should help you to appreciate what totalitarianism is.

Remember that a totalitarian government is one that seeks to use its power fully to control every aspect of life. Think about what you would write in the spaces below.

A How strong was totalitarian control?

Germany   *Russia*

Both Nazi Germany and Stalinist Russia used the following three main methods of asserting their power over the people.

The one-party organisation

Stalin always ensured that the Communist Party was in control of every part of central and local government and the civil service. It dominated Russia very effectively. The Communist Party itself was totally under Stalin's personal control, purged regularly to ensure its total loyalty.

Terror

Hitler's terror was very extensive. The SS and the Gestapo had absolute control over spying and violence, and interfered in everything. The main method of terror was the concentration camp, where about 100,000 Germans were killed before the war. All opponents were dealt with brutally to ensure that opposition was effectively crushed.

Propaganda and indoctrination

The whole of the media and the arts were taken over by the state. Every item of news and opinion was controlled, concentrating on what the Party wanted, such as economic achievements and the glorification of Stalin. Censorship was very tight indeed.

Special attention was paid to the indoctrination of children and youth, both at school and in the various youth movements. The communist message was everywhere.

Opposition

Stalin removed all political opposition parties, groups and unions including even potential leaders within the party. All alternative sources of power and influence were removed or persecuted.

Germany   *Russia*

Ideas and beliefs

Hitler, by terror and especially by propaganda, tried to make *all* Germans into true Nazis. It is impossible to assess how successful he was as there is not enough evidence. However, it is unlikely that most adult Germans fully accepted everything that he stood for. People with strong alternative religions and political values certainly kept quiet, but did not change their beliefs.

Society and race

Hitler removed German Jews by persecution and the handicapped by his euthanasia policy. The Nazis tried to control the life and role of women, workers, youth and the peasants. It is very difficult to assess how effective this control was.

The economy

Stalin took over every part of the economy. All industry and trade was completely nationalised. Stalin nationalised agriculture by collectivising the farms. The economy was totally controlled by the state in a series of Five-Year Plans.

Q

1a What would you write in the spaces above? Do not simply write the same as what it says in the other column. There will be some similarities and some differences. Write a paragraph under each heading, comparing the two systems.

b Conclude by saying which was the more totalitarian, and why.

THE SECOND WORLD WAR

Why did war break out in 1939?

Historians have identified several causes of the Second World War, but disagree about their relative importance. You must decide for yourselves which were the main causes of the war.

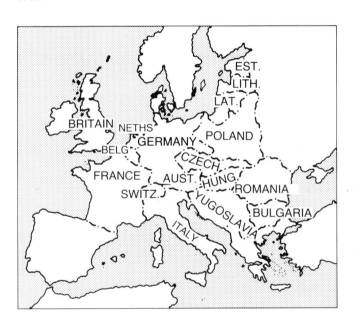

Europe in 1939

A The basic problem of Germany

The problem was that Germany was the most powerful country in Europe, situated right in the middle of the continent. As such, it wanted to assert its power. The Treaty of Versailles had failed to deal with this problem. In fact it had made the problem much worse, causing Germany to feel very resentful. The Treaty also left Germany in a much stronger position for the future by creating weak new states around Germany in the South and the East. By the early

1930s, Britain and France had altered many parts of the Treaty of Versailles by actions such as the cancelling of reparations. However, Germany's lost lands were still under the control of other nations. Any German government, whether it was Nazi or democratic, would want to alter this state of affairs, but not necessarily by war.

B The non-co-operation between the former allies

In order to defeat Germany in the war, co-operation would be needed between the countries which had defeated Germany in the Great War. There was no such co-operation. **America** was isolationist and was determined never again to join in another war in Europe. **Russia**, the only communist power, was regarded by all as an outcast. No-one would trust or co-operate with her. **Britain** was too involved in her own huge Empire to want to be involved on the Continent again. Only **France** was willing to act against Germany, but was too weak to do so alone. She had tried, and failed, in 1923 when she had invaded the Ruhr, and would not try again. France had terrible problems of her own in the 1930s and was becoming more divided within herself, as Germany became stronger and more united under Hitler.

C The failure of the League of Nations

The League of Nations failed to deal with any major problems that arose between the two World Wars. In 1931 Japan, growing more aggressive, invaded Manchuria in China, but the League of Nations was forced to allow Japan to stay. The worst blow came in 1935 when the Italian Fascist dictator, Mussolini, invaded Abyssinia in Africa. The League could do nothing at all against Italy and was virtually ignored from then onwards. Some people had seen the League's weaknesses from the time it was set up in 1919, but by the late 1930s they were obvious to everyone.

D The Depression

The Depression hit the world very badly and put an end to good relations which were beginning to develop between Germany, Britain and France. It made countries think only of their own problems and look after only their own interests. All governments put higher taxes on foreign goods, causing the relations between countries to become much more tense. The Depression also enabled Hitler to come to power in Germany.

E Hitler's foreign policy

Of the three aggressive powers in the 1930s—Germany, Italy and Japan—Germany was the most powerful and therefore the most dangerous. From 1933, Hitler was in charge of Germany's foreign policy and had several aggressive aims. He wanted to overturn the Treaty of Versailles. In 1935 he openly declared that he would break the Treaty by rearming Germany, but most of all he wanted Germany's

lost lands to be returned, especially those given to Poland. In addition he wanted all German speakers to be part of the Third Reich, even those who had never lived in Germany, such as the Austrians and the Germans in the Sudetenland, part of Czechoslovakia. Hitler also talked a great deal about *Lebensraum*—living space—for Germany in Eastern Europe. There and in Russia he could gain vast economic resources to make Germany really self-sufficient. Russia, too, was communist as well as being Germany's traditional enemy in the East.

In 1936 Hitler took a risk and sent German troops into the Rhineland, the part of Germany de-militarised by the Treaty of Versailles. He was ready to pull back his troops if Britain and France acted against Germany, but they did nothing. In March 1938 he sent troops into neighbouring Austria, also prohibited by the Treaty of Versailles. No-one objected. Next was Czechoslovakia's turn, when Hitler claimed the Sudetenland for Germany. This time the British Prime Minister, Neville Chamberlain, visited Hitler in Munich and, in return for a promise not to take any more land, allowed Hitler to take the Sudetenland in 1938.

F Appeasing Hitler

Appeasement is the word used to describe British and French policy towards Germany in the late 1930s, although it was mainly a British policy. It means that they allowed Hitler certain gains in the hope that he would go no further. It is easy nowadays to criticise the British Government for appeasement, but at the time there seemed some very good reasons for it, as you can see below:

1 Britain was too harsh towards Germany in the Treaty of Versailles, especially by taking land from Germany. If Britain allowed Germany to have some lands back, Hitler would stop demanding so much.

2 Public opinion was against any war, especially so soon after the Great War.

3 The Depression was still not over. Britain had too many economic problems and felt it had to deal with these first.

4 Britain's forces were not ready. They would take several years to build up.

5 Britain had no real interests in Eastern Europe. Its own safety was not threatened by Hitler at that time.

The Germans enter Czechoslovakia

6 If Britain acted in a friendly manner towards Hitler, he might turn his attack onto Communist Russia. This would suit Britain, especially as it would weaken both Germany and Russia.

There is no doubt that appeasement led Hitler on and encouraged him to take more land and to become more aggressive.

The outbreak of war—1939

Up to March 1939 Britain and France appeased Hitler. However, at that time Hitler invaded the remainder of Czechoslovakia, which he had not yet taken. Immediately the mood in Britain and France turned to war. This time they were determined not to 'give in' again. Hitler, however, still hoped that they would continue to do so. In case they did not, he made an agreement with Russia known as the Nazi–Soviet Pact. By this agreement Germany and Russia agreed not to fight one another. This

Entering Czechoslovakia

suited Hitler perfectly. In August 1939 he invaded Poland. This was the last straw for Britain and France. On 1 September they declared war on Germany.

―――――Q―――――

1 Which of the causes of war were started or worsened by the Treaty of Versailles?
2 Which of the causes of war were
a circumstances that no-one could do anything about;
b the actions or decisions of individuals or groups, who might have acted differently?
3 Which, in your opinion, are the three most convincing reasons for appeasement? Explain your choice.

4 Arrange the causes of war in order of importance. Give the reasons for your choice.
5 Why was the Nazi–Soviet Pact such a success for Germany?
6 Both pictures were taken when the German Army entered Czechoslovakia. One was taken in the Sudetenland in 1938, the other in Prague, the capital, in 1939. Which is which? Give your reasons.

Making sense of the Second World War in Europe

The Second World War can be confusing because so many events took place in so many different places. However, to make sense of it, we can divide the war into two parts.

Up to the winter of 1942–1943

In this half of the war the Germans and their allies expanded rapidly in three directions—in Western Europe, in the Mediterranean, and in Russia.

The turning point of the war came in the winter of 1942–1943. In two important battles the Germans were defeated while at the furthest extent of their power. These were the battles of El Alamein and Stalingrad.

From the winter of 1942–1943 to the end of the war

After these two battles, the Allies (Britain, France and, after 1941, America) pushed the Germans back, in the Mediterranean, in Western Europe and in Russia.

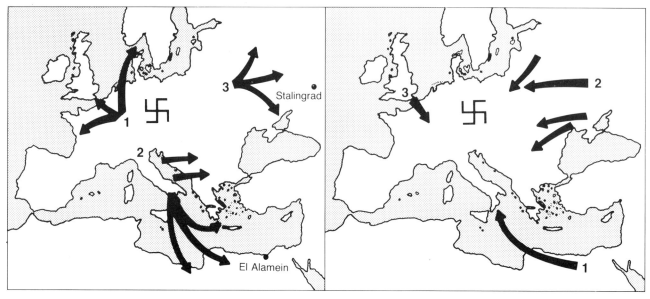

German expansion 1939–42/3

German retreat 1942/3–45

Up to May 1940

The main campaigns of the Second World War began in May 1940, when Germany invaded France. Before that time, Germany with its new *Blitzkrieg* tactics, easily defeated Poland. Russia too invaded Poland and took her share, as arranged in the Nazi-Soviet Pact of August 1939. The British and French could do nothing to help Poland. Their armies waited in France and began to build up their strength. They had long expected the German Air Force, the *Luftwaffe*, to bomb their cities but the attack never came.

Only at sea was there some action, as German surface raiders like the *Graf Spee* and U-boats began to sink British merchant ships. Hitler ordered an attack on France in November 1939 but bad weather prevented it. The British called this part of the war the 'Phoney War'.

In April 1940 Germany invaded Denmark and Norway. This ensured that the route for the vital iron ore supplies from Sweden via Narvik in Norway remained in German hands. The British and French sent troops and ships to help the Norwegians, but after two weeks of useless effort they were forced to withdraw.

The invasion of Western Europe, May–June 1940

Blitzkrieg in action

Comparing the two sides before and during the invasion of Western Europe will enable you to assess why the Germans won so easily.

The table on the following two pages compares the two sides under different headings.

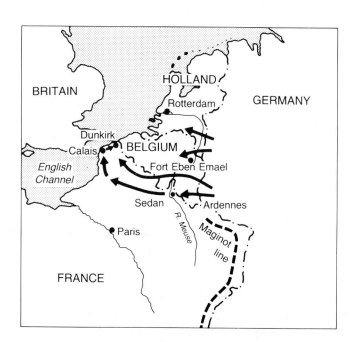

The invasion of Western Europe, 1940

| *Britain and France* | *Germany* |

Armed forces

Divisions. 135 divisions comprising about one million French soldiers and over 300,000 British. There were 4 armoured divisions, 3 French and 1 British.

Tanks. 2,500 tanks, mostly French, including 260 of the Somua, the best tank in Europe. However the French tanks were not fitted with radio. The British had about 230 fairly inferior tanks.

Aircraft. 2,600 planes, of which 1,600 were British. Only 500 of these were modern, capable fighters.

Divisions. Germany was not quite ready for war, but had about one million men in 134 divisions. 10 of these were armoured divisions.

Tanks. 2,250 tanks, only 600 of which were really satisfactory, the Panzers III and IV. All of these were fitted with radio.

Aircraft. 4,500 aircraft, only about 2,250 of which were modern and capable. Their main duty was to support the Army, being fighters and dive bombers.

Strategy

French strategy was to wait behind the Maginot Line, a system of strong forts and guns supplied by underground railways. This line only ran from the Swiss frontier to the Belgian frontier. The frontier between Belgium and France would be protected by the Ardennes Mountains and by the best divisions of French troops.

The French used their tanks spread out and moving at the slow speed of the infantry who accompanied them, as they had done in the Great War.

British strategy. The British did not have a clearly worked out strategy, expecting, wrongly, that the war would be an air or naval war.

Germany's *Plan Yellow*, developed in 1940 and favoured by Hitler, was to invade through the Ardennes and move to the Channel, seizing part of Northern France. Germany's tactics were offensive, known as *Blitzkrieg* — Lightning War. Armoured divisions would thrust deeply and quickly into enemy territory. Their main weapons were tanks, preceded by dive bomb attacks and followed by all their own artillery, infantry and supplies, *all* motorised. These divisions moved very fast indeed.

Leadership

The French Prime Minister, Paul Reynaud, was a fighting figure but the rest of the Cabinet was rather hesitant. The French military leaders thought in old-fashioned terms as if they were fighting the Great War.
Winston Churchill became the British Prime Minister in May 1940. He was a very positive war leader. The British military leadership was cautious. It could not afford to lose the British Army in France, known as the British Expeditionary Force (BEF), completely.

Hitler was an utterly confident and inspiring leader. He favoured young generals like Guderian and Manstein, who had developed Blitzkrieg warfare.

Daily Mirror cartoon, 1940.

ALL BEHIND YOU, WINSTON

Britain and France   *Germany*

Morale

Morale is very difficult to assess.
France was certainly not very confident, even
though she was fighting for her survival. She
had too many problems which had divided her
and made her unsure of herself.

German morale was extremely high, especially
after the early and easy conquests of Poland,
Denmark and Norway.

VOILA CE QUI NOUS ATTEND, SI
LE GOUVERNEMENT N'EST PAS CAPABLE
DE SORTIR L'AVIATION FRANÇAISE DE LA
SITUATION DRAMATIQUE OÙ L'A PLACÉE
LE FRONT POPULAIRE!

French poster demanding that the government provide more
aircraft

British morale was at a high level, especially after
Churchill's appointment, when a small War
Cabinet was formed containing members of all
political parties.

With this comparison in mind, we can now go on to see what actually happened.

―Q―

1 Why could the British not afford to lose the BEF in
Northern France?
2 What does the cartoon suggest about British morale
at the time? What other evidence would you like to
have to be more certain about this?

3 How useful is the poster in telling you about the
state of the French Air Force?
4 Under each of the headings armed forces, strategy,
leadership and morale, make a list of points, indicating
where the Allies were superior, inferior or equal to
Germany.

The fall of France 1940

The German army began a two pronged offensive on 10 May; one section of the army attacking Holland and Belgium while the main *Blitzkrieg* divisions attacked through the Ardennes. They took the Allies by surprise and showed how useless the Maginot Line was by going around it. The allied forces were split in two and were unable to prevent the rapid German advance.

By 20 May, only ten days after the first attack, the Germans had reached the coast. The Allies were in confusion and acted separately. The Belgian Army surrendered and France concentrated on the defence of Paris. Lord Gort, the British Commander-in-Chief, decided to save the BEF from capture by evacuating it from France.

Dunkirk

Churchill, realising that further resistance was pointless, code-named the evacuation Operation Dynamo. The German advance was so rapid that Dunkirk was the only port left. A vast fleet of over 700 ferries, pleasure cruisers, even large barges and small yachts made its way to the Belgian coast. For some reason the German Army halted for two days outside Dunkirk. These two extra days allowed the BEF and the ten French divisions to defend the town more successfully and to evacuate large numbers of troops. The evacuation began on 27 May and went on for nine days until 4 June. The *Luftwaffe* bombed the troops and ships but bad weather

Troops wading out to a rescue steamer, Dunkirk 1940

hindered it, as did continuous attacks by Spitfires and Hurricanes from British airfields.

Nearly 340,000 troops including virtually the whole of the BEF and 140,000 French soldiers were saved. The British Army however was badly demoralised. Most of its equipment, including vast numbers of vehicles and guns and 474 aircraft, was lost. Without these the defence of Britain itself was seriously hindered.

Churchill spoke on the BBC, 'In the midst of our defeat, glory came to the island people, united and unconquerable. There was a white glow, over-powering, sublime, which ran through our island from end to end. The tale of the Dunkirk beaches will shine in whatever records are preserved of our affairs.' The newspapers talked of the 'Dunkirk Spirit'. Churchill also said elsewhere, 'Wars are not won by evacuations'.

Meanwhile the German army wheeled southwards. On 14 June Paris fell and on 16 June Marshal Pétain took over and requested an armistice from Germany. Hitler took great delight in signing the armistice in the same railway carriage as was used on 11 November 1918.

Troops being evacuated from beaches, Dunkirk 1940

1 Using your knowledge of the two sides, both before and during the fall of France, arrange the following in order of their importance to the German victory. Give your reasons.
armies   leadership   strategy and tactics   morale

2a What do you think were the dangers and difficulties of evacuating armies from beaches?
b What do the pictures suggest about the way the British carried on the evacuation?
3 The newspapers treated the evacuation as a victory. In what way was it a victory? In what way was it a defeat?

The Battle of Britain 1940

Now it was Britain's turn. Hitler set the date for the invasion—15 September—and code-named the operation 'Sea Lion'. He gathered together a large fleet to transport his *Blitzkrieg* army across the Channel to Britain. However, first he had to clear the skies of British planes and he ordered the *Luftwaffe* to do this.

Britain, too, speeded up her preparations. The South coast was heavily fortified, its people evacuated, roadsigns taken up and obstacles placed on open stretches of roads and fields to prevent the landing of German planes. Operation 'Cromwell' was drawn up for the defence of Britain area by area. The Home Guard, 'Dad's Army', was founded. The Dunkirk Spirit was still strong, but the people were very anxious.

Comparing the two sides

On the German side, the *Luftwaffe* was equipped with 1,000 fighters and 1,600 bombers and had over 6,000 available pilots. The RAF had 820 fighters, mostly Spitfires, the best fighter of all, and 1,500 pilots including some Poles and Czechs. They also had the advantage of the use of radar which had just been invented.

The Battle

Stage 1. 8–15 August

The *Luftwaffe* carried out intensive attacks on British shipping in the Channel.

Stage 2. 15 August–7 September

Göring concentrated the *Luftwaffe* attack on RAF bases, mostly around London, such as North Weald, Biggin Hill, Debden and Croydon. The *Luftwaffe* destroyed so many planes, installations and fuel reserves that, although Dowding only used fighters and pilots when necessary in small numbers, the British were almost defeated. They could not have gone on for much longer.

Stage 3. 7 September–end of September

On 7 September Hitler directed the *Luftwaffe*'s attacks away from the airfields to the cities, especially to London. This may have been because he thought the RAF was already defeated, as Göring told him, or because he was retaliating against a British bombing attack on Berlin. Whatever the reason, it saved the British, even though the blitz on British cities caused terrible devastation. The important fact was that British airfields were no longer under attack and could recoup their losses. The bombing and the British counter-attacks went on for several weeks but in fact the Battle of Britain was over. Hitler dismissed his invasion fleet and gave up all thoughts of invading Britain for the time being. He turned his attention to Russia instead.

1a Why did Britain win the Battle?
b Why was the Battle so important?

The Mediterranean Campaigns 1940–1942

Italian offensives

In 1940 Hitler's ally, the Italian dictator Mussolini, launched two offensives to extend Italy's power and to reach the Suez Canal and oil reserves. One offensive was in North Africa, where Marshal Graziani, with 200,000 troops invaded Egypt. 35,000 British troops under General Wavell managed to stop them reaching the Nile, and turned them back into Libya, capturing Tobruk and Benghazi in January 1941, along with 100,000 Italian troops and 400 tanks.

The other attack was in the Balkans in October 1940, where the Greeks withstood the Italians. Mussolini turned to Hitler for help.

The German invasion of the Balkans

The Germans forced Hungary, Romania and Bulgaria to join them as allies, and quickly defeated Yugoslavia and Greece in April 1941. In Greece they fought British troops, whom Churchill had transferred from Egypt, and forced them to retreat to Crete. In May 1941 35,000 German paratroops successfully drove the British from Crete back to Egypt at a heavy cost in German lives.

The German invasion of North Africa — the desert campaign

Hitler chose the tank commander Erwin Rommel to lead the brand new *Afrika Korps* to the Suez Canal. Rommel now used *Blitzkrieg* tactics all over the desert. Arriving in March 1941, he soon won back the whole of Libya and defeated Wavell at Halfaya Pass. He could go no further, however, as his supply lines were over-stretched. The British Eighth Army under their new leader General Auchinleck, counter-attacked in December 1941 and re-captured Libya as far as Benghazi. Rommel, reinforced by Hitler, struck again in May 1942. Although outnumbered in men and tanks, he won a major victory over the British at Gazala and pushed them back into Egypt. Churchill now sacked Auchinleck and replaced him with General Bernard Montgomery.

Montgomery's personal leadership and the reinforcement of the Eighth Army with American Sherman tanks uplifted British morale. Montgomery drew up his forces at El Alamein in October 1942. The British had superiority in tanks and in air power, but even so Rommel, with only 90 tanks, tried to break through. In a three day battle Rommel was defeated and retreated westwards. Germany had reached its furthest extent. In this area of the war the turning point had come at El Alamein.

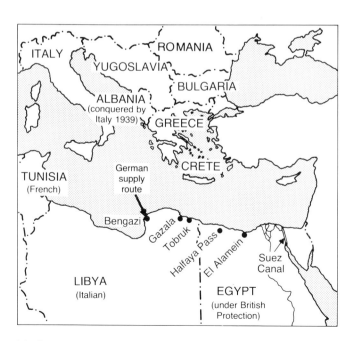

Mediterranean campaigns, 1940–42

British troops capture an enemy tank

The Russian Campaign June 1941–January 1943

Hitler knew that he had to avoid a two-front war, fighting in both East and West. Such a war had defeated Germany in 1918. However Hitler decided that, although the British had not been defeated, he would take a calculated risk.

On 22 June 1941 Operation Barbarossa began. It was the biggest *Blitzkrieg* of all and was planned to knock out the Red Army and to capture Moscow. It was to be a short war lasting eight months. A *total*, long term war, which actually happened, was not planned.

Russia was simply not ready for this surprise attack. The *Luftwaffe* destroyed many Russian planes on the ground and captured vast numbers of troops. The German advance took place on three fronts.

The north

Manstein's Northern Army Group quickly made its way to Leningrad and besieged the city. In the most terrible siege in history, Leningrad was cut off from the rest of Russia, apart from a winter ice-road across Lake Ladoga. The people suffered severely and were reduced to eating their pets, rats and even the glue from the wallpaper before they died. Over one million people perished in this siege.

The centre

Here two immense columns [under Generals Guderian and Hoth] tore through the Ukraine, encircling over 300,000 Russian troops at Minsk, and doing the same again at Smolensk. The Generals then wanted to strike immediately at Moscow before the winter began, but Hitler forbade this. He decided to divert German forces southwards to help in the capture of Kiev. Only in December 1941 — too late — did the two columns again try to encircle Moscow. They were unprepared for a winter campaign and became bogged down in the frozen mud.

By now Stalin had geared up the Russian economy for total warfare and was turning out an increasing number of arms, helped also by British and American aid. Stalin's 'scorched earth' policy of destroying the land and everything on it as Russian troops retreated, deprived the Germans of food and equipment. In December 1941 the Red Army under Marshal Zhukov was ready to attack, equipped with winter clothing and trained to survive without shelter. Behind German lines the Russian Partisans, resistance fighters, used guerrilla tactics to sabotage German supply lines and to ambush German troops. Zhukov managed to stop the German encirclement of Moscow and

The Eastern Front, 1941–43

brought the German Army to a halt. The Germans had actually reached the bus terminus on the outer edges of the city.

The south

German armies under General Kleist encircled hundreds of thousands of Russian troops at Uman. At Kiev Stalin refused to let the Red Army withdraw, despite the most appalling slaughter and the capture of three quarters of a million Russian soldiers. The southern armies then made their way southward to Kharkov in December 1941.

Stalingrad

In 1942 both the Germans and Russians put most of their effort into the southern campaign. German divisions entered the Caucasus but found the oil wells, which they so badly needed, destroyed. It became obvious that if the Germans were to stay in the Caucasus they would have to capture the city of Stalingrad. In August 1942 Field Marshal von Paulus and his Sixth Army began to attack the city. Everyone knew that this would be *the* decisive battle of the whole war. Both Hitler and Stalin refused to allow any retreat whatsoever and ordered their troops to fight to the death. The German Army was in fact in a very exposed position and was in danger of being encircled at Stalingrad by a Russian pincer movement from north and south. The city centre was the scene of the most tenacious fighting as each house and sewer became the scene of bitter battles.

More Russian soldiers died defending this one city than Americans died in the entire war. Even when the Red Army began to encircle Stalingrad, Hitler still refused to let the Sixth Army retreat. Paulus fought on for long enough to let the German Panzer divisions escape from the Caucasus before being blocked in, but in February 1943 he disobeyed the Führer and surrendered with a third of a million troops. Hitler had been stopped at last. The war was turning. From now on Hitler could only retreat.

— Q —

1 Why was Hitler's decision to invade Russia a calculated risk?

2 Mark on the map arrows showing the various German advances through Russia.
3 Why was the Battle of Stalingrad so important?

The war at sea

Even though Britain had the largest navy in the world, it was still very vulnerable to the smaller German Navy. Britain had a huge empire and 21 million tons of merchant ships to protect on the high seas. The German Navy consisted of two modern battle ships, the *Bismarck* and the *Tirpitz*, three pocket battleships, such as the *Graf Spee*, and, most dangerous of all, a large fleet of U-boats. The main purpose of each navy was not to fight major battles but to blockade the enemy. This meant destroying enemy ships carrying food and materials before they reached home. This situation was much harder for Britain, who had to import so much to survive.

Churchill said after the war . . .

the only thing that ever really frightened me during the war was the U-boat peril.

In spite of engagements between the British fleet and the *Graf Spee* and the *Bismarck*, naval warfare was not really about surface battles but about U-boats, and merchant shipping was the U-boats' real target. To combat the loss of one million tons in the first few months of the war, the British navy adopted the convoy system, in which large groups of 20–50 ships sailed together. Destroyers protected them, fitted with detectors to search out the U-boats. In response the Germans began to hunt in 'wolf-packs' sailing on the surface to avoid detection. Up to 1943 the U-boats were winning, destroying over 2,000 ships amounting to 12 million tons.

By 1943 the Allies had developed better radar and faster frigates, but it was really longer-range planes, better radar systems and more accurate depth charges that finally defeated the U-boat menace. In May 1943, 41 U-boats were sunk and Germany called off its U-boat campaign.

Inside a German submarine

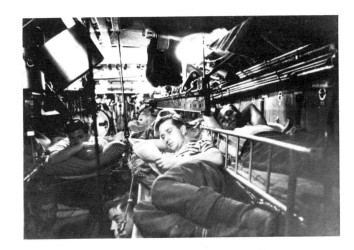

The Mediterranean

Throughout 1942 the British lost control of the Mediterranean altogether due to U-boat attacks, and their island base at Malta was left unprotected. However, despite terrible damage caused by Italian air-raids and by virtual starvation, the island held out and the British gradually regained control of the Mediterranean.

Q

1 What does the photograph tell you about being a sub-mariner? What other evidence would you need to re-create a better understanding?

2 What did Churchill mean by the quotation on page 119?

Extension

Why did Germany win the war up to the winter of 1942–1943?

During the first part of the war Germany won almost continuous victories. Most of Europe was in German hands. France, Britain and Russia had been fully or partly defeated.

The Allies managed to stop the German advance but had not really begun the counter-attack. Britain had avoided invasion in 1940 and had stopped the Germans at El Alamein in North Africa. Russia had been devastated, but had stopped the Germans at Stalingrad. America, joining the Allies in December 1941, had hardly yet begun to assert herself in full force.

Why were the Germans able to achieve such spectacular advances in this part of the war? Below are a list of reasons, not arranged in any particular order. It is your task to arrange them in the most convincing order, explaining your choice and how the reasons are linked together.

● Hitler was able to defeat his enemies separately, mainly by avoiding fighting on two fronts at once.
● Germany's enemies, Britain, France and Russia were weak or unprepared for war.
● Hitler and his generals were effective war leaders at this stage.
● Germany's *Blitzkrieg* tactics and surprise attacks were superior to the enemies' tactics.
● The German economy was very well prepared for war, at least for a *Blitzkrieg* type of war.
● German morale was always very high, and increased with so many easy victories.

The Nazi Occupation of Europe

Racial policy: The Holocaust

Hitler's obsession with race is shown in his treatment of Europe, especially of Jews and Slavs. Genocide, the murder of whole races of people, was certainly attempted. Historians disagree about whether Hitler deliberately planned the 'final solution', or whether it suddenly became possible with the invasion of Russia, where so many Jews lived. At first the Jews were rounded up into ghettos and camps where they were murdered and persecuted at will. Only in 1942 did extermination camps, using gas chambers and mass cremation, come into operation. Auschwitz became the most notorious of these, although there were several others, mostly in Eastern Europe. Jews were herded into cattle trucks from all over the continent for their last journey. Over *six million* Jews died in this Holocaust.

Slavs too were treated as 'sub-human'. Most of the Polish upper and middle classes were immediately slaughtered, and Polish language and culture was stamped upon. Almost six million Poles, too, perished in the war, and countless millions of Russians. Half a million gypsies were exterminated with similar savagery.

In Western Europe, where the races were not regarded by the Nazis as so inferior, there was less harsh treatment. However, here too the most brutal repression was used if it was thought necessary or desirable.

Economic policy

The Nazi occupiers had planned a short *Blitzkrieg* war. When total war actually happened, they never fully coped with it. Even though the whole of Europe's economy was in their hands, the Nazis did not make the best use of it. Hitler's economic adviser, Albert Speer, did his best to organise Germany and occupied Europe for total war but Eastern Europe was hardly allowed to have any industry at all and most of the Nazis' economic effort was centred on Germany itself.

Collaboration

Each of the defeated countries was treated differently, depending on what suited Hitler at

A baby found murdered by Nazis in Russia

'The Prayer of the Killed' by Bronislaw Linke. Jewish prayers in the rubble of Warsaw

the time. Some parts of Czechoslovakia and Poland became part of the Third Reich itself. Other nations in Eastern Europe were ruled directly by the SS or by the military authorities. In Western Europe Hitler preferred to rule through collaborators. It was not the local Fascist leaders whom Hitler chose to rule the defeated countries, but more traditional figures such as Marshal Pétain of France or King Leopold of Belgium. In fact Hitler allowed Pétain to rule one third of France as an un-occupied zone, known as 'Vichy' France, for two years because it suited him to allow this instead of forcing France to go on fighting in 1940.

Resistance

Who resisted?

In Western Europe resistance was quite limited to begin with. In France few people supported the Resistance and most supported Marshal Pétain, although by 1945 there were over 50,000 French men and women in resistance groups. In Eastern Europe the only choice was to resist or to submit. Consequently the Polish Resistance, the Yugoslav Partisans and the Russian Partisans were immense underground organisations. Many people did feel strongly enough to take the crucial step to become a resister. Many of these were patriots, democrats, socialists, communists and people of strong religious beliefs.

What did resisters do?

Some types of resistance were of more use to the Allied war effort than others. Most of these were controlled by the Allied Secret Services such as the Russian KGB, the American OSS and the British Special Operations Executive (SOE), MI6 and MI9.

Escape was one form of resistance. Escape routes were set up in Western Europe by MI9. The sole purpose of these networks was to rescue pilots, escaped prisoners and refugees.

Intelligence was another type of resistance. Spies would report back on troop movements, proposed bombing targets or any information that would help the Allied war effort.

Anti-German subversion was yet another type of resistance action. This was the largest category of all. Some resistance movements carried on large scale guerrilla operations against Germany, especially in Russia, Yugoslavia and Poland. The

Somewhere in Russia

Yugoslav Partisans liberated their own country without any Allied support. The French Resistance helped to liberate Paris, and the Italian Partisans helped to free Northern Italy too.

Sabotage was another subversive activity, involving the blowing up of railway lines and factories connected with the manufacture of war materials, or disrupting German troop movements.

The publication of resistance posters, hand-bills and even newspapers could have an inspiring affect on an occupied population.

Lastly there was **indirect resistance**. The Dutch developed the habit of walking out of cafes and shops whenever Germans entered. The King of Denmark wore a yellow star when Danish Jews were ordered to do so. Nightly, millions listened to the BBC news, the penalty for which could be death. One old lady delighted in tripping up Germans as she sat in the park, which was a kind of resistance!

---

1 Make a list of things that were 'typically Nazi' in the treatment of occupied Europe. Use the photographs as well as the text.

2 What sort of personal qualities were needed by different types of resisters? Would you make a good resister? Which type of resistance would you choose, if you had to do so?

3 Which of the different types of resistance helped the Allied war effort, and how? Start with the most helpful.

4 Examine the painting by Bronislaw Linke and the photographs in this section. What thoughts do they raise in your mind?

The Home Front

Fighting a total war

The war dominated people's lives. For years afterwards many people spoke of nothing else. More than in any other war, people were organised, controlled, regulated, inspired, conscripted, rationed and programmed. It was TOTAL war. The whole economy and population was geared to provide war needs and to back up the armed forces, supporting them with the will to win.

Most people, most of the time, kept up their spirits. Propaganda was continuous and all-embracing through the media and through posters. Propaganda, however, was not everything. For most people there was a genuine, automatic sense of 'pulling together' and of helping one another. Morale was high. For six years people put up with the suffering, the hardships and the inconveniences, like those in the photograph.

The appointment of Winston Churchill proved a very successful choice. He was a most effective war leader who earned people's affection and admiration by his own 'bulldog' spirit. The country was fighting for its survival, especially when it was really alone in 1940 and 1941.

The Blitz

The worst aspect of life during the war was the Blitz. 60,000 people were killed by bombs and two and a half million made homeless. Coventry was the town worst hit, losing over 4,000 of its people in a single raid in November 1940. London, however, took the brunt of the Blitz, especially the docks areas in the East End. Yet, despite individual heartbreak, the public spirit remained defiant and determined.

The economy

It was the needs of the economy that forced the government to regulate almost every aspect of life. Conscription was applied not just to the armed forces, but to every sort of work. Ernest Bevin, the Socialist Minister of Labour, was in charge of this. He conscripted millions of women to do what was normally regarded as men's work—driving buses and ambulances, piloting civil aircraft, and most important of all,

Bombed out—the morning after

producing war goods. Millions joined the Land Army and 'Bevin Boys' were conscripted to work down the mines instead of joining the army.

The whole economy concentrated on the technology of war—on tanks and guns, on ships and submarines and, most of all, on aircraft and bombs for the strategic bombing of Germany. Britain's economic war effort provided about one sixth of the total Allied war effort. Yet, by 1945, the civilian industries were backward and ground down, exports had fallen to only 40% of pre-war levels, and Britain had spent most of its huge overseas investments to pay for the war. The economy was in serious trouble.

Rules and regulations

Early in the war people became used to being ordered and controlled. Within a few days of the

Posters for the Home Front

outbreak, over two million children had been evacuated from the cities to safer areas. The Blackout was in effect, and new groups of people—ARP wardens, fire wardens, Home Guards—enforced the new rules.

The shortages of goods, fuel and raw materials in 1940 led to more and more regulations. Homeless families had to be rehoused, by government order, with other families. It was unthinkable to build new houses 'for the duration'. The U-boat menace cut down food supplies and brought in severe rationing. Petrol rationing forced private cars off the roads. Clothing regulations dictated that hems should be higher and that pleats should disappear—all

to save material. Some foods were restricted to minute proportions—half a pound of meat per week. Pasture-land, parks, lawns and gardens were ploughed up to grow crops.

Despite all this hardship the government was concerned about the people's welfare. Children and expectant mothers were given free milk and orange juice. There was continuous education about better eating and better health. The diet of the poorest classes actually improved during the war. And there was a growing sense that all classes, rich and poor, were treated more fairly and equally. By 1945 people wanted more and more improvements, not to go back to the depression of the 1930s.

Q

1a Construct a questionnaire for people who can remember the war. Get your ideas from the topics on this page.
b After your survey, note down what different experiences and reactions people had to the war. What do you find most interesting?
c What are the drawbacks of using remembered evidence?

2 Despite hardships, like those of the men looking at their bombed-out home on the previous page, people coped with the war. Using the photograph, explain how people would react to their problems.
3 How would each of the posters help the war effort?

The turning point of the war 1942–1943

The time for decisions— Casablanca 1943

It was during the winter of 1942–1943 that the Battles of El Alamein and Stalingrad marked the

turning point of the war. At this time President Roosevelt and Winston Churchill met in a conference at Casablanca in North Africa and came to a crucial decision. The Americans really wanted to invade Europe across the English Channel. Stalin too was demanding that they should do this in order to take the terrible pressure off Russia. Churchill, however, would only invade directly across the Channel when he was sure of success. He persuaded Roosevelt that the best way to attack Germany would be through Italy. This decision meant that a direct attack across the English Channel would only be possible in mid-1944. Therefore, for another 18 months the main campaigns of the war would be fought in the Mediterranean and, especially, in Russia.

The Mediterranean Campaign

The desert

After the Battle of El Alamein in October 1942, Rommel retreated to Tunisia and defended it strongly. The British approached from the East and the Americans from the West, but only in March 1943 did the American General Patton and the British General Montgomery break through the Mareth Line and drive Rommel out of of Tunis, which finally fell in May 1943.

Sicily

Operation 'Husky', the campaign to capture Sicily, was very well organised. Over 150,000 men and 3,000 landing craft were used on the first day, 10 July 1943, and within 39 days Patton and Montgomery had captured the island and reached the Straits of Messina.

Italy

Italy, about to be invaded, now tried to get out of the war. The Italian people had turned against Mussolini, and the King of Italy dismissed him. However, German paratroopers daringly rescued him and restored him to power. Hitler poured huge reinforcements into Italy. In September 1943, the Allies managed to gain a foothold on the Italian mainland, but could not get beyond the German defence line, the Gustav Line, at Monte Cassino. The Americans had never been interested in Italy and now began to withdraw men to take part in the cross-Channel invasion which was being prepared. Only in May 1944, when Monte Cassino fell, did the Allied advance continue. Rome was liberated but the Allies soon lost their momentum after breaking through another defence line, the Gothic Line. Torrential rains held them back, and more and more

Desert and Italian campaigns

divisions were withdrawn to fight in France, where the cross-Channel invasion had now taken place. In April 1945 the Allies pressed forward again, and the Italian resistance fighters, the Partisans, rose up against the German Army and helped to liberate their country. Mussolini was captured, shot and mutilated, and, in May 1945, the German armies in Italy surrendered. They were the first to do so as the war came to an end.

The 30 Allied divisions fighting in Italy successfully liberated the country, but they had a long and hard struggle in doing so, in the mountainous countryside and winter weather.

Q

1 Why did Churchill want to be absolutely certain of success in crossing the Channel?

2 What do you think Stalin's response was when he heard that his allies would not attack directly across the Channel?

The Eastern Front 1943–1945

After the Battle of Stalingrad, Marshal Zhukov's armies quickly re-captured Orel and Rostov. In the north the siege of Leningrad was relieved. By this time the Russians had vast amounts of war equipment pouring out of their own factories.

At Kursk Hitler decided to stop the Red advance. He gathered over 2,000 tanks, backed up by huge armies. The Russians responded with even more tanks and one and half million men. The battle lasted for six weeks over a front hundreds of miles long. It proved to be a devastating defeat for Germany, one of the biggest battles in history.

The Red Army moved westwards in a series of offensives without pause. The only hope for Germany was to withdraw and to re-group her forces as necessary, but Hitler would not allow this. The Germans lost men by the hundred thousand, but their tenacious fighting could only slow down, and not halt, the Russian advance. Stopping outside Warsaw in 1944, Stalin encouraged the Polish Resistance to rise up against the Nazis. He then deliberately held back and left them to terrible reprisals. This cleared the way for a communist government, as did the Russian conquest of Romania and Hungary. Yugoslavia, under its Partisan leader Marshal Tito, liberated itself.

Despite falling war production and manpower, Hitler still kept 200 divisions in the East. Both sides fought with the utmost stubbornness, but slowly the Russians advanced, capturing German troops in huge encirclements.

The battle for Berlin

Early in 1945 the Red Army entered Germany itself, but Berlin had been surrounded by seven defence lines, dug by civilians and guarded by fanatical members of the Hitler Youth as well as by German troops. In a superhuman effort on both sides, two and a half million Russians engaged one million Germans. After two weeks the German defences collapsed. Hitler killed himself on 30 April, and on 1 May, Russian soldiers hoisted the Red Flag on the Reichstag building.

The importance of the Russian Front

'It was the Red Army that tore the guts out of the German war machine.' This was the tribute of Winston Churchill. Of the 675 divisions raised by Germany and her allies during the war, 500 were defeated on the Russian Front. There Germany lost three quarters of its tanks, aircraft and artillery and three quarters of its dead. What enabled Russia to achieve this?

1 The heroism of the Russian army and people

The Russian people were fighting for survival. They called the Second World War 'The Great Patriotic War'. About 20 million Russians died in the war.

2 Russia's economic war effort

After the initial devastation of 1941–1942, the Soviet war machine was soon under way, and production soared upwards to provide the vast resources needed for total war.

3 Natural factors. Size and climate

Russia is an immense country and has never been successfully invaded. Its size creates too many problems of supply and communication for its enemies. The Russian winter, too, helped to break the Germans.

Q

1 Arrange the reasons for Russia's victory in order of importance, explaining your views.
2 Do you agree with Churchill's tribute? Give your reasons.

D-Day and the Second Front 1944–1945

6 June 1944 was D-Day, the day the Allies launched a new offensive by opening the Second Front in Europe along the French coast. By this time Churchill could be reasonably sure of success.

Before 6 June

Rommel was in charge of the German defences, known as the 'Atlantic Wall'. He realised that the enemy should be pinned down on the beaches, and he strengthened the 'wall' in order to do this. All sorts of obstacles were created as well as the usual fortifications and heavy guns, but Rommel was not allowed to complete the wall because of disagreements in the German High Command.

On the Allied side the Supreme Allied Commander was the American General Eisenhower, with another American, General Bradley, and the British General, Montgomery, as his deputies. Eisenhower controlled his vast forces of three and a half million men very effectively. By June they were encamped all over Southern England, ready to go.

A huge fleet of ships, including 3,000 landing craft was also waiting along the south and east coast, ready to converge on France. New weapons had been invented to ensure that the first wave of troops actually got off the beaches. Two prefabricated concrete harbours, and PLUTO (Pipe Line Under The Ocean) were used to ensure the continuous transportation of troops and supplies. For weeks beforehand, over 3,000 aircraft, with complete air superiority, had destroyed the railway network of Northern France and cut the enemy forces into two.

The Normandy Landings

'OK, we'll go,' announced Eisenhower on 6 June. Gales had delayed D-Day for 24 hours. The invasion ships left southern England on their intricately time-tabled approach to the Normandy beaches. On the same day two airborne divisions landed on either flank of the beaches. By the end of the day over 156,000 troops had landed along a 30 mile front, but Caen had not been captured as planned.

Omaha Beach, 6 June

Landing, 7 June

A tank with flails to detonate mines

The breakout of Normandy and the advance to Germany

The Germans held back the Allies for several weeks. Only in late June did the British take Caen and the Americans take the Cotentin Peninsula and Cherbourg. On 3 July General

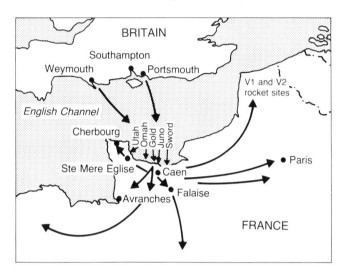

D-day and later campaigns

Patton broke out southwards and as the two Allies moved together, they encircled and captured 50,000 Germans around Falaise.

The British now moved northwards towards Belgium, and the Americans moved westwards towards Germany itself. Paris was liberated on 25 August by a rising of the French Resistance, but the city was only saved by the German Commander's disobedience of Hitler's order to destroy it. As the Allies approached Germany from the west, the Red Army entered it from the east. Who would win the race to Berlin?

The German recovery, winter 1944–1945

General Model was now in command of German troops after Rommel's suicide, ordered because of his involvement in a bomb plot to assassinate Hitler. Model's clever use of troops helped to revitalise the German war effort, as did three major last-ditch attempts to defeat Germany. One of these was at Arnhem, when three Allied airborne divisions were sent to seize the Rhine bridges in advance of the British Army but were attacked by a nearby German Panzer division. Although the British paratroops held out for 10

A collaborator with her head shaved is hounded out of her village, carrying her German baby

days, this was not long enough for the army to reach them.

A further counter-attack was the Battle of the Bulge in December 1944. 20 German divisions caught the Americans by surprise as they broke through the Ardennes, but an American division held on to Bastogne, and the Bulge was bloodily forced back.

Another German retaliation was the use of missiles. Ever since June 1944 thousands had caused terrible damage to British cities. Now came the more powerful V2 guided missiles which could not be heard before they hit their marks. They caused even more devastation and alarm, but their launching-pads were captured early in 1945. Fortunately, German scientists had not developed the atom bomb in time.

The invasion of Germany

As the Red Army approached Berlin, Eisenhower ordered the Allies to cross the River Rhine in February 1945. German resistance was beginning to crumble. Already millions of Germans were pouring westwards so that they would be captured not by the Russians but by the British and the Americans. Hitler still refused to accept defeat and was preparing to take everything and everyone down with him. British and American troops crossed the River Elbe and met up there with Russian soldiers on 29 April. On 7 May the German High Command surrendered unconditionally to Montgomery on Luneberg Heath.

Q

1a How well prepared were the Allies for D-Day? Give examples.
b What mistakes, if any, did the Germans and the Allies make in the D-Day landings?

2 Imagine you are a war correspondent. Describe for listeners back home the events and features of the photographs of the landings.
3 What do you think were the attitudes of the French villagers in the photograph?

Air warfare

Air superiority

Everyone agreed that air superiority was essential in the Second World War. This was achieved by fighter planes. Their purpose was to destroy enemy fighters and bombers and to protect their own bombers. Air superiority was also essential in providing support for armies and navies in achieving their objectives. The British first achieved it over Britain and the English Channel in 1940, but it was only in March 1944 that the Allies gained air superiority over Germany's own airspace.

Strategic bombing

This aspect of air warfare caused great disagreement during the war and has done so ever since.

Strategic bombing had two possible purposes. One was the destruction of the enemy's resources by bombing economic targets like oil reserves and factories. The other was the

destruction of civilian morale by 'area' bombing or 'terror' bombing of homes and cities in general.

The RAF found both of these tasks impossible in the first part of the war. Instruments for guiding planes to target areas and for actually targetting bombs were hopelessly inadequate at this time. In 1942 only one bomb in three actually reached within five miles of its target. Because of this, Churchill came to believe more and more in area bombing instead. When vast numbers of bombers and favourable weather conditions coincided with one another, a most terrifying result could be achieved. A fire storm would happen, producing hurricane force winds, which sucked people into a vast inferno. This happened at Hamburg in 1943 when 50,000 people were killed in one night. Up to 100,000 died in the Dresden firestorm in 1945, more than were killed by the atom bomb at Hiroshima shortly afterwards.

The bombing of Darmstadt, a medium sized

town of 100,000 people, was typical of area bombing. One man told of how he was forced out of a shelter by the intense heat . . .

> More bombs were already falling in the garden. We crouched low, each of us beating out the small flames flickering on the clothes of the one in front. Phosphorus clinging to the trees dripped down on us. The heat was terrible. Burning people raced passed us like live torches, and I listened to their unforgettable final screams.

By this time the asphalt, metal and glass in the centre of the fire storm was melting. Another man told of his experiences . . .

> I went to lie under a big advertising hoarding. For perhaps 15 minutes I stayed among the children there trying to make them feel safe, wrapping them in blankets. Then I went to look for a better place for us. When I returned to the hoarding it was in flames. With one child in my arms and leading another by the hand, I took 20 people to the wall. It was not death that was terrible that night, but the fear of death, the whimpering, the shrieks, the screams.

Rescued after an air-raid on a German city

About 11,000 people were killed on that night in Darmstadt. About half of the dwellings were destroyed and some of the town's industry.

The American Eighth Air Force preferred day-time raids on specific targets to night-time area bombing. These raids were not successful at first as German fighters, which still had air superiority over Germany, could pick off the bombers. However, gradually, specific targetting became more successful and navigational aids improved. More and more bombers were produced and the Mustang fighter, protecting them, gained superiority over Germany.

By the spring of 1945 immense damage was being done to the German economy, particularly to selected targets like the German oil reserves, which almost brought German tanks to a halt. Even so, the Germans were able to minimise the economic damage by concentrating their fire-fighting forces on industrial targets and letting their houses burn. German industry was by no means totally destroyed in the Second World War.

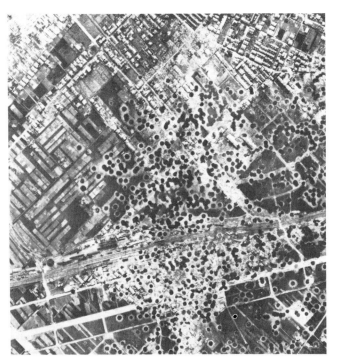

Photograph taken to assess the damage of a bombing raid on a railway and railway yard, 1945

Q

1a Use the first picture and the extracts of the eyewitnesses to show how different people reacted to air-raids.
b How do you account for the fact that, apart from the firestorms, air-raids did not seem to cause a breakdown in civilian morale?

2 From the second photograph, assess the economic damage caused by bombing. The purpose of the raid was to destroy the railway line and its yards.
3 Give several examples of air superiority that you have come across in this chapter.

Case study
Was strategic bombing worthwhile?

Did it achieve its aims?

Was the cost too great?

For

Strategic bombing helped to put German industry out of action for considerable periods of time. It was very effective in 1945, when targetting became more successful and German resources became scarce.

Area bombing, especially when it led to fire storms, probably helped destroy German morale, at least in the later stages.

Against

It did not really upset Germany's economic capacity to wage war on a large scale, except possibly in the very late stages of the war. It did not destroy German industry.

Normally morale was increased, not destroyed by enemy bombing, even on a large scale.

For

No. In the absence of other, more certain, methods of warfare, the technological and financial effort was essential.

In total war, enemy lives cannot be considered as being of the same value as one's own. 'Bomber' Harris said, 'I would not regard the whole of the remaining cities of Germany as worth the bones of one British soldier.'

Civilians contributed to the war effort as much as soldiers.

Against

The amount of money and technological effort spent on planes and bombs was more than the results were worth, diverting all the effort from other equipment. Replacing bombers was very expensive, especially when hundreds were lost in individual raids.

Over 590,000 German civilians died in the Second World War including women and children. They were non-combatants. This was not morally right and losses of pilots and crew were also very high and not worthwhile. Almost 60,000 British airmen lost their lives during the war.

Q

1 Was strategic bombing worthwhile? Use the arguments for and against in coming to your conclusion.

Why Germany lost the war

Below is a list of reasons why Germany lost the war. They are not listed in order of importance, because historians disagree about this. You must make your own mind up about the relative importance of these reasons . . .

Resistance movements. The importance of guerrilla warfare, especially in Eastern Europe.
Air warfare. The strategic bombing of Germany.
The contribution of USA. The huge economic effort, amounting to over half the total Allied effort; human effort and high morale, especially in the Second Front.
Naval warfare. The defeat of the U-boats.
The contribution of Britain. Preventing invasion in 1940; the great economic effort, providing over one sixth of the total Allied effort; the high morale and human effort, especially in the Desert and Italian Campaigns and the Second Front.

German failings. Germany, despite the most incredible human and economic efforts, was simply not strong enough for its enemies; its failure to organise its economic resources for total war.
The contribution of Russia. The high morale and immense human effort and sacrifice throughout the war; the economic effort, amounting to over one third of the total Allied effort; Russia's size and climate.
The Two-Front war. The Grand Alliance of Britain, America and Russia was simply too much for Germany. Germany could not win a war on two sides.

Q

1 Arrange the causes for the Allied victory in order of importance. Give your reasons.

The Second World War in the Far East

Pearl Harbor—victory or blunder?

For years Japan had been expanding its territory by force in East Asia. First of all it took Manchuria from China in 1931. In 1936 the Japanese Army seized and occupied large parts of China herself and, in July 1940, French Indo-China. Japan under the military rule of General Tojo was in a confident and aggressive mood and wished to expand even further, especially to the Dutch East Indies and to the Philippines, where there were rich reserves of oil and raw materials, which Japan so badly needed.

Japan was an ally of Germany and Italy and, with the Tripartite Pact of 1940, the two European dictatorships recognised Japan's leadership in eastern Asia. But America, in possession of the Philippines and owning huge interests in China, stood in the way of Japan.

America, however, was very reluctant to go to war. The people were in an isolationist mood, and President Roosevelt, although he wanted to go to war with Hitler, tried his best to avoid a war with Japan. Only something really catastrophic would force the American people into two wars at once.

In 1941 the Japanese took a calculated risk. They decided to knock out the American fleet based at Pearl Harbor, Hawaii, calculating that the task of re-building the fleet and then waging war across such a large area as the Pacific would be impossible. Even if the Americans tried to do this, the Japanese hoped to make it too difficult for them in the end by seizing and defending most of the islands in the South Pacific.

The Japanese Fleet, accompanied by five aircraft carriers, left Japan in secret and, on 7 December, 1941, made a massive surprise attack on Pearl Harbor which had many consequences. . . .

American losses

Three battleships were sunk in the attack, the *California*, the *Arizona* and the *Oklahoma*, along with 16 other ships, 188 planes and great loss of life. However, the Japanese missed America's three major aircraft carriers which happened to be carrying out exercises at sea, and huge stores of oil. Most of the crippled warships were soon repaired and in action again.

The American reaction

For several months America could do nothing at all against the Japanese. However, the American public was outraged and determined to defeat Japan unconditionally, whatever the cost. In the following year America was recovering and began to cross the Pacific. Japan could not possibly hope to defeat America in a full-scale war.

The German reaction

The Americans did not declare war on Germany at this point, and it is possible that they would not have done so. Hitler, however, not realising that America would ultimately join in a European war on an immense scale, declared war on 11 December 1941. Once this happened, Germany too, was bound to be defeated by the combined might of America, Russia and Britain.

Japanese expansion 1941–1942

Japan followed the Pearl Harbor attack by the rapid invasion of many countries. One drive was to South China, Hongkong and Thailand, which were easily captured. Another was to the Philippines, where the Japanese crushed the American defenders. Another was towards Malaya where the Japanese with air superiority sank British battleships. They easily captured the naval base at Singapore and 100,000 British troops. Yet another Japanese thrust was to the Dutch East Indies. By mid-1942 the Japanese had conquered Burma, another British possession, and seemed poised to enter India. The Japanese fleet even bombarded Ceylon. In the Pacific the Japanese defended their immense empire by taking outlying islands from America.

The fight back

In the Pacific it was the Americans who virtually defeated the Japanese on their own. The

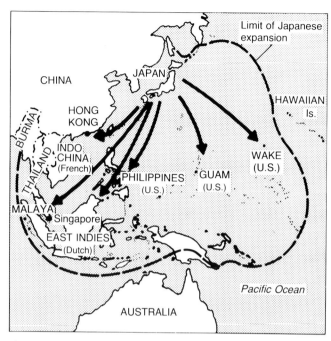

Japanese expansion 1941–42

Russians did not take part in the war against Japan and the British were occupied in Europe, although they did defeat the Japanese on land in Burma. China, too, took part in the war against Japan, but was not instrumental in defeating her.

In the middle of 1942 Japanese expansion was checked by two important battles, the Battle of the Coral Sea and the Battle of Midway Island. This was a crippling blow from which the Japanese never recovered. Then came the Battle of Guadalcanal, a six month engagement involving several sea battles and terrible fighting on the Island of Guadalcanal, which the Americans finally captured in February 1943.

Island hopping

After several months the Americans were ready to begin their two main drives towards Japan. One drive was to reach the Philippines from Guadalcanal through the East Indies. The other drive came across the Central Pacific, with huge numbers of marines and a large accompanying Task Force of 16 aircraft carriers carrying 1,000 aircraft. Japanese resistance was intense and losses were always heavier than American losses because of the Japanese code of honour. The Japanese fleet could hardly cope with so much American war technology. The Gilbert Islands were the first to fall in November 1943, followed by the Marshall Islands in February 1944. Then came the capture of Guam in August 1944 after

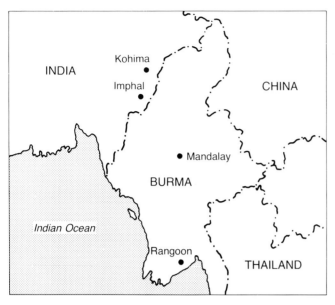

Burma campaign

the Battle of the Philippine Sea, which took place between aircraft carriers and aeroplanes.

In October 1944 the Fifth Fleet sailed almost 2,000 miles to the Philippines, and immediately on its arrival fought the four day Battle of Leyte Gulf with three Japanese fleets. It was the biggest naval battle in history. The American advance continued as the Fifth Fleet joined up with the armed forces to re-take the Philippines.

Pacific campaign

It was at this time that the Japanese first used *Kamikaze* suicide pilots against American ships, but these were desperate tactics and could not stop the American onslaught. In February 1945 American marines took Iwo Jima Island with the loss of 4,000 American and 28,000 Japanese lives. Even more Japanese died in defending Okinawa Island. From these captured islands the American bombers could easily reach the Japanese mainland, which they now bombed with the most terrible devastation. Several major cities were virtually destroyed.

The Burma campaign

On land the Japanese objective had been India, which it had invaded in March 1944 through the towns of Imphal and Kohima. There the Fourteenth British Army held out for four months. Their success was the turning point of the war there, because the Japanese now had no alternative but to retreat, pursued by the British and the Chinese. The rapid British advance through the jungles and hills of Burma surprised the Japanese who lost the city of Mandalay in March 1945 and the capital city of Rangoon in May 1945.

The atom bomb

At this point, in the summer of 1945, the Americans were preparing for an invasion of the Japanese mainland itself. The Japanese had been defeated on land and at sea, their navy and airforce had been virtually destroyed and Japanese cities had been devastated by American bombers. The Russians, who had up to this point fought only against Germany, now threatened to attack Japan. The Japanese requested an armistice, but refused to accept the unconditional surrender that the Allies demanded. They feared that their Emperor would be deposed if they surrendered unconditionally.

On 6 August 1945, the Americans dropped an atom bomb on Hiroshima, killing about 70,000 people. On 8 August Russia declared war against Japan, and on 9 August another atom bomb was dropped on Nagasaki, killing 40,000 people. Only then, when Tokyo itself was threatened with a third atom bomb, did the Japanese Emperor overrule his Cabinet and order unconditional surrender.

Extension

Why did America drop the atom bomb?

At the time and ever since there has been great disagreement about whether the Japanese were about to give in, or whether they would fight on with fanaticism to the bitter end, especially if Japan herself were invaded. The question was never put to the test. Instead, the dropping of the two atom bombs ended the war for Japan.

Why were the atom bombs dropped? Read the following two pieces of evidence to find some clues to this question.

In 1955 President Truman, who ordered the dropping of the atom bombs, wrote about his decision in his memoirs . . .

In all, it had been estimated that it would require until the autumn of late 1946 to bring Japan to her knees. All of us realised that the fighting would be fierce and the losses heavy. General Marshall told me it might cost half a million lives to force the enemy's surrender on his home ground. We laboured to construct a weapon of such over-powering force that the enemy would be forced to give in swiftly. This was the main aim of our secret and vast effort. Let there be no mistake about it. The final decision was up to me. I regarded the

bomb as a military weapon and never had any doubt that it should be used. The top military advisers recommended its use, and when I talked to Churchill, he told me that he favoured the use of the bomb if it might aid to end the war.

In 1954 Churchill wrote in his book on the Second World War . . .

To crush the Japanese resistance man by man might require the loss of a million American lives and half that number of British. With the invention of the bomb, this nightmarish picture had vanished. Also, we should not need the Russians. We had no need to ask favours of them. A few days later I wrote to the British Foreign Secretary, 'It is quite clear that the US do not at present desire Russia joining in the war against Japan.' We seemed suddenly to possess the means of ending the slaughter in the Far East and of a better future in Europe against Russia. I have no doubt that these thoughts were in the minds of our American friends. The final decision lay with President Truman, but I never doubted what it would be, nor have I ever doubted that he was right. There was unanimous, automatic, unquestioned agreement at our meeting.

Q

1 The results of Pearl Harbor.

a Which of the results of the Japanese attack were long term and which were short term?

b Which of the results of the attack were correctly forseen? Which were a miscalculation? Which were unforseen?

2 Mark on the maps opposite the main movements, with basic information such as dates, of:

a Japanese expansion; b The fight back.

3 Give examples of behaviour resulting from the Japanese code of honour.

4 The atom bomb.

a Do you have any bias in your own mind about the dropping of the atom bomb? If so, what is your bias?

b What is the reason given by Truman? What are the two reasons given by Churchill?

c How reliable is each piece of evidence about reasons for dropping the bomb?

d Write down your own conclusions about why the bomb was dropped, based on the evidence.

e Was the dropping of the bomb necessary?

Discussion topics

1 Do you think that our attitudes to other nations are still influenced by what happened in the war?

2 Do you think that the Second World War was a 'just war'?

3 Do you think that the atom bomb should have been used in 1945?

Essays

1 Why did the Second World War break out in 1945?

2 Outline the main events of the war between 1939 and January 1943. Why did the Germans win this part of the war?

3 Outline the main events of the war after the Battle of Stalingrad.

4 Outline the main events of the war in the Pacific.

5 Briefly describe and explain the importance of three of the following: Dunkirk; The Battle of Stalingrad; The Italian campaign; Strategic bombing.

THE COLD WAR

What is the Cold War?

When the Second World War—the 'hot' war—ended in 1945, the 'Cold' War began. The Cold War is the phrase we use to describe the hostility between East and West. By East we mean Russia and her allies, all communist states. By West we mean America and her allies, including Britain; mostly democratic states.

Another term we use for this hostility is 'super-power rivalry'. Both Russia and America are known as 'super-powers', states whose power and influence are so much greater than other powers that they are in a class of their own.

In 1945 Russia, America and Britain were allied to one another against Germany. All genuinely admired one another's heroism, and were grateful for one another's help in the fight against Nazism. Yet within a very few years they were almost fighting one another. How had this hostility, tension and suspicion come about?

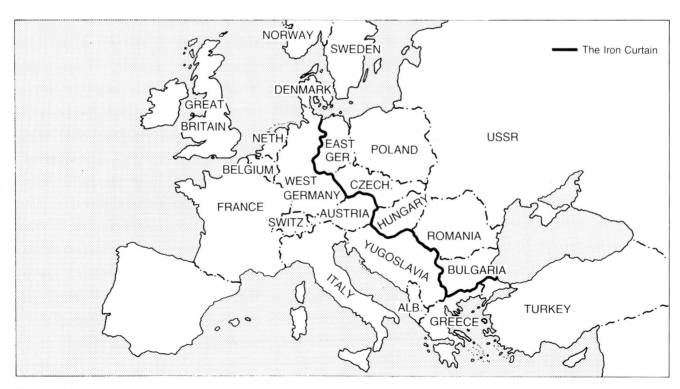

Europe in 1945

The causes of the Cold War

Some people think that the Cold War is mainly a clash of very strongly held ideals such as communism and democracy. Others think that it is the conflict of the different nations looking after their own interests. Whichever are the more important, these causes were strong in 1945 and are still the same now. They are very difficult to separate from one another.

The East

The West

The ideals of the two sides

Belief in communism

Communists strongly believe that communism is right and is bound to come to power all over the world. Most Russian communists believe, as Stalin did, that Russia is the saviour of communism for the whole world. They regarded the Second World War as a fight for communism, which must be followed up by the victory of communism everywhere.

Belief in democracy

Most people in the West strongly believe in parliamentary democracy and all its freedoms. They think it is true and right that all countries should have democracy. Democrats regarded the Second World War as a fight for democracy, and were not going to let it slide afterwards.

Anti-capitalism and anti-democracy

Ever since Karl Marx, communists have hated the capitalism of the West. They think it is an evil system which exploits people. The parliamentary democracy of the West is, to communists, a confidence-trick. They think that in democracy a few people possess real power while the majority do not have any power or freedom at all, even though they think they do. Communists are convinced that capitalism will try to stamp them out if possible.

Anti-communism and anti-totalitarianism

Most people in the West detest communism as a totalitarian system. They feel that they have fought against one form of totalitarianism, Nazism, and should continue the struggle against communism. Ever since the 1917 Russian Revolution many people in the West have been fearful of a communist revolution in their own countries.

The National interests of the powers

1 Security

Russia

Russia's main national interest is its own *security*. Russians feel very insecure indeed, having been invaded and almost defeated twice in the twentieth century. In the Second World War they lost twenty million and certainly suffered more than any other nation. Russia fears being encircled by hostile nations and feels vulnerable, so prefers to have smaller communist states all around it, especially in Eastern Europe. These can act as a 'buffer' between Russia and its potential enemies.

America

America's main national interest is not its own security. America is a very secure and self-sufficient country, protected mainly by oceans from its enemies. America does not feel vulnerable in the same way that Russia does. Many countries, especially Britain, have always encouraged America to take up the leadership of the West. The European countries fear for their own security if America does not do this.

The East

The West

2 Status

Russia has always been one of the world's greatest nations and, since 1945, has been a super-power. Russians are a very nationalistic people, proud of their history and of their own character and way of life. They are particularly proud of their contribution to the defeat of Germany in the Second World War. After the war they wanted to take a leading role in the affairs of the world and began to take over other countries.

America is the most powerful nation in the world, and many Americans feel that America should take the leading role in world affairs and behave like a super-power. Americans are conscious of their power and are very nationalistic, believing very strongly in their own character and in 'the American way of life'.

3 Economic interests

Russia is not concerned mainly with economic interests. It has immense economic resources of its own and does not export many goods to outside nations.

America has many economic interests all over the globe and has always needed to invest money abroad, especially in Europe. This clearly would not be possible if Russia dominated other countries.

Russia sees America as its main enemy, standing in the way of all its national interests.

America sees Russia as its main potential enemy, standing in the way of all its national interests.

Why the Cold War is so frightening and dangerous

Although the Cold War has never broken out into a hot war, it has created some of the most tense and frightening situations of all time. Why?

1 The nuclear arms race

At first only America had the atom bomb, making Russia feel insecure and determined to get one of its own. This it did in 1949. In the early 1950s both nations developed hydrogen bombs. Then came the *ICBMs* (Inter-Continental Ballistic Missiles) which both sides built up into huge arsenals. Although America was superior to Russia in nuclear weapons until the late 1960s, equality in nuclear arms is not really important. It is enough to be able to destroy the enemy ten times over. Both sides possess this capacity. As tensions increased almost to breaking-point on occasion, a nuclear arms race threatened to destroy the world. It could still do so.

2 Never back down

Both sides learned the same lesson from their dealings with Germany in the 1930s. They had tried to come to terms with Hitler in the hope that he would be satisfied. He never was. Therefore, they still thought that if one side backed down, the other side, like Hitler, would take advantage of it. Therefore, neither side could ever back down.

Soviet cartoon showing General Eisenhower (right) and other Western leaders

Stalin said in 1946 . . .

> Mr Churchill now takes his stand among the warmongers. A point to be noticed in this respect is that Mr Churchill and his friends bear a striking resemblance to Hitler and his friends.

President John F. Kennedy said in 1962 . . .

> The 1930s taught us a clear lesson; aggressive conduct, if allowed to grow unchecked and unchallenged, ultimately leads to war. We will not necessarily risk the cost of a world wide nuclear war, but neither will we shrink from that risk if at any time it must be faced.

In the 1950s this tendency never to back down but to go on to the brink of war was known as 'brinkmanship'.

3 Misunderstandings

'Know your enemy.' It is obviously important that policy makers should understand their enemies well. There is evidence that the leaders and people on both sides do not always appreciate the ideals and the national interests of the other side. Unless one side has had the same experiences as the other, real understanding will become very difficult, if not impossible. Misunderstandings have certainly led to some of the crises of the Cold War.

— Q —

1 Do you find it easy or difficult to reach an unbiased view on the Cold War? Do you sympathise with any of the ideals or national interests of the super-powers?
2a Which is more important, in your opinion, on each side—the ideals or the national interests? Are they basically the same, or different?
b Why is it so difficult to separate ideals from national interests?

3 What point is the Russian cartoon making about the Western leaders? How does it make its point? Do you think it represents a genuine belief?
4 Of the three reasons given above for the Cold War being so frightening, which one is the most dangerous? How are the three reasons linked together?

The best way to deal with an enemy

Options—deterrence or détente

Each government has the duty to achieve its own national interests and to follow its own ideals, but it has a choice about how best to do this . . .
1 **Deterrence.** This means that a nation will serve its own interests by building up its strength to deter its enemy from attacking it.
2 **Détente.** This means that a nation will serve its own interests by improving relations with its enemy so that tension and hostility will decrease.
3 **A combination of deterrence and détente.**

Ways of achieving deterrence and détente

You can see from the following list the different ways of achieving deterrence and détente:

Cultural and sporting exchanges.
Making defence alliances with other nations.
Arms limitation or arms reduction agreements.
Insulting and provoking propaganda.
Supporting friendly governments of small nations with arms or finance.
Encircling the enemy with military bases.
Promoting economic links, especially trade and investment.
Promoting the settlement of local conflict in various parts of the world.
Economic boycott and other sanctions.
Building up equality or superiority in arms.
Seizing the territory of states friendly to the 'enemy'.
Expressions of friendship and goodwill.
Supporting guerrilla movements against governments friendly to the enemy.

—— Q ——

1 Make two columns, headed deterrence and détente. Sort out the list on page 139 into the relevant columns.

You will come across examples of all these types of deterrence and détente during your study of the Cold War. Fortunately the Cold War has never broken out into a hot war, but it has gone through several stages of deterrence and détente. You can follow the various stages and crises of the Cold War during the rest of this chapter . . .

The stages of the Cold War

Germany, Eastern Europe and the Iron Curtain, 1945–1947

Even before the Second World War was over, it was clear that Russia, America and Britain were unlikely to remain allies for long. In 1945 two conferences were held between the Big Three. One, just before the war ended, was at Yalta and the other, just after the end of the war, at Potsdam. Churchill and Stalin were deeply suspicious of one another's intentions, but the American President—first of all Roosevelt and then his successor Truman—still believed in co-operating with Russia and in coming to terms with Stalin over the matters of Poland and Germany. First Stalin promised to hold free elections in Poland, but soon made it clear that these would never actually be held. The Big Three also agreed to split Germany into zones, but disagreed about how exactly to deal with the zones. The Americans began to agree with Churchill that Stalin was taking advantage of their goodwill.

By 1946 Russia had set up communist governments in Poland, East Germany, Hungary, Romania and Bulgaria. Czechoslovakia followed shortly afterwards in 1948. Winston Churchill, visiting America, spoke of an 'Iron Curtain' across Europe and between East and West. In Eastern Europe only Greece withstood the communists through the help of Allied troops.

In 1947 the American President made clear America's intention by announcing the *Truman Doctrine*. This said that America would help any non-communist country to resist pressure with military aid. Backing up this policy was the *Marshall Plan*. By this scheme vast amounts of American money poured into Europe to help the non-communist world to recover from the war.

—— Q ——

1 Was the Soviet take-over of Eastern Europe defensive or aggressive or both? Give your reasons. Refer back to the causes of the Cold War.

2 Was the Truman Doctrine defensive or aggressive or both? Give your reasons. Refer back to the causes of the Cold War.

Target Berlin, 1948–1949

It was obvious that the two sides would not agree on Germany. Russia was firmly in power in the eastern third of Germany, while America, Britain and France each had a zone in the western two thirds. America and Britain realised that West Germany must be allowed to rise again and be used as the front line of defence against the Soviet Union.

Stalin, terrified of a revival of Germany, a country he feared more than any other, was determined to prevent its re-appearance and to push the Allies out of Germany. He chose Berlin as his target.

The Berlin blockade was the first really serious confrontation of the Cold War. Berlin itself was a city divided into four zones, although it lay 100 miles into the Russian zone of East Germany. In April 1949 the two sides quarrelled about whether the new currency of West Germany should be allowed to be used in Berlin. The Russians began to halt road and rail transport on their way to Berlin.

America and the other Western powers decided that the only response was an airlift. Virtually every transport plane and pilot in the West was brought to Germany to airlift all goods—food, medicine, even coal from West Germany to Berlin. Over 8,000 tons a day were transported and a plane landed in Berlin every three minutes. For eleven months a war of nerves, of dramatic events and crises continued, but it soon became clear that the airlift could work.

It was a terrifying time for Berliners; a time of cold, poor rations, hardship and fear. However, neither America nor Russia was prepared to use force. In May the Russians called off their blockade and transport resumed as normal.

After Berlin—The results of the blockade

The Berlin episode was important. In the following years, several events and developments took place. Some were caused by the Berlin confrontation, others were speeded up and still others would have happened anyway.

1 Germany and Berlin were permanently split

Now Germany was split into two distinct parts, a development which the Powers had tried to prevent. The same thing happened to Berlin. Very soon after the airlift started West Germany was set up as a separate state, with West Berlin detached from it but still a part of it. The Russian zone became the German Democratic Republic.

2 Tension, suspicion and hostility increased between the two sides

This continued for several years at a very high pitch. America immediately moved its bombers to Europe to threaten Moscow for the first time.

3 The arms race increased on both sides

Russia developed the atom bomb in the following year and increased its already large armaments. Both America and Britain increased their spending on arms by large amounts. Germany was allowed to rearm in 1955, though some were worried about this, as you can see in the photograph. This arms race did not stop for many, many years.

A demonstration in London

4 Both sides sought defence alliances

The North Atlantic Treaty Organisation (NATO) was set up in 1949 after the ending of the blockade. It included most of the major powers of Europe, as well as America and Canada. When Germany rearmed in 1955, she was allowed to join NATO. From Norway to Turkey, Russia was encircled in Europe. Russia's response to this was to set up the Warsaw Pact, an alliance of the communist powers of Europe, in 1955.

5 After Berlin there was no further major confrontation in Europe

In the following year America and Russia turned their attention to the Far East, to the Korean war.

Q

1 Explain the attitude of different Berliners, such as an ex-Nazi, a democrat and a communist, to the air lift.
2 In your opinion which of the consequences of the Berlin airlift were caused entirely by the airlift? Which were speeded up by the airlift? Which might have happened anyway?
3 Why do you think that neither side used force against the other?

The Korean War, 1950–1953

Almost as soon as the Berlin crisis was over, the world's attention moved to the Far East. There the Korean War broke out in 1950. Korea had been ruled for many years by Japan, but in 1945 Russia and America had split it into two along the 38th Parallel—a line on a map—for convenience. As in the case of Germany, there was no question of uniting North and South Korea, but both super-powers withdrew their troops and handed over to separate Korean leaders. You can see from the summaries below and from the outline of the war, the part played by each of the countries concerned.

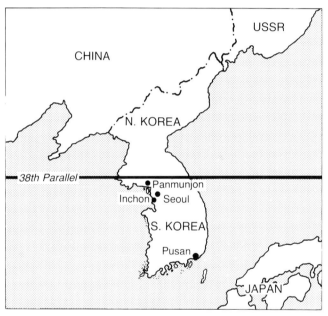

Korea

South Korea was not a very stable country, nor was it well armed. Its new leader, Syngman Rhee, was very strongly anti-communist. Fearing a communist rising from the South Korean peasants, he wanted American support for his government. He claimed to rule the whole of Korea.

North Korea was under the control of the Communist Party Leader, Kim Il Sung, who also claimed to represent the whole of Korea and had much support from the peasants of the South. North Korea was very well-armed with Russian equipment.

Russia would be glad to see its puppet neighbour of North Korea extend its influence over the whole country. This would threaten American interests in nearby Japan.

America was not anticipating trouble in Korea and had not stated that she would protect South Korea. President Truman however was determined to act in the face of a communist takeover.

China came under the communist control of Mao Zedong in 1949. The Chinese were very nationalistic and anti-American, and were determined not to be taken advantage of. They had to protect their own security.

The United Nations was officially in charge of holding elections in Korea to ensure that Korea became a united, democratic country. It had the responsibility for doing this because it had taken over Korea, along with Japan's other colonial territories, after the war.

The events of the war

25 June, 1950. After several skirmishes between the troops of both sides on the border, the North Korean army invaded South Korea. With its massive amounts of Russian equipment it took the South completely by surprise and quickly captured the capital, Seoul, and moved far into South Korea. It is not known what was the Russian involvement, if any, in this decision.

By the end of June President Truman had ordered American troops to support South Korea. Fortunately for America, the United Nations called on North Korea to withdraw and decided to send an army. It put the American General MacArthur in charge of the UN Army. American troops provided most of this UN Army. Other UN members, such as Britain and Australia, also provided troops.

August 1950. Within a few weeks North Korean troops had smashed the American UN forces and had taken almost the whole of South Korea except for the Port of Pusan.

15 September 1950. General MacArthur at last broke out of Pusan and landed at Inchon. The Americans returned to the 38th Parallel. Soon the North Korean army had collapsed and the whole of South Korea was reoccupied.

2 October 1950. China warned America that if they entered North Korea, China would resist. President Truman took MacArthur's advice that Chinese resistance was unlikely. He allowed MacArthur to move beyond the 38th Parallel. The UN recommended the holding of elections in North Korea.

By the end of October the Americans had occupied most of North Korea and were on the Chinese border.

26 November. Two huge Chinese armies counter-attacked and surrounded the American troops.

January 1951. MacArthur was forced out of North Korea and back into South Korea, leaving Seoul once again in enemy hands. However, when MacArthur advised President Truman to atom-bomb China itself and risk a nuclear war, he was dismissed.

During the rest of 1951 both sides dug in and held their lines along the 38th Parallel for the next two years. There was the most appalling loss of life, particularly on the Chinese side.

1953. A ceasefire was arranged at Panmunjon, only after President Eisenhower threatened to bomb China again. Korea was divided into two along the 38th Parallel, exactly the same border as before the war began. This border still remains. About two million people died in the war, mostly Korean peasants and North Korean and Chinese soldiers. The war led to an increase in the arms race, especially in the United States. But the Korean War was always a limited war. It was never allowed to develop into a general war.

Q

1 Point out the part played by each of the participants in starting or worsening the war. Make clear which points you are sure about and which you would like to know more about.

2 Why did the Korean War, in your opinion, not become a general war?

3 Mark on the map the main movements and incidents of the war.

1953–1962: Deterrence or détente?

In 1953 the Korean War ended, Stalin died and a new American President, Dwight D. Eisenhower took over. During this period there were no wars, like the Korean War, in which one or more super-powers were involved, and no major crises until 1962. The Cold War, with its mixture of deterrence and détente, was still on in earnest.

The arms race

America

In the 1950s the American army increased to 3.5 million men and the American Air Force doubled. More and more American air bases were set up overseas, especially in Europe.

Nuclear weapons

More sophisticated weapons were also invented including first and second strike weapons. America easily had superiority in nuclear weapons.

Russia

Russia increased its non-nuclear forces to a level higher than America's in this period, but its nuclear forces were inferior. Even so they were still capable of devastating America. By an immense technological effort Russia won the first round of the space race by launching the Sputnik in 1958. This made it possible for nuclear weapons to be launched from submarines and from the ground as well as being dropped by air.

The search for allies

The West

The work of NATO increased as the rearmed Germany joined it in 1955. America continued to make similar treaties throughout the world in order to encircle Russia. However, none of these were as powerful as NATO. One of them was SEATO in South East Asia, another was CENTO in the Middle East, while close ties with Japan, Australia and New Zealand were also developed.

The East

Russia too sought allies. China was one of these, potentially another super-power but at the time involved in her own problems. The Eastern European states, formed into the Warsaw Pact in 1955, were also allies. However Russia's allies were much weaker than America's.

The Russian control of Eastern Europe

After Stalin's death several Eastern European countries tried to take advantage of the new Russian leader, Khrushchev, and to weaken Russian control. The first to try were the people of East Berlin. In June 1955 many workers went on strike and demonstrated against their own leaders. Immediately the government, led by Walter Ulbricht, responded by force and soon cleared the streets. The same thing happened in June 1956 in Poznan in Poland. There the people also went on strike and a major demonstration occurred. Once again tanks and the police bloodily crushed the demonstrators.

West German cartoon of the Hungarian Rising, 1956

By far the most serious rising in Eastern Europe was in Hungary. In October 1956 the Hungarian people rioted on a large scale and managed to get the moderate, patriotic communist Imre Nagy appointed as Prime Minister. Suddenly there was a tremendous upsurge of anti-Russian and anti-communist feeling. People tore down symbols of communism and attacked their own hated Secret Police. However, when it became obvious that Hungary would break away from the Warsaw Pact, its fate was sealed. The Red Army thundered into Budapest and cruelly supressed

the rising. 20,000 Hungarians were killed, thousands arrested and almost a quarter of a million fled to the West.

The West listened to the last broadcast from Hungary on Free Hungarian radio . . .

> Civilised peoples of the world! We implore you in the name of justice, freedom and the binding moral principles of active solidarity to help us. Our ship is sinking. The shadows grow darker every hour over the soil of Hungary. Extend to us your brotherly aid!

The West did nothing, however much it sympathised with the Hungarian rebels.

Russian foreign policy towards the West

In 1955 the new Russian leader Nikita Khrushchev began to talk of 'peaceful co-existence', saying that East and West should agree to live together. He began to travel in the West, visiting Europe and America, and to offer reductions in nuclear weapons.

American foreign policy toward the East

President Eisenhower and his Secretary of State J. F. Dulles were strongly anti-communist and anti-Russian, supported by American public opinion which wanted a very positive anti-Russian policy. Eisenhower and Dulles extended the Truman doctrine to the even stronger policy of 'massive retaliation', a promise that they would always respond to any Russian action. Dulles said that he was even in favour of helping Eastern European anti-communist risings. He believed in the 'domino theory', that is, that the communists would take over one country after another in the way a domino, when it falls, knocks down all the others.

Summit meetings

For the first time since the Second World War the leaders of America and Russia met in America and in Geneva. They were due to meet at the Paris Summit in 1960, but the shooting down by Russia of an American spy plane prevented them from meeting.

Disarmament discussions

These were regularly held at Geneva and in 1955 Russia accepted most of the West's demands. It is not known whether this was a serious move or simply propaganda. In any case America rejected it.

Agreement on Austria

After the war Austria was split up into zones just as Germany was, but in 1955 both sides agreed to let it develop into a democratic state. However it was not allowed to join NATO but was to remain neutral. The solution of this problem was a minor success.

Germany—The Berlin Wall 1961

The two sides had never agreed on how to deal with Germany. In 1961 they still disagreed. Khrushchev was determined that Berlin would never be the capital of a reunified Germany. He feared that this would happen if the West had its way. Moreover, since 1945, over two million East Germans had crossed over to the West. Khrushchev's first action was to take away the rights of Berliners to cross the city from East to West to go to work or to visit their families. This was against Russia's own agreement to keep the city open. The new American President, Kennedy, was under pressure from Berliners and from West Germany to prevent Khrushchev from closing the city. Kennedy however wanted to improve East–West relations.

In September, 1961 the East Germans closed the border in Berlin and created a barbed wire fence which prevented all East Germans from crossing the border. Checkpoints were set up and soon a huge concrete wall was erected. President Kennedy did not act to prevent the city from being divided. The frequent shootings of escapees roused public opinion in the West. Relations between the super-powers deteriorated.

East German border guards retrieve a shot escapee

Q

1 What would be the response of a) a Russian b) a West European c) a Hungarian to the cartoon and the radio broadcast of the Hungarian Rising?
2 Under two headings Deterrence and Détente, list the events and features of this period according to whether they encouraged deterrence or détente. Conclude by assessing whether this period was mainly one of deterrence or of détente.
3 What is your response to the picture of the dead East German?

Cuba 1962: Case study

In October 1962 came the most frightening crisis of the nuclear age. Cuba, until 1959, was under the rule of a dictator supported by America. In that year he was overthrown by the Marxist Fidel Castro. America was only 90 miles away from Cuba and did its best to undermine and overthrow Castro.

In 1961 President Kennedy supported a disastrous attempt by anti-communist Cubans to invade Cuba at the Bay of Pigs. Cuba turned more and more to Russia, who was pleased to take advantage of her request.

In October 1962 an American U2 spy-plane photographed a Russian missile base being prepared in Cuba, from which American cities could be bombed. Russian ships carrying missiles were also spotted crossing the Atlantic towards Cuba. President Kennedy's policy was to set up a blockade of American war ships to prevent the Russian ships from reaching the island of Cuba.

The whole world waited with mounting and terrified anxiety. The tension increased as another American plane was shot down over Cuba and as American marines boarded a Russian ship and opened the crates carrying the missiles.

The crisis ends

Everything depended upon the two leaders. Both Khrushchev and Kennedy realised the need

British demonstration over Cuba, 1962

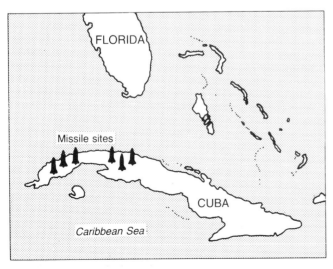

Cuba

not to cause a nuclear war, but neither could easily back down.

A correspondence took place between the two men. In his first letter Khrushchev offered to withdraw the missiles if the Americans would agree not to attack Cuba in the future. Yet before Kennedy answered this letter came Khrushchev's second letter, which said . . .

I understand your concern for the security of the United States, Mr President, because this is your first duty, and I have the same duty.

Our aim has been, and still is to help Cuba. And no-one can deny the humaneness of our motives, which are to enable Cuba to live in peace and to develop in the way its people desires.

All countries want to make themselves safe. But how are we to assess your actions since you have surrounded the Soviet Union with military bases—in Britain, in Italy, in Turkey. You are worried by Cuba because it is a distance of 90 miles by sea, but Turkey is next to us. Do you consider then that you have the right to demand security for your country and do not admit the same right for us?

Khrushchev now added another condition to his demand that America should promise not to attack Cuba. He suggested that Russia would remove its missiles from Cuba if America removed its missiles from Turkey.

President Kennedy replied publicly to the first letter, agreeing not to invade Cuba in the future. To the second letter he agreed privately and secretly to remove the missiles from Turkey. The crisis was over. The ships turned back to Russia. The leaders and the whole world breathed a sigh of relief. Russia, it appeared, had backed down.

Two years later, in 1964, Khrushchev wrote another account of the Cuba crisis in his book of memoirs.

I will explain what the Cuba crisis was all about. We intensified our military aid to Cuba. We were quite sure that the Americans would never accept a communist Cuba. The fate of Cuba and the

upkeep of Soviet bases in that part of the world concerned us. We had to set up a real effective deterrent to American interference in the Caribbean area. The logical answer was missiles. I had the idea of setting up missiles in Cuba without letting the US find out they were there until it was too late to do anything about them. We had no desire to start a war.

We sent the Americans a letter saying that we agreed to move our missiles on condition that the President promised there would be no invasion of Cuba. Finally Kennedy gave in and agreed to make such a promise. It was a great victory for us, though, a triumph of Soviet foreign policy. A spectacular success without having to fire a single shot.

Western historians tend not to agree with Khrushchev, as in the following examples of their views . . .

1 Mr Khrushchev had backed down. The world was safe from war. In the end a compromise was reached. Russia agreed to withdraw all missiles from Cuba. USA promised not to invade Cuba.
2 The outcome was a Soviet defeat: Khrushchev was forced to withdraw his missiles.
3 Kennedy refused at first to withdraw his missiles from Turkey, but secretly he agreed to remove them 'soon' (in fact they were already out of date). Khrushchev backed down and the Russian ships were taken away.

Q

1 What do you think are the views and fears of the British demonstration in the photograph?
2 How reliable is Khrushchev's letter in revealing his true intentions? Compare it with his later account.

3 Do you agree with the general opinion of the Western historians that Cuba was a defeat for Russia? What further evidence would you like to have to make up your mind?

1962–1979 The decline of the Cold War

The super-powers face other issues

After the terrible fears aroused by the Cuban crisis of 1962, there was a considerable relaxation

of tension and hostility. This was not only because Russia and America were determined not to repeat such a near disaster. The world was also changing and the relations between the two super-powers were becoming less important.

There were three main reasons for the decline

of the Cold War in this period. One was the rise of China, potentially a third super-power. Another was the refusal of many new nations in the world to join either one side or the other. A third reason was that both Russia and America faced serious problems of their own at this time, which took their attention away from their own rivalry.

1 The rise of China

An old Chinese proverb runs, 'My enemy's enemy is my friend.' Whose side would China be on?

1949–1961. China, as the second most important communist power in the world, took advice and aid from Russia in making China communist. America was regarded as the deadly enemy and had fought a bitter war with China in Korea. America protected the former ruler of China, Chiang Kaishek, in his island fortress of Taiwan and refused to recognise the communists' right to rule China.

1961–1974. China and Russia quarrelled bitterly about the different types of communism they were following. China claimed back large parts of territory which Russia had seized in the nineteenth century. China also competed with Russia for the leadership of many Asian countries, which China wished to dominate. Because of these quarrels China and America began to come together. America gave less support to Taiwan, and recognised China in 1979. In the late 1970s and 1980s agreements were made for more and more American money to be invested in China.

It is clear that super-power rivalry is now between three and not two super-powers. However, China is not a stable, settled country and is often thrown into confusion. She does not possess the *military* might of Russia and America. Whose side, if any, will China be on in the future?

2 The non-aligned world

A non-aligned country is one which refuses to join either the Russian or the American side in the Cold War. Before the 1960s there were very few of these. However, in the 1950s and 1960s many parts of the world became independent and the number of countries grew from under 50 to over 150. Most of these countries belong to the Third World; the poorer, developing nations. They have many problems of their own and in spite of pressure, refuse to join the super-powers. These non-aligned countries do not feel strongly about democracy or communism and resent being dominated by the super-powers.

With so much non-alignment, the super-powers failed to bring the Cold War to the rest of the world.

3 The weaknesses and problems of the two super-powers

America's problem—Vietnam

Vietnam, like Korea, was split into two. In the South was a military dictator, Diem, supported by America. In the North was a communist state under Ho Chi Minh. The communists also had a lot of support among the peasants of South Vietnam. There they supported the communist guerrilla movement, the Vietcong.

Several American presidents, including President Kennedy, gave considerable aid to South Vietnam. In 1965 President Johnson sent a full-scale American army of nearly half a million men, backed up by thousands of bombers and horrifying chemical weapons like napalm. The Americans found that all their military might did not help them against a guerrilla movement. The Vietcong, merging into the jungle and into the peasant population, could not be defeated. America also lost the battle for the support of the South Vietnamese people by their devastation and slaughter of both innocent and guilty.

Vietnam became the most bombed country in the world, yet it was always a 'limited' war. In America itself the 'hawks', fiercely nationalistic and anti-communist, wanted to fight the war even more strongly. The 'doves' wanted to withdraw gradually and to hand over to the South Vietnamese. It was the American President who in the end decided what should happen. By 1969 America was sickened by the war. Public opposition increased. Over 40,000 Americans had died. Immense American wealth had been spent, but nothing had been gained. President Nixon was elected on the understanding that he would end the war with as much honour as possible. Slowly America withdrew from the war, and in 1975 South Vietnam was occupied by the communists. The war commanded almost the whole of America's attention for years and left her confidence badly weakened.

Russia's problems—Eastern Europe

Russia's Eastern European 'satellite' allies had never really accepted Russian domination and had always shown signs of resistance. By the 1960s trouble was brewing again. This time

Graffiti on a Prague statue

Street cartoons in Prague, 1968

Czechoslovakia was the flash-point. There the standards of living of the people were poor, and their leader Novotny was holding back economic development.

In March 1968 the new Czechoslovakian leader, Alexander Dubcek, began what became known as the 'Prague Spring'. Dubcek talked about 'socialism with a human face', involving less censorship, less control over the economy by the government, even allowing non-communist political activity. His programme became immensely popular with the Czech people, although Dubcek made it clear that he would never leave the Warsaw Pact.

The Russian leader Brezhnev and the other Eastern European leaders were less certain. They feared that what was happening in Czechoslovakia would, if allowed to go on, happen in their own countries. They watched for months as the protests of the anti-communist Czech people flourished. Then, realising that the Eastern Bloc had to be united, they acted. On 20 August 1968 Russian tanks rolled into Prague, all the changes were stopped and Dubcek was replaced. The Czechs could not resist, but you can see their reaction from the photographs on this page. Yet even though the Soviet leaders had 'won' against the Czechs they were continually worried about Eastern Europe.

The two super-powers, therefore, increasingly preoccupied with their own problems, had less taste for confrontation with one another.

Lenin weeps at the invasion of Czechoslovakia

Russian troops listen to Czech protesters, 1968

1 'My enemy's enemy is my friend.' Explain what this means and give examples of it in action between China, Russia and America.

2 Which of the three issues described on the previous page do you think was most important in causing the decline of the Cold War? Give your reasons.

3 Many Russian soldiers had thought that they were being sent to Berlin, not to Prague. They saw the street cartoons, and spoke and argued with Czech protesters, as you can see in the photograph. What attitudes and views do you think each side expressed in such a discussion?

Events and developments 1962–1979

Deterrence and détente

You can see from the columns below how the super-powers continued to develop both deterrence and détente in their relations with one another. In fact the 1970s are often called *'The* détente'.

Deterrence	Date	Détente
The basic hostility remained and the main means of deterring the enemy – arms and alliances – remained strong.	1962 to 1979	The super-powers realised the need to improve relations and to understand one another better. Tension certainly decreased during this period as both sides took measures to reach an understanding. They attempted to solve some of the problems between them, especially the problem of the arms race.
The *arms race* continued, with each side developing new weapons. The Space Race began on a large scale between the two super-powers. Both super-powers found it essential to win the Space Race for two reasons. One was the great status that was gained by being the most advanced power. The other was the potential military use of space. Up to the 1960s the main method of delivering nuclear weapons was to drop them from bombers. The Space Race has meant that land and submarine launching can also be used. Space also allows each side to spy on the other and even to begin to develop space weapons.		Basically the two powers did their best to avoid confrontation with one another. They had learned some of the lessons of the Cuban crisis, which had nearly brought the world to war.
		There were good reasons for détente. In many ways both super-powers had already achieved security by being able to destroy one another many times over. Making fewer weapons was also much less expensive.
Alliances too remained strong and intact in this period, especially NATO. The super-powers continued to find safety in numbers.		It also enabled the super-powers to appear to world opinion as great peace-makers. In addition, some of the leaders on both sides actually believed that peaceful methods would increase their security as much as confrontation did.
America possessed 50 nuclear weapons and Russia had 35.	1960	
The Americans completed the first Polaris nuclear submarines, as did the Russians.	1963	A 'hot-line' was set up to link the two super-powers by telephone in case of emergency.
		A Test Ban Treaty was signed, banning nuclear tests on land, sea and air.

Deterrence	Date	Détente
America now possessed about 2,000 nuclear weapons, while Russia had 500.	1965	
	1967	A Test Ban Treaty, banning nuclear tests in space, was signed.
	1968	The Nuclear Non-proliferation Treaty was signed, preventing smaller countries from possessing nuclear weapons. It has not been very successful.
Both sides developed missiles which could shoot down other missiles. These are known as anti-ballistic missiles.	1969	Both sides made clear that they wanted the arms race to slow down. President Nixon and President Brezhnev made more friendly speeches. The Strategic Arms Limitation Talks (SALT) began.
It was clear that both sides did deter one another, yet still forced one another to build more and more weapons. By now America possessed 2,300 while Russia had 1,500.	1970	
	1972	Trade links increased between Russia and America, in particular a Wheat Deal, in which America sold huge amounts of surplus wheat cheaply to Russia. President Nixon visited Moscow. *SALT I.* In this treaty both sides agreed to limit their weapons to existing levels for five years.
In 1975 America possessed 2,200 nuclear weapons, while Russia possessed 2,500. America, however, had more warheads. Still new weapons were developed by both sides. Cruise Missiles were developed on the American side and SS22s on the Russian side.	1975 to 1979	Presidents Carter and Brezhnev stimulated a more friendly relationship. President Carter was very committed to a policy of détente. In 1975 the Helsinki Agreement was made. By this agreement both sides agreed that the existing European borders between states should become permanent. The Helsinki Agreement also stated that all those states which signed it should recognise *human rights* for their subjects. This confirmed freedom of thought, religion and movement. Under this agreement more and more pressure was brought to bear on the Russian government by President Carter to be less repressive towards its own people. It began to allow Russian Jews to emigrate to Israel in much greater numbers. In 1979 the SALT II talks came to an end with another treaty limiting arms.

1 Looking back at the time chart, which years would you identify as highlights of détente? Give examples.

2 Do leaders pursue détente because they believe in peace and harmony *or* because it suits them *or* both? Give reasons for your views.

1979–1990: The Cold War rises – and falls

After the late 1970s the relationship between the two super-powers became more hostile and tense once again. Détente decreased and deterrence became much more important. As you read through the following events and features of this phase of the Cold War, you will be reminded of similar events from earlier stages.

1979 – The Soviet invasion of Afghanistan

There were several possible reasons for this . . .
1 Afghanistan was friendly to Russia but politically unstable, and in danger of collapsing. It was important to the Soviet Union that Afghanistan, its neighbour, should be in friendly hands.
2 Russia itself has a huge Muslim population in the areas neighbouring Afghanistan. During this period fanatical Muslims, spreading their ideas from Iran, began to reach Afghanistan. If these ideas reached Russia itself, Russia's own Muslim population might become affected.

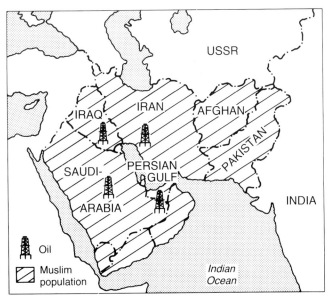

Afghanistan and Gulf area

3 The Persian Gulf, through which oil was transported from the Arab states to Western countries, was crucially important to the West. Taking over Afghanistan would extend Russia's power and importance towards the Gulf at the expense of the West.

The response of President Carter in 1979 to the invasion was to cancel the SALT II agreement and to begin economic sanctions against Russia. America refused to sell wheat and technological goods to Russia.

Whatever the reason for invasion, Russia only kept control of Afghanistan with great difficulty and with a very high cost in soldiers' lives. In 1988 the Russian leader, Mikhail Gorbachev, signed an agreement with President Reagan to gradually withdraw Soviet troops from Afghanistan. All were withdrawn by February 1989.

The election of President Reagan – 1980

President Reagan was elected to 'make America great again'. Many Americans thought that Carter had been weak towards the Soviet Union. Reagan appealed to the very strong anti-communism and nationalism of many Americans. He wanted America to 'walk tall' again and be feared and respected in the world. It is thought that, at first, Reagan and his advisers wanted not only to stop Russian expansion but actually to make Russia unstable by undermining its allies like Poland and its economy by sanctions. This, it was thought, would force the Russians to spend more and more on arms, which they could not afford, thus creating discontent within Russia.

The arms race

After the failure of the SALT II treaty both sides took up the arms race once again. Both sides

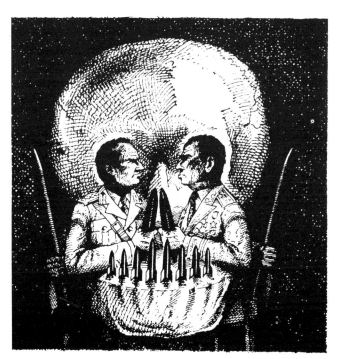

British cartoon, 1979

deployed more and more missiles in Europe. America was in the lead, because of its technological superiority. In 1984 the Americans destroyed a missile from space, making a real possibility of the Strategic Defence Initiative, popularly known as Star Wars. Also, very small nuclear weapons were invented, known as 'battle field' weapons. These were regarded as very dangerous indeed as there might be a great temptation to use such small weapons, especially in Europe, while not risking the use of large warheads. Another weapon to be developed by America was the neutron bomb, which killed people while not devastating property. Strategic Arms Reduction Talks (START) were held throughout this period and in 1987 Reagan and Gorbachev signed an agreement to reduce nuclear weapons and to withdraw them from Europe.

Alliances

Both NATO and the Warsaw Pact remained strong, but there were weaknesses. In Europe there was considerable dissatisfaction about American aims and a rising feeling of anti-Americanism, as shown in the growth of the CND movement. On the other side there was a tendency of some Eastern European states, such as Romania, to give less help to the Warsaw Pact.

Russia and Eastern Europe

The Soviet Union continued to have problems with its satellite states. Poland, the most anti-Russian of all, was the largest and potentially most troublesome of these. There a free Trade Union movement, *Solidarity*, led by Lech Walesa, was formed in the Gdansk shipyards. It began to make demands for political changes, particularly less control by the communist government. There was also a very strong anti-Russian feeling. Although the new leader, General Jaruzelski, was favourable to Russia and banned Solidarity from 1984 to 1988, Poland remained a problem. Russia hesitated to interfere in Poland, the largest of her allies.

Romania too, under President Ceaucescu, began to draw away from Russian control.

American intervention in other countries

Like Russia, America too is prepared to interfere in the affairs of other countries, even to invade, if it regards its security to be in danger. In 1983 American troops invaded the West Indian island of Grenada and removed a pro-Cuban government. America still fears that the domino theory will operate in Central America and the Caribbean, and that, one by one, states there will become communist. America regards this area as its own 'back-yard'. Nicaragua has already elected a Marxist government. American policy is

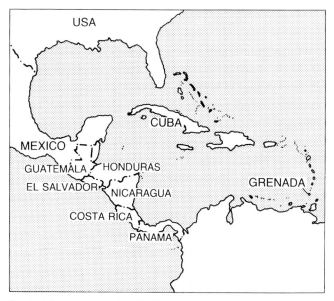

Central America and the Caribbean

to support the non-communist Contra guerrillas against the Nicaraguan government, and to support the non-communist governments of Central America in crushing their Marxist guerrillas. America is terrified of a Marxist revolution spreading nearer and nearer to its own neighbour, Mexico, and to itself.

The fall of the Cold War

By 1987 it seemed that the tension was declining again. Mr Gorbachev no longer wished to increase spending on arms, and he became more friendly with the West. His policies of *Glasnost* (openness) and *Perestroika* (restructuring) granted more rights to the Russian people. Soon, various Soviet peoples were demanding more rights, even their independence. The Baltic states (Latvia, Lithuania and Estonia) were quickly

followed in this by Georgia, Armenia and the Muslim peoples of Central Asia.

It was in Eastern Europe that the Cold War was most affected. Gorbachev, openly refusing to send troops to Eastern Europe, allowed drastic changes to occur. In Poland, Hungary and Czechoslovakia the communist governments were forced to share power with opposition groups.

The most important change took place in East Germany. There the government began to collapse after massive demonstrations. In November 1989, the government, with Gorbachev's support, began to pull down the Berlin Wall.

The Western governments welcomed the improvements in international relations, realising the need to prevent Russia from feeling insecure. But the biggest challenge came with the realisation that the reunification of Germany was now on the international agenda.

---

1 Explain the meaning of the cartoon from 1979. Does it still apply today?
2 Why do you think Russia took over Afghanistan? Write a paragraph arranging the reasons in the most sensible order.
3 Did détente fade away in 1979–1980 because of the Russian invasion of Afghanistan or the election of President Reagan, or both?
4 Which of the events and features of this stage of the Cold War have you not come across at earlier stages? Give examples.
5 Do the ideals and interests of the Cold War, stated at the beginning of this chapter, still hold true today? Construct a questionnaire asking several people for their views and beliefs about the USA and USSR.
6 What signs were there that détente increased in the late 1980s?

Discussion topics

1 What developments are now taking place in the relationship between East and West? Are you hopeful or not about the future?

Essays

1 What were the causes of the Cold War? Describe one important cause of super-power confrontation and assess its importance.
2 Describe and briefly explain how any four of the following influenced the relationship between the super-powers: the Berlin Airlift; The Korean War; The Hungarian Rising; The Berlin Wall; The Cuban Crisis; SALT; Afghanistan.

THE ARAB-ISRAELI CONFLICT
since 1948

The problem—two peoples, one land

Up to the First World War, Palestine was ruled by Turkey as part of her large empire. In 1919 the mandate (right) to rule Palestine was given by the League of Nations to Britain.

As you can see on the map, Palestine was a small, poor country with a tiny population. Even so two peoples, the Arabs and the Jews, claimed the country as their own. Both peoples belonged to the same racial group, the Semitic race, but had different religious and cultural traditions. Up to 1919 the Arabs and Jews lived in relative peace with one another, but their antagonism soon increased. They began to compete for possession of the land which the Arabs called Palestine and the Jews called Israel. Why should such a small land be the cause of one of the world's major problems?

The Middle East in 1948

The Jews

In Roman times the Jews had been expelled from their homeland in Israel and had spread over large parts of North Africa, the Middle East, Europe and America. They kept alive their separate religion, identity and culture, especially in Europe where they were often cruelly persecuted. In the late nineteenth century the Zionist Organisation was formed to create a sense of pride and nationhood for Jews everywhere, to sponsor migration to Palestine and to work for a Jewish homeland. In 1917 the Zionist Organisation managed to get the support of the British government. In the Balfour Declaration the British government agreed that the Jews should have their homeland in Palestine.

Under the British mandate the Jews were favoured and Jewish migration to Palestine, mostly from Europe and America, increased so much that by 1948 there were approximately 650,000 Jews in Palestine. This was about one third of the population. They now wanted to rule their old biblical homeland and its capital Jerusalem, the centre of their religion.

The Arabs

In the seventh century AD the Arabs had moved out of their original homeland, Arabia, and had quickly spread across the Middle East and North Africa. In 1919 there were about 50 million of them, a single people with a common language, a common culture and a common religion, Islam. Only a small proportion of the Arabs, 1,350,000, lived in Palestine. During the Great War the

Arabs had been promised their independence from Turkey by Britain and France, and had helped the Allied war effort. However, in 1919 the Arabs were not allowed to become a single independent nation. Instead they were split into several nations, mostly under British and French mandates. The main Arab nations were Syria, Iraq, Transjordan (now Jordan), Egypt and Saudi-Arabia. Even so they claimed to act as a single race and they supported the claims of the Palestinian Arabs to control Palestine. They felt that, as they were in possession, they had the right to rule the country. They particularly wanted to control Jerusalem, which was one of the centres of their religion.

The outside powers

The British were the main outside power in the area. As well as having the mandate to rule Palestine, Britain was a world power with huge interests in the Middle East. Britain owned most of the oil companies in the area, especially in Iraq, which it needed for economic and military reasons. The British also part-owned the Suez Canal, which controlled the route to the British Empire in the East. These interests had to be protected at all costs.

America too was becoming much more interested in the Middle East, mainly for economic reasons and was developing its oil interests in Arabia very quickly. **France** also had great interests in the area, especially in Syria and Lebanon, and as part owner of the Suez Canal. **Russia** had no economic interests in the Middle East but, like America, was becoming increasingly interested in all parts of the globe.

Since 1948 wars have been fought between the Arabs and the Jews, making the Middle East one of the world's most dangerous trouble spots. We shall follow the progress of these wars from before 1948 up to the present day, working out their causes and their consequences.

Q

1 If Palestine is so small and poor, why does it raise such powerful emotions among various peoples? Identify some of these strong emotions.

2 Mark on the map, using different colours, the interests of the different nations and peoples.

The first war, 1948–1949

Causes of the war

Jewish nationalism

During the 1920s and 1930s the British rulers of Palestine favoured the Jews by allowing Jewish immigration on quite a large scale. They also allowed the Jews to buy up large areas of land from absent Arab landowners. However, in 1939 the British began to restrict Jewish immigration from Europe, at the very time when Hitler was beginning his most atrocious persecution. The Jews became bitterly opposed to the British, and their hostility increased ten-fold during and after the Second World War. Surviving Jews realised the full horror of the Holocaust and were determined to set up a separate Jewish State to make themselves safe from such atrocities.

More and more Jews set out to settle in Israel, but the British turned them back, even from the beaches themselves. The most famous incident was when the British turned back the ship *Exodus*, shown in the photograph, and transported its 4,500 illegal entrants to displaced persons' camps in Germany! Up to this point the leader of the Jews was the moderate Zionist Chaim Weizmann, but he now lost his influence to the more demanding Ben Gurion. For most Jews now, nothing but a separate Jewish State would do. This seemed within their grasp for the first time since the Roman Empire, and they were not going to lose it. The majority of Jews even began to sympathise with two terrorist groups, known as Irgun and the Stern Gang, which carried on a campaign of bombing and ambushing to force the British to agree to a Jewish State. In 1946 they blew up the British Headquarters at the King David Hotel in Jerusalem, killing 88 people. By 1948 the Jews were intent on setting up a State of Israel with Jerusalem as its capital. They were determined to fight for it to the bitter end.

The *Exodus* arrives in Palestine only to be sent away again

The outside powers

British policy. The British were trying in vain to look after their own interests—Middle Eastern oil and the Suez Canal—while trying to solve the Palestinian problem. Not really knowing what to do, they changed their minds and made serious mistakes. Up to 1939 they favoured the Jews, then realised that, during the Second World War, they would need Middle Eastern oil, which depended on Arab support. Of course they failed to convince the Arabs that they were really sympathetic to the Arab cause, and they also lost the support of the Jews. Both sides deeply distrusted the British.

After 1945 the man in charge of the Palestinian problem was the new Labour Foreign Secretary, Ernest Bevin. He wanted in the future to divide the British mandate into two parts, one Jewish and one Arab, but his immediate problem was Jewish violence against British rule. He sent in commandos to crush Irgun and the Stern Gang, but their harsh commando methods caused terrible reprisals and antagonised the Jews. In 1947 he realised that the British could simply cope no longer with the problem. He decided that he would hand the mandate back to the United Nations, which had taken over all the League of Nation's mandates. Even so, Britain refused to allow a UN administrator into Palestine to enable an orderly transfer of power

Arab nationalism

Under the British mandate the Palestinian Arabs increasingly resented Jewish immigration and the buying of land from absent Arab landowners. Occasional violence broke out between the two peoples, but in 1937 a full-scale civil war erupted until the British ruthlessly suppressed the Arabs. Even though the British became more sympathetic to the Arabs in 1939, the Arabs hated both Jews and British.

Under their extremely nationalistic religious leader, the Mufti of Jerusalem, they began to plan a holy war against Jews and British. If the Arab cause had been left to the Palestinian Arabs there would have been simply a civil war. But the Arab states surrounding Israel were a more serious matter for the Jews. In 1941 they formed the Arab League. Although there were many divisions and rivalries between them, they were united in their hatred of the Jews and of a separate Jewish State. They were determined to keep Palestine an Arab country and to keep control of Jerusalem.

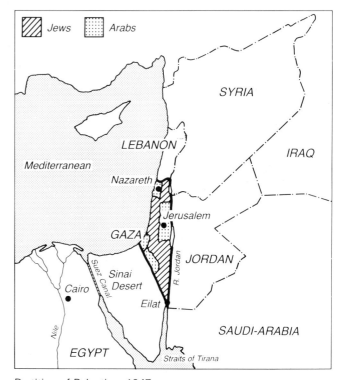

Partition of Palestine, 1947

to take place. The British allowed King Abdullah of Jordan to put troops into the Arab parts of Palestine, then suddenly ordered them to withdraw.

The United Nations sent a Special Committee to Palestine in 1947. This recommended splitting the country into two, as shown in the map, with Jerusalem as an international area. Neither side was willing to accept this. It was not a sensible idea but there was little else that the UN could think of. War was now inevitable.

The fighting

The war began in March 1948 with the ferocious Battle of Qastel near Jerusalem, even before the British left on 14 May 1948. On that same day the Jews proclaimed the State of Israel and found themselves at war with Jordan, Egypt, Syria, Iraq and Lebanon. Egypt successfully invaded from the South and almost reached Jerusalem, but was thrown back in December. The Jews seized the Southern Arab area adjoining Gaza.

In the centre the Jews prevented the armies of Jordan, Lebanon, Syria and Iraq from overrunning the Jewish areas of Palestine and the new city of Jerusalem. However, they failed to keep the old city of Jerusalem, which Jordan captured, although they did take several Arab lands on the West Bank adjoining Jewish territories.

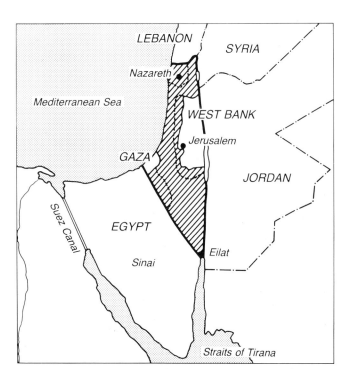

Gains made by Israel, 1948

In the North the Jews gained the Arab area centred on Nazareth. It was a brutal war. Even the official Israeli Army terrorised Arabs, although the most notorious event was the massacre of the inhabitants of the Arab village of Dir Yassin by the Irgun and the Stern Gang. The Stern Gang also murdered the UN official Count Bernadotte.

Results of the war

Israel

An Israeli victory was won for the time being. New land was gained for Israel, as you can see in the map, and the Jews refused to hand it back.

The Arabs

The Arab territory – the reduced Arab area on the West Bank of the Jordan – was declared independent by the Mufti of Jerusalem, but he was soon deposed and his territory was seized by King Abdullah of Jordan. The Gaza Strip in the South was seized by Egypt.

The Arab nations themselves were defeated. Their divisions were clear to see. Their pride was hurt and their hatred of Israel increased.

Palestinian refugees

Fearing more reprisals from the Jewish terrorist gangs and the Israeli Army, most Palestinian Arabs left the Jewish areas and fled to the West Bank and the Gaza Strip. Their terrible bitterness was soon to become a major problem.

Why did the Arabs leave after the massacre of Dir Yassin? There is some doubt about the exact reasons why the Arabs fled in such numbers.

A Red Cross official, who investigated the massacre, wrote . . .

> The press and radio spread the news everywhere. In this way a general terror was built up among the Arabs. Driven by fear, the Arabs left their homes.

The Irgun and Stern Gang issued a statement at the time . . .

> The village was attacked because it was mistakenly thought to be an Arab Headquarters.

After the war the Palestinian Arab Leaders declared . . .

> The flight of the Arabs was a deliberate policy. They will return with our later victory

The United Nations

It had failed in its first attempt to sort out a problem. Officially it was in charge of Palestine but in fact it was the least important party involved in the real situation. In the future it would have no alternative but to stand by its original division of Palestine into two parts, even though the Jews had seized more than the UN had allotted them.

Q

1 What would be the attitude of the following to the incident shown in the picture on page 157 . . .
- a would-be immigrant on board the *Exodus*?
- a Palestinian Arab?
- a British sailor preventing the *Exodus* from arriving?

2 Draw a map showing clearly the growth of Israel during the 1948 war with relevant information.

3 Arrange the reasons given for the war in order of importance, linking them together where necessary.

4 Do you think that this war was bound to happen or might have been avoided? Give your reasons.

5 Assessing the reliability of the three pieces of evidence, state your views about why so many Arabs fled after the massacre of Dir Yassin.

6 Which of the consequences of the war were not final and would, in your opinion, continue to develop into a later war?

The second war, 1956–1957

The Suez Crisis

This war was not just a war between Israel and an Arab power, Egypt. It was also part of a war between Britain, France and Egypt.

Causes of the war

Israeli nationalism

Israeli nationalism was just as strong as before, if not stronger. The new state of Israel knew that not only its success but its very existence depended on its own military efforts. If the Arabs were once successful, that would be the end of Israel.

Israel was a democracy with the enthusiastic support of its own inhabitants, the financial support of Jews all over the world, especially in America, and a strong, well-led army. Since the first war almost three quarters of a million extra Jews had migrated to Israel, mostly from the Arab states of the Middle East and North Africa. The Israeli economy was developing fast, both in industry and agriculture. The Israeli government would not wait to be attacked, but deliberately prepared to confront Arab nations if they threatened Israel any further. For example, Israeli troops attacked Egyptian Headquarters in the Gaza Strip in 1955. By 1956 the Israelis were ready to use any opportunity to act with force to protect their own security.

Arab nationalism

This too had increased since the first war. All the Arab nations felt humiliated by the first war and were determined to get their revenge on Israel and to destroy the Jews. The most advanced and aggressive Arab nation was Egypt. In 1952 some Egyptian Army officers, under the leadership of Colonel Abdul Nasser, overthrew the corrupt King Farouk. They began to modernise Egypt much more quickly and to make it into the leading power in the Middle East. More than anything else they wanted to get rid of British influence and troops in the Middle East. After this they planned to deal with Israel.

Colonel Nasser built up the Egyptian Army with Russian arms and equipment and then took several actions that provoked Israel. He began to organise and supply the Palestinian Arabs with arms for terrorist raids into Israel. These refugees had not merged into the Arab populations of the other Arab nations. They were kept in refugee camps, especially in the Gaza Strip. Their poverty and deprivation made them even more resentful of Israel, although they were not well organised. Supplied by the Arab nations, in particular by Egypt, they organised bands of *fedayeen*, terrorists who carried out bombing raids into Israel.

Then, in 1956 Egypt blockaded the Straits of Tirana to prevent ships from reaching Israel's port of Eilat. At the same time Nasser seized his opportunity to act against Britain and France. He announced that Egypt would nationalise the Suez Canal.

The outside powers. Britain and France

The British and French governments, the owners of the Suez Canal, were outraged. The British Prime Minister, Sir Anthony Eden, was determined to get back the canal and to protect British interests by insuring that no other Arabs tried to act in a similar fashion against Britain. Even though America warned Britain and France against taking military action, by October the British and French were ready to fight.

The fighting

The fighting took place between Israel, Britain and France on one side and Egypt on the other. The other Arab nations were not involved. On 29 October 1956, the Israelis attacked under the command of General Moshe Dayan, invading Egypt across the Sinai Desert. On the following day Britain and France ordered both sides to leave the Canal area. Egypt of course refused, as it was Egyptian territory, and Israel was not there anyway. On 31 October Britain and France began bombing Egyptian military targets, and on 5 November landed troops at Port Said. The immediate Egyptian response was to block the Suez Canal by sinking ships all along it.

Israel had achieved all she wanted. She had taught Nasser a lesson and had ended the blockade of the Tirana Straits. She had also gained the whole of Sinai. The war however was a disaster for the British and French. President Eisenhower of America furiously and publicly denounced their invasion and led the criticism of them in the United Nations. The Russians threatened to use force, even nuclear force,

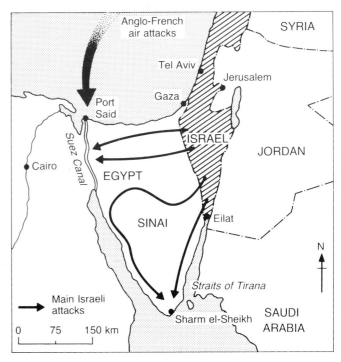

1956 War

against Britain and France. Without American support, the two Western powers could do nothing. On 6 November they accepted a ceasefire and withdrew.

Results of the war

Israel

Israel had won another victory and had achieved everything it wanted. Having taught Nasser a lesson and stopped the Palestinian *fedayeen* raids for the time being, Israel decided to hand back the whole of Sinai to Egypt shortly afterwards. It did not want this territory.

The Arabs

Although defeated by Israel, Nasser was now the hero of the Arab world. He had stood up to Britain and France and had gained the Suez Canal. He began to feel that, if Britain and France had not been involved, he might have defeated Israel.

The outside powers

For the two European powers the war was a disaster, especially for Britain. They were publicly humiliated and their status sank very low indeed. Britain was now virtually finished as

This *Daily Mail* cartoon shows the restrictions that the Labour Party wanted to place on Eden's actions in Egypt

a world power. The Arab world's distrust of Britain deepened. Soon British interests all over the Middle East, especially the oil interests in Iraq, were in danger. Public opinion in Britain was deeply divided on the Suez affair, as you can see from the cartoon.

The two super-powers, America and Russia, took care not to become too involved. Russia did not allow Egypt to use its new Russian planes in the war and America did not support Britain and France, her NATO allies.

The United Nations

The United Nations sent a peace-keeping force to Sinai to patrol the border and to ensure that the Straits of Tirana remained open. However they had no power to prevent a war.

Q

---

1 Draw a map to show the main events of the war.
2 Arrange the reasons given for the war into a convincing explanation of its causes. Make clear whether the war was mainly an Arab–Israeli war or an Egyptian–British/French war.

3 What does the cartoon show about British public opinion?
4 Who gained and lost most from the war? Explain your views.
5 Did the war improve or worsen the Arab–Israeli problem? How?

The third war—1967
The Six Day War

Causes of the war

Jewish nationalism

Israel became wealthier and stronger after the 1956 war. Her people, now 2.5 million strong, were united and becoming increasingly prosperous. Israeli industry was developing in oil refining, chemicals and ship building, and agriculture was prospering with the growth of the fruit and wine industries. There is no doubt that Israelis had an intense sense of patriotism in their new, successful country. Yet they felt more and more insecure as the Arab nations and the

Palestinian Arabs began to increase the guerrilla raids inside Israel. In the North, Syria began to shell Israeli settlements from the surrounding higher areas. The Israelis always retaliated with great force against their Arab neighbours, backed up by a growing supply of sophisticated American weapons and equipment. They were ready for war at any time.

Arab nationalism

The Arabs as a people were beginning to feel more and more confidence in themselves, yet they were still divided. Two of Israel's Arab neighbours, Egypt and Syria, were left-wing republics, quickly developing their industries and improving the conditions of their people. Both of them accepted large amounts of Russian military and financial aid, but they competed with one another for the leadership of the Arab cause.

Israel's other Arab neighbour was Jordan, whose young King Hussein did not want to wage war on Israel in case Israel seized his land on the West Bank of the Jordan.

Despite these divisions, the Arabs were still united in their hatred of Israel and there was a growing war fever in most Arab nations.

The Palestinian Arabs

The Palestinian Arabs were beginning to develop their own organisations, after being so long disorganised. In the 1950s they had set up bands of freedom fighters, or guerrillas like Al Fatah, run by Yasser Arafat. Finally, in 1964, the Palestine Liberation Organisation (PLO) was set up under Ahmed Shukairy. Its purpose was to return Palestinian Arabs to their homeland. Its weapons were anti-Israeli propaganda and guerrilla raids from the West Bank.

The outside powers

The super-powers, America and Russia, deliberately supported different sides in the Arab–Israeli conflict and competed with one another for power and influence in the area.

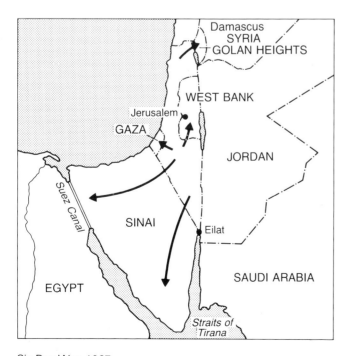

Six Day War, 1967

American Jews poured money into Israel and the American government sold large amounts of government equipment to the Israeli Army. The Russians supported both Syria, their main ally in the area, and Egypt with weapons and aid.

The immediate causes of war

In 1967 war did not seem to be about to break out; the combination of several immediate causes made it happen.

The PLO increased its guerrilla raids from the West Bank, for which Israel wanted to punish Jordan.

Syria from its high position on the Golan Heights increased its shelling of the Israeli coastal strip. When Israel retaliated, several Syrian fighter planes were shot down. The Arab world called on Egypt to help Syria.

In **Egypt** Colonel Nasser was not keen on war, but he felt he had to keep up Egypt's position as the leader of the Arab world. He also felt that, this time, he might be able to defeat Israel, who was without allies. In May 1967 he ordered United Nations troops to leave Sinai where they had been since 1956. He also once again blockaded the Straits of Tirana to prevent ships reaching Israel. This he did under pressure from the other Arab nations, but probably intended to go no further.

Jordan too was not really willing to fight. Many of King Hussein's subjects of the West Bank were Palestinians. They were out of his control and he could not prevent the raids into Israel. He was pressurised unwillingly into making an alliance with Egypt on 30 May 1967.

The **UN** Secretary-General hastily agreed to move the United Nations troops out of Sinai at Nasser's request. He failed to consult the major powers about this. Russia and America, who had been pouring weapons into the Middle East, now tried to calm the situation, but it was too late.

Israel, genuinely expecting war at any moment, decided to make a pre-emptive strike. They would not wait to be attacked.

The fighting

The war lasted for only six days and ended in complete victory for Israel. In the first few hours of war, on 5 June 1967, Israel destroyed the Egyptian, Jordanian and Syrian Air Forces in surprise attacks. This gained them control of the air and ensured that the victory would be theirs. For the next three days Israel turned on Egypt

Israeli troops at the newly-captured Wailing Wall of the Temple during the Six Day War, 1967

and Jordan at the same time. Swiftly moving her tanks, backed up by aircraft in sole command of the skies, Israel quickly took the Gaza Strip and the whole of the Sinai up to the Suez Canal. The Israeli army also repelled a Jordanian attack on the Jewish part of Jerusalem, then went on to capture not only the Old City of Jerusalem but the whole of the West Bank. Israeli soldiers raced to be the first to reach the only remaining part of the old Temple, the Wailing Wall. It was now in Jewish hands for the first time since the Roman Empire, a source of great delight, as you can see from the photograph.

Israel then attacked Syria. Syria had not attempted to invade Israel, but had looked down from her powerful defences on the Golan Heights. In the last two days of the war Israel easily took the Golan Heights.

By 10 June all the powers had accepted the United Nations call for a ceasefire. The war was over.

Results of the war

Israel

The war was an outstanding military victory for Israel. She had captured the whole of the former country of Palestine and had regained her old biblical territories. Israel now had securely defended borders. From the Golan Heights Israeli guns now looked down on the Syrian capital of Damascus instead of Syrian guns bombing Israel. She had taken the West Bank from Jordan and Gaza and the whole of Sinai from Egypt. Israel was at her fullest extent.

Yet there were serious problems. The West Bank and Gaza were, according to the original UN decision, Arab territories. The UN insisted that they should remain so. Israel would face serious problems in ruling these newly-conquered Arabs. The Golan Heights had never belonged to Palestine anyway, and Syria still claimed them.

The Arabs

There was still no peace. The Arab nations felt humiliated, and could not even bring themselves to recognise Israel's right to exist. Egypt, Jordan and Syria refused to accept the loss of their lands. The Arab world wanted revenge, but the separate nations could not agree on how to proceed. Some leaders like King Hussein of Jordan wanted less violent methods of dealing with Israel, while others remained more aggressive.

The Palestinians

The Palestinians now left the West Bank in further waves of emigration. They had come to the conclusion that the Arab nations had let them down and that it would be better to regain their homeland by their own efforts. The PLO and other Palestinian groups now determined to step up their raids on Israeli territory. So far their propaganda had been ineffective in convincing the rest of the world to support their cause. Now they would force the world to hear them and to give them what they wanted. Terrorism would be carried far beyond Israel.

The two super-powers

The two super-powers had realised the need not to get involved in a war in the Middle East, which might become a global conflict. Yet both had interests there which had to be protected. Both were still deeply involved with the two opposite sides. Russia at once replaced all the lost Arab weapons, and America continued its supplies to Israel.

The UN

The UN was again discredited by the decision taken by the Secretary-General to leave Sinai so hastily. It now called upon Israel to withdraw from the occupied territories, but Israel refused. It also called upon the Arabs to recognise Israel, but they refused. No one seemed to listen to the United Nations.

1 Make clear on a map the five gains made by Israel.
2 In this war it seems that the immediate causes were very important.
a Which of these immediate causes were avoidable?
b Should we blame the individual people concerned for making mistakes?

3 Which of the consequences of the war would go on developing or increasing, in your opinion?
4 How would the following react to the photograph on the previous page:
● An Israeli soldier.
● A Palestinian Arab.
● Yourself.

The fourth war—1973
The Yom Kippur War

Causes of the war

Jewish nationalism

Israel now felt safe for the first time since 1948. She continually refused to give up the five distinct territories that she had seized since 1967, defying the United Nations order to do so. These were: the Old City of Jerusalem, the West Bank of the Jordan, the Golan Heights, the Gaza Strip and the Sinai Desert. Israel now occupied these territories and ruled by military force. Jerusalem, the site of the Temple, she would never give up. The Golan Heights and the Sinai Desert were not Jewish territory even though they were useful as a buffer between Israel and her enemies Syria and Egypt. The other two territories, the West Bank and the Gaza Strip, were within the old biblical land of Israel. The Israeli government certainly did not want to let them go, but they did contain a terrible problem, the one and a half million discontented, rebellious and deprived Arabs. The West Bank was the most troublesome of the two areas. On the West Bank Israel now began to confiscate Arab land and to build her own fortress-like settlements. Then more Zionist Jews who regarded the West Bank as Israel's own land, began to move into these settlements. Trouble was bound to erupt there.

The Arabs

The Arab powers, and particularly ordinary public opinion, felt humiliated by the Six Day War. Some of their leaders, however, were prepared to negotiate with Israel, and even to recognise Israel's right to exist. Colonel Nasser of Egypt was one of these, as was King Hussein of Jordan. After Nasser's death, the leader of the more moderate Arabs was Anwar Sadat, the new Egyptian President. He and King Hussein realised that they would have to act fairly quickly, otherwise the Israelis would not give up the occupied territories. The best way to achieve this would be to persuade America to force Israel to give up these lands.

Sadat turned out his Russian advisers, although he kept their weapons. However the Americans were slow to be convinced that he really was serious. Frustrated by his failure to win over America, Sadat made a close alliance with the more aggressive Syria in 1973. Secretly the Arab leaders once again prepared for war.

The Palestianian Arabs

The PLO was taken over in 1968 by Yasser Arafat. The Palestinians, now better organised and more powerful, began to rely less on the Arab powers and more on their own efforts. Outside Israel, their bases were in Lebanon and in Jordan. From there they carried out bombing and guerrilla raids into Israel itself but with little effect.

The Palestinians' main base was in Jordan. There were so many of them that they were almost out of King Hussein's control and treated large parts of the country as their own. King Hussein feared Israeli retaliation and in 1970 decided to assert his authority. He used his own army against the Palestinian refugee camps. About 10,000 Palestinians were killed and many others left Jordan in large numbers. Most of them made their way to Lebanon. Up to this point Lebanon had played little part in the Arab–Israeli conflict, but now its government was weak and could not keep the Palestinians out.

Several more militant and violent Palestinian groups broke away from the PLO. One of these was called Black September and another was the

British newspaper headline, 1972

Popular Democratic Front for the Liberation of Palestine. They carried terrorism to the rest of the world, bombing Israeli targets in other nations. Their most notorious act was the murder of several Israeli athletes at the 1972 Munich Olympics, as illustrated in the newspaper headline.

Palestinian terrorist campaigns and propaganda kept the tensions high between Israel and the Arabs, and made Israel more determined to deal very firmly with the occupied lands.

The outside powers

Neither super-power realised that a fourth war was about to break out, although both were determined to help their favourites in the Middle East. Even Russia, turned out by Egypt, provided close support for its ally Syria and arms for Egypt. The area was still important for the super-powers, even though their own relationship was becoming less tense and hostile in the 1970s.

The immediate causes of the war

As with the previous war, the situation suddenly deteriorated into open warfare. Syria's President Assad was preparing to fight to get back the Golan Heights, which overlooked his own capital Damascus. Arab public opinion was also becoming so strong that Sadat felt pressurised to do something and prove that he was still the leader of the Arab world. He had failed to convince America of his willingness to deal with Israel. Now, with better military equipment, he felt that he would be successful, especially if he had surprise on his side. He did.

The fighting

Egypt and Syria chose 6 October 1973 as the day to strike. It was Yom Kippur, the Jewish Day of Atonement. The Israelis, on holiday, really were taken by surprise when Egypt crossed the Suez Canal and Syria, with Jordanian support, invaded the Golan Heights. Moshe Dayan, now the Minister of Defence, concentrated first of all on repelling Syria from the Golan Heights. He then drove the Israelis back across Sinai and over the Suez Canal. By 24 October the war was over, but mainly because the super-powers forced their allies in the Middle East to accept a cease-fire. The Russians encouraged Syria and Egypt to end the war in case they lost even more. The Americans were frightened when the Saudi-Arabian government banned the export of oil to America. They could not do without Arab oil. They forced Israel to stop.

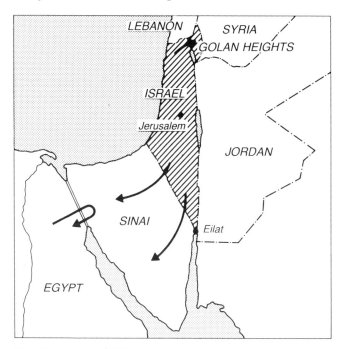

Yom Kippur War, 1974

Results of the war

Israel

Once again Israel had won the war and had kept the occupied territories. However Israel was not so obviously superior this time in arms and leadership, and had been genuinely surprised.

The Arabs

Once again the Arab nations had lost the war. They had regained no territories but, for the first time, they had not been so humiliated by Israel. Now, with greater self-respect and confidence, they might be prepared either to wage war yet again or, as an alternative, to come to terms with Israel. It would all depend upon what would happen in the next few years.

The oil-producing Arab nations, led by Saudi-Arabia, also gained in confidence by using their new found weapon of the oil embargo against the rich nations of America and Europe. At last they realised the power they had over the rich, advanced countries of the world. Now they raised the price of oil, causing terrible inflation and recession in the Western world for the next few years.

The Palestinians

Once again the Arab powers had failed to make any progress for the Palestinians. The only thing that the PLO and the other more extremist splinter groups could do was to step up their campaign of terrorism.

The super-powers

Already Russia and America were coming together with their policy of détente in Europe. America was now vulnerable to the Arab oil boycott, and Russia was less influential in Egypt. Both super-powers now tried to find a solution to the Middle Eastern problem. They began to encourage the two sides to come together.

Q

1 Mark clearly on a map the main events of the war.
2 Why did Israel refuse to give up the five areas?
3 How important were the immediate causes in this war? Or was this war the inevitable result of the basic causes?

4 Which of the consequences of the war favoured a further war? Which favoured peace?
5 What would be the attitude of the average British newspaper reader to the headline on page 165? Do you think that Palestinian terrorism puts people off or makes them think the Palestinians have a cause?

Peace not war

The Sadat peace initiative 1977–1979

There have been no Arab–Israeli wars since 1973. The dispute about who should live in the various parts of Israel has not been solved, nor has the question of the occupied territories. However in 1979 an important agreement was reached between Israel and Egypt.

The causes of the agreement

Israeli support

Israel had several reasons for coming to terms with the Arabs:

1 Israel had always wanted to negotiate an agreement with the Arabs, as it would mean that the Arabs recognised her right to exist.

2 Israel was now in a very strong position and could afford to give back some of the areas which it had seized from Egypt and which were not in Israel.
3 Israel was being pressurised by America to come to terms with the Arabs.
4 The Israeli economy was being hit by world-wide inflation and depression, yet the government was having to spend vast amounts of its income on more advanced technological weapons like missiles.
5 In future wars Israel would find it increasingly difficult to defeat the Arabs as it had done in the past. Their weapon technology was improving too.
6 An agreement with Egypt would weaken the Arabs and benefit Israel by dividing her enemies.

Israel was always prepared to fight if necessary, but for these reasons welcomed an approach from the Arabs.

Egyptian support

Although the Arabs as a whole were still strongly opposed to Israel, Egypt realised that there were good reasons for coming to terms with her:

1 Egypt did not feel so humiliated after the 1973 war and her feeling for revenge was less strong. As it would be difficult, in a future war, to cross the Suez Canal and to regain the Sinai Desert before getting anywhere near Israel, Egypt preferred other methods of dealing with Israel.
2 President Sadat wanted to gain more American rather than Russian help, and could only do this if he came to terms with Israel.
3 Sadat wanted Sinai back, and coming to terms with Israel would give it to him.
4 Sadat wanted to make a start at last on settling the Palestinian problem by persuasion rather than by force. He hoped that Israel would agree to set up a separate Palestinian Arab state on the West Bank.
5 Egypt was spending too much money on arms, and the Egyptian economy was being held back.

The super-powers

America wanted to prevent another Arab–Israeli war from breaking out because the Arabs might refuse to sell oil to America and Europe again. Russia and America wanted the Middle East to calm down so that it would not endanger the improving relationship between them at the time.

The agreement

In 1977 President Sadat visited Jerusalem and the Israeli Prime Minister Menachem Begin visited Cairo. In 1978 President Carter of America invited them both to Camp David to help along their negotiations. In 1979 both leaders signed two agreements in Washington. One was a definite peace treaty between Israel and Egypt; the other was not a final agreement but a list of proposals to settle the Palestinian problem.

The peace treaty between Israel and Egypt had several important terms:

1 Both countries at last made peace after four wars, and recognised one another's right to exist.
2 Israel agreed to leave Sinai, but not Gaza, to Egypt.
3 Egypt agreed officially to open the Straits of Tirana to ships sailing to and from Israel.

The other, less definite, agreement made several proposals to settle the Palestinian problem. The main one of these was that the West Bank Arabs were to be allowed to have some local government and that their future should be decided by Israel, Jordan and Egypt.

The results of the peace initiative

Israel had gained a great success. It was now recognised by an Arab power, something that it had wanted ever since 1948, yet had made no promises to give up any Palestinian territory.
Egypt also gained its own security and its land back again. However it lost the support of the Arab world.
The other Arab powers bitterly criticised Egypt for deserting the Palestinians and dividing the Arab cause.
The Palestinian Arabs refused to accept the agreement and continued their campaign of terrorism. Yet some of their more moderate leaders began to be prepared to accept a smaller Palestinian state. They realised they would never regain the whole of Palestine.

Q

1 Who gained most from the Sadat Peace Initiative?

2 Which of the consequences of the agreement still endangered peace?

The 1980s—War or peace?

More and more complications in the Middle East

Since 1979 there have been no wars in the Middle East. There have been no more peace developments either. In the future will there be further peace, or will there be a fifth Arab–Israeli war? On this page are a list of causes. But causes of what? Some seem to point towards war, some to peace.

Israel

It is still a very nationalistic country, determined to fight for its existence if necessary. However Israel does feel more secure than ever before and wishes to be recognised by the Arab powers.

Israel has very serious economic problems and wishes to spend less money on arms.

Israel has declared that, for security reasons, she will never give back the Golan Heights to Syria. In the occupied territory of the West Bank, Israel tried to let the Arabs have their own town councils, but did not allow any larger Arab administration. Most of the West Bank Arabs are law abiding citizens and many of them work in Israel itself. However, in 1988, many young Arabs started to riot and demonstrate against Israel. Israeli troops dealt harshly with them, causing world public opinion to turn against themselves.

Many Israelis claim that the West Bank should become part of Israel. The government has never announced this, as it would upset American, UN and world opinion. It is not known what the Israeli government intends to do in the future with the West Bank. It has set up 120 fortified settlements containing 6,000 Jews, dominating West Bank territory. If it does decide to give up the West Bank it will face terrible opposition from many Jews.

The Iran–Iraq war

Throughout the 1980s this bloody war raged, confusing an already complicated situation until it ended in 1988. Iran is not an Arab nation, but is deeply anti-Israeli and is involved in the problems of the area.

The Palestinians

Most Palestinian Arabs live in the West Bank and the Gaza Strip and became increasingly violent in the late 1980s. The others, chased from Jordan and then from Lebanon, are now scattered throughout the Middle East. The PLO is badly divided. Yasser Arafat, the leader of the moderate Palestinians, has agreed to accept a smaller Palestine state, probably comprising only the West Bank. The more extreme parts of the PLO and the other Palestinian organisations still resort to terrorism throughout the world. It is Arafat whom most of the world recognises as the leader of the Palestinians and who seems to be convincing world opinion of the Palestinian case.

The super-powers

In the 1980s President Reagan was not as interested in solving the Palestinian problem as President Carter had been. America kept Israel very well supplied with arms. American troops were used in the Lebanon partly to help Israel and partly to bring peace, but they were withdrawn when they failed to do so. Russia was keen to reach a settlement in the 1980s, but did not always calm down the situation and kept the PLO and Syria very well armed.

The Arab powers

The Arab nations continue to hate Israel, but are still very divided amongst themselves. **Egypt** remains the only Arab country to have come to terms with Israel. Egypt continues to recognise Israel and to avoid war with her. However many Egyptians want to change this peaceful policy. One group of fanatically religious Egyptians assassinated President Sadat in 1981. Sadat's successor, President Mubarak, continues Sadat's policies, although he has many enemies.

Syria is aggressively opposed to Israel and is determined to regain the Golan Heights. Syria is well armed by Russia.

Jordan declared in 1988 that it no longer wanted the West Bank. King Hussein did not want war with Israel. Yet he could not risk going against the other Arab nations in case they worked up his own people against him and caused him to lose his throne.

Lebanon was never really involved in the Arab–Israeli conflict until recently. However, when the Palestinian Arabs found a refuge there in the 1970s, they behaved as if it was their own country and began to attack Israel from there. Israel retaliated by invading Lebanon in 1978 and again in 1982. Gradually the Palestinians have been forced to leave Lebanon. However they have left it in a state of civil war. Different religious groups including Christians, Druses and various types of Muslims all indulge in open warfare and terrorism against one another. Syria, Lebanon's big neighbour, also moved in to the northern part of the country to expand its power and influence there. In 1985 Israel, finding Lebanon too much to handle, began to pull out. Lebanon remains divided and ruined. If anti-Israeli groups win the civil war there, they will be a serious menace to Israel.

─── Q ───

1a Make two columns headed Pointers to Peace and Pointers to War. In these columns note down the relevant points described in this section.
b Conclude by stating your own view of the future.
2 *Comparing 1948 with now.* Some of the following features of the Arab–Israeli conflict are the same as in 1948, others have changed. Identify these under two headings—CHANGE and CONTINUITY, explaining your views.
Israeli nationalism   The role of Britain   The role of USA   The Palestinian Arabs   The attitude of the Arab nations to Israel
Conclude by stating whether the problem is basically one of change or one of continuity.

Discussion topics

1 What are the latest developments in the Arab–Israeli conflict? Do they indicate peace or war?
2 What will have to happen on both sides if peace is to become more certain?

Essays

1 Why are Arabs and Jews so hostile to one another?
2 Describe the course and results of the wars of 1948 and 1956–1957.
3 Outline the main developments in the Arab–Israeli conflict since the mid-1960s.

CHINA

since 1925

China in 1925

In 1925 China was in one of the saddest and most confusing periods of her history. In every way she was beset by severe problems.

Political problems

Ever since the last Emperor of China had been overthrown in 1911, China had had no proper government in Beijing. The various provinces of China fell under the control of war lords. There were five main war lords and many lesser ones. They were generals whose armies dominated each area with cruelty and corruption. Only in one part of China, in the provinces near Guangzhou in the South, was there a government that wanted to unite China and to modernise the country. Here the Kuomintang, the Nationalist Party of China, ruled. Its leader was Doctor Sun Yatsen. Although Sun believed in democracy, he had made an agreement with the Russian government and the small Chinese Communist Party to work together and to reunite China.

Economic and social problems

Chinese society had changed little for thousands of years. It was as if the Roman Empire still existed in Europe in the twentieth century. China was an agricultural country. At the highest level of society were the landowners, who rented land out in small plots to hundreds of millions of peasants. China did not produce enough food to feed itself. Droughts and floods regularly killed millions of people.

There were many large cities in China, producing industrial goods for the huge population, but they were mostly made by hand, not by industrial machinery in large factories.

There was only a very small amount of modern industry, and most of it was owned by foreigners. Famine, poverty, the unequal treatment of women, and the absence of any social reforms were the main features of Chinese life. The huge and rising population of about five hundred million dragged back any developments that might have occurred.

International problems

Being such a backward nation, China was no match for powerful foreign countries. Most of the world's major powers seized territories and interests in China, and made unequal treaties with her. Japan, China's neighbour in the Far East, was the power with the most interests in China. Japan controlled several Chinese provinces and owned many rights there, especially in the North. Britain and America too had large economic interests, centred on Shanghai which had almost become a British-controlled city.

The Chinese looked down on all foreigners and resented being treated so arrogantly. They were determined to cancel the unequal treaties and to expel the foreign powers.

China, then, was at its lowest ebb. Still, many Chinese were determined that she should reassert herself and overcome her problems. China needed to expel the foreigners, to modernise her industry and agriculture, to cure her social problems, to unite the nation and to give it strong government. It was a daunting task, but many forward-looking Chinese knew that it had to be attempted. At the end of this chapter you will be able to judge how successfully China has dealt with these problems.

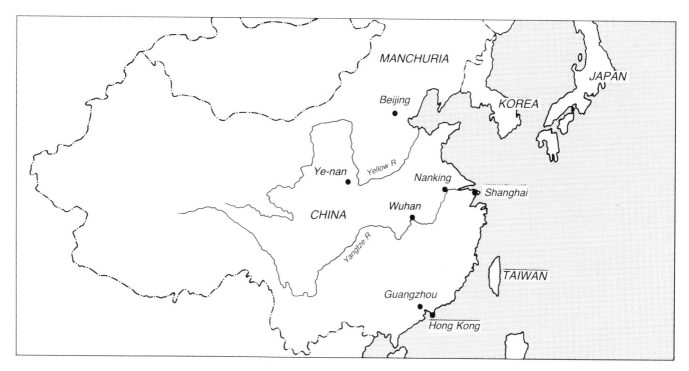

China

―Q―

1 Of all of China's problems, the need for unity and strong government was the greatest because unless it was solved first, the others could never be solved. Do you agree with this view? Explain your answer.

The rule of the Kuomintang 1926–1947

The Three Principles of the People

The Kuomintang (KMT), also known as the Nationalist Party, was led by Doctor Sun Yatsen. Its aim was to solve the problems facing China, which you read about on the previous page. Its method of doing this was to put into practice the Three Principles of the People. Sun had been inspired by these three principles for several years, but only now did it seem possible that he might put them into action.

The first principle of the people— nationalism

This meant two things. First of all it meant reuniting China by imposing strong, effective KMT government on the whole country. This would mean dealing with the war lords and the communists. Secondly it meant turning the foreign powers out of China.

The second principle of the people— democracy

Many KMT members believed in democracy as the fairest way of ruling China.

The third principle of the people— The people's livelihood

This meant sharing out the wealth of China more fairly, especially by giving land to the peasants, and by improving living standards. It also meant making China industrially strong and prosperous.

To achieve these aims Sun made an agreement with the Russian government, who sent advisers and aid, and with the small, new Chinese Communist Party (CCP), which was allowed to join the KMT. However when Sun died in 1925 the communists and the more traditional wing of the KMT began to clash over who should lead the party. The problem was solved in 1926 when a KMT officer, Chiang Kaishek seized the leadership of the party in Guangzhou. Chiang and the KMT were to rule China for over twenty years. How successful would they be in achieving the Three Principles of the People?

The first principle of the people—nationalism

Reuniting China

In 1926 Chiang Kaishek started on his Northern Expedition to reunite China. Within a year he had reached the Yangtse River and had captured Wuhan, and Shanghai. By 1928 he had set up his new capital at Nanking and had defeated several hostile war lords on his march northwards. In June 1928 Chiang marched into Beijing, the old capital, and in December 1928 Manchuria came officially under KMT control.

Providing strong, effective government over the whole country

Not all the war lords had to be defeated in battle. Many, especially in North China and Manchuria, joined up with the KMT. Although they accepted the Nanking government as the government of China, they still wielded immense power in their own provinces. The most powerful of these war lords was Chang Hsuehliang, in Manchuria. Some of these war lords were virtually independent.

The KMT began to govern China from Nanking, but soon found that China was simply too large and too populous to control. The KMT was simply not well-organised enough. In Nanking, power was shared between Chiang Kaishek, who controlled the army, and a civilian leader Wang Chingwei. The leadership was not strong enough and did not have enough officials and party members to rule such a vast country properly, although it was always powerful in the cities. It was the backward, rural, agricultural areas that the KMT could not reach.

The main problem for the KMT was the Communist Party. The communists' purpose was originally to let the KMT reunite China and then to seize power from it. Chiang Kaishek realised this well enough. Even as he marched

northwards he turned on the communists. He not only expelled them from the party but massacred thousands of them in Shanghai and in other cities in 1927. The communists fled from the towns to the country areas, especially in South China, and set up a Red Army and soviets to control the rural areas. In 1930 the communists, under their leader Li Lisan, tried to recapture the cities of South China but were badly defeated by KMT troops.

Chiang fully realised the danger from the communists and was determined to stamp them out completely. In 1931 his troops seemed about to defeat the Red Army, but, before either side won, KMT troops had to be withdrawn to deal with the Japanese invasion of Manchuria. However, by 1934, several campaigns to exterminate the communists had succeeded in defeating the Red Army in open battle at Kuangchang. The communists were now restricted to Kiangsi province and seemed about to be crushed.

The Long March

The communists had no alternative but to flee from Kiangsi. They had no idea where to go but, in October 1934, about one hundred thousand of them secretly escaped westwards and then northwards. For a whole year the Red columns were bombed and attacked by KMT and war lord troops. Nevertheless they moved over 18 mountain ranges, across 24 major rivers and through countless natural and manmade

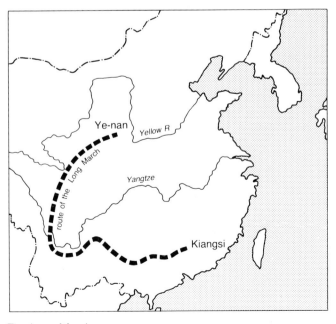

The Long March

Recent propaganda poster showing the end of the Long March

hazards. In October 1935, under the command of their new leader Mao Zedong, less than twenty thousand surviving communists arrived at Yenan in the remote north of China.

At the time and ever since, Chinese communists have always glorified the Long March. The propaganda picture, painted in recent times, shows the arrival of the Long March at its final destination. Is the picture a true portrayal of the Long March? Read three other pieces of evidence on the same subject.

Mao's own servant, who was present at the end of the Long March, wrote . . .

> Large snowflakes were falling. Although we weren't wearing too many clothes, nobody felt the cold as we trudged over the rough mountain paths. From a distance we could see a large gathering at the entrance to the village. The people were waiting to welcome the Chairman. As soon as they caught sight of him, they cheered madly. Amidst a tremendous din of gongs and drums, the crowd rushed up waving banners bearing words of welcome.

Edgar Snow, an American journalist who admired the communists and who visited them immediately after the Long March wrote . . .

> Foot-sore, weary and at the limit of human endurance, they finally arrived. The Red Army finally reached its objective with its core still intact, and its morale and political will evidently as strong as ever.

Harrison Salisbury, a journalist who has travelled the route of the Long March and interviewed many of its survivors, wrote in 1985 . . .

> The Red Army was home. The people turned out to welcome the tough, tired, thin men and women. They greeted the Red Army with cheers and smiles and food. Mao's force, compact, united, combat-hard, shared a spirit and purpose in common. They would provide the force for the revolution that all believed they would bring to China.

After the Long March the communists began again to win support among the peasants of Northern China. They were helped by the fact that the Japanese had just invaded North China. In large parts of Northern China the CCP carried on guerrilla warfare against the Japanese with well organised Red Army units and with the strong support of the peasants who were given their own land. By 1947 they controlled vast areas of the countryside of Northern China and a hundred million people.

Turning the foreign powers out of China

As Chiang moved northwards in his Northern Expedition, he forced the foreign powers to give up some of their rights and to begin to renegotiate the unequal treaties. By the beginning of the Second World War, all the major powers except Japan had given up their rights in China.

Japan. Japan however was the gravest threat to China. Japan was determined not to let a strong, united China threaten her dominance in the Far East. In addition, Japan wanted China's food and raw materials for herself. Already Japan was the power with the most rights and territories in China, particularly in Manchuria, and she continually interfered in China's affairs. As soon as the KMT reached Manchuria, Japan acted.

In September 1931 the Japanese Army invaded Manchuria. China appealed to the League of Nations for help, but it could do nothing. Nor could Chiang himself cope with such a powerful neighbour, and he was forced to withdraw. In 1933 the Japanese set up the last Emperor of China, Pu Y'i, who had been deposed in 1911, as Emperor of the new state of Manchukuo. In the following year the Japanese moved gradually into large areas of Northern China. Chiang's top priority was to defeat the communists on their Long March to Yenan, and he realised that he could never defeat the Japanese if they did invade in force. However, in 1936, Chiang was arrested by Chang Hsueh-liang, on a visit to the North. He was forced to agree to form a United Front against the Japanese threat. When Japan actually invaded North China in full force in August 1937, Chiang and the communists co-operated against them. Unfortunately they could not prevent a Japanese Army of one million soldiers from occupying most of Northern China and the coast of all China. The KMT fought bravely and effectively to defend Shanghai and Nanking, but failed to stop the Japanese advance inland. Chiang was forced to flee into Chongqing in remote Szechuan province, far beyond the reach of Japan. From there Chiang ordered Nationalist troops to wage guerrilla warfare in the countryside. This was very successful in South China, as were the Communist Party's similar efforts in North China.

In 1941 Japan went to war with America and Britain, who immediately became China's allies and donated vast amounts of money and equipment to Chiang. Chiang continued to defend his lands against further Japanese attacks, but rarely attacked Japanese troops directly. As the war went on he held back most of his equipment and his best troops. These he kept on the border with the communists, not against the Japanese. The communists too avoided battle with Japan and prepared to cope with the Nationalist attack which they expected as soon as the Second World War was over. It was the Americans, not the Chinese, who finally defeated Japan in 1945, forcing them to withdraw from China.

It was unfortunate that, throughout the war against Japan, China faced the enemy divided, with antagonism and distrust between the Kuomintang and the communists.

The second principle of the people—democracy

The KMT made several genuine and sound attempts to make life in China fairer and easier for people. The courts of China were improved and cruel punishments were abolished. The KMT tried to introduce democratic ideas into local government, but made no real attempt to introduce democracy into central government. This was not entirely because they did not want to, but because they were not really well enough organised to do so. Also there seemed so many more urgent problems to deal with. The KMT became more and more under the control of the army, and the army was under the control of Chiang Kaishek. The war against Japan made any progress towards democracy impossible. Chiang tried to continue with the democratic changes in local areas, but not enough money was made available to develop this policy. China was now ruled as a military dictatorship and Chiang was known as Generalissimo.

The third principle of the people—the people's livelihood

The Kuomintang made several attempts to

improve the wealth and living standards of the people. In the cities they made a good start in trying to turn China into a modern, industrialised nation. The government improved China's transport and communications, reformed the tax laws and improved the Chinese banking system. They lessened the economic power of foreign countries and encouraged the building up of Chinese-owned businesses and modern factories. Laws were passed to improve the conditions of workers in factories, to build schools and to encourage trade unions. Yet most of these changes took place only in Central China and in the cities there, where the KMT had real power, not in the North and the South.

As for most of China, comprised of the countryside where the peasants lived, the KMT did try to grant money to groups of peasants who would join their farms into a co-operative farm. However the KMT never really had the organisation to deal with agriculture. It did not take the land away from the rich landowners and give it to the peasants, as Sun Yatsen had earlier promised. China was simply too big for the KMT to cope with in such a short time.

Q

1 Is the propaganda picture of the end of the Long March accurate? Use all three written sources of evidence in coming to your conclusion.

2 Do you think that the communists were wise to win the support of the peasants in communist areas by giving them their own land rather than seizing all the land? Give reasons.

3 Do you think that Chiang was wise to concentrate on defeating the communists rather than the Japanese? Give reasons for your answer.

4 How successfully had the KMT brought about the Three Principles of the People? Deal with each heading separately. In each case consider the problems involved before reaching your conclusion.

The Civil War 1947–1949

After the Japanese surrender in 1945 it was obvious that a civil war would break out between the Kuomintang and the Chinese Communist Party. There was some fighting in 1945 and 1946, but from 1947 to 1949 a full scale civil war was fought for the future of China.

Most of the fighting was in Manchuria and Northern China. The Nationalists did win several battles, even capturing Yenan. However they never controlled the countryside, nor the roads and railways, and had to be supplied by air-lifts to the cities. In 1948 the Red Army, now known as the People's Liberation Army (PLA) managed to capture all the cities in Manchuria and the neighbouring provinces, including the best Nationalist armies and, more importantly, their modern American equipment. By November 1948 the PLA felt strong enough to risk a full scale open battle instead of guerrilla warfare. This was the Battle of Huai Hai. After this Beijing fell in January 1949, and the PLA advance southwards was very swift as the KMT armies gave little resistance. In April the Yangtse was crossed and soon the whole of South China was taken. In October 1949 the Peoples' Republic of China was proclaimed. Chiang Kaishek fled with the remaining Kuomintang officials and armies to Taiwan. To this day, the Nationalists rule Taiwan.

Case study
Why did the communists win the Civil War?

Comparing the two sides

KMT	Communists
### Size and state of army	
The two to three million men were not organised in a united army. Large sections were still controlled by war lords. Many of the KMT soldiers were conscripts, badly trained and poorly treated by their officers. There were many desertions and the army had low morale.	A half to one million men, very well disciplined and fed and cared for, with high morale and efficient organisation.
### Equipment	
Huge reserves of American equipment, but not replenished when lost. The modern Air Force was useful for dropping supplies to Nationalist cities, but was useless against guerrillas.	Some captured Japanese and American equipment. No air power, which would have helped against the Nationalist cities.
### Tactics	
KMT tactics were to entice the communists into open battle, which they failed to do. Their modern equipment was not of much use against small bands of guerrillas.	Guerrilla warfare, fought in small groups against specific targets and towns. No open battle was risked until late 1948, when it was victorious.
### Leadership	
Chiang Kaishek often ignored American advice, and refused to deal with known faults. Many KMT generals were not respected and did not have effective control over their armies.	Extremely good leaders like Chu Teh and Lin Biao had very effective control and good tactical sense.
### Popular support	
At the beginning of the war the Nationalists controlled four hundred million people and four fifths of the land. Chiang Kaishek had little popular support in Northern China. Kuomintang troops treated the peasants and townspeople badly, looting and raping. KMT generals and officials were corrupt and arrogant. In Central China, where they had been strongest before the Japanese invasion, the returning KMT officials were detested. The Kuomintang was not well organised enough, and law and order began to break down all over China.	At the beginning of the war the communists controlled one hundred million people and one fifth of the land. They were popular in Northern China. They cared for the peasants and did not take their land away from them, even from land owners and richer peasants. Nor did they take businesses from their owners. They began to win over many people outside their own areas. They always treated the population fairly, with equal rationing, and kept firm law and order.

KMT

There was terrible inflation in the KMT areas, which ruined many families and turned even the middle classes against Chiang.

Chiang was blamed for not having fought strongly enough against Japan. This counted heavily against him.

Communists

Their currency had no inflation and prices were kept very low.

Communists were regarded as having fought bravely against the Japanese throughout the war.

Q

1 In what ways did the KMT have superiority?
2 In what ways did the communists have superiority?

3 Why did the communists win the Civil War? Deal with the most important reasons first. Explain your views.

China under communist rule

China in 1949 — Still a country of problems

Many of the problems that had faced the Kuomintang in 1925 still remained. In fact they had been worsened by years of war. It was the communist task to deal with these problems.

Political problems and solutions

China was now united, but still needed extremely strong government to control such a large area and population. This had never really been achieved in the history of China. On top of this, Mao and the Communist Party wished to get rid of all the old beliefs, traditions, attitudes and values which China had inherited from its long past and which were very deep-rooted. The oldest and strongest of these were the ideas of Confucius, which supported the traditional idea of obedience to authority — to government, to family, to the father, the husband, the teacher. Mao wanted to overturn all these ideas and replace them with his own brand of communism.

Economic problems and solutions

China was still a very backward country with very little industry. She needed to develop modern industries to create more power and wealth. Her agriculture too was also very backward and simply did not produce enough food to feed the population. Mao wanted to

make China more efficient. This would involve the building of huge new flood control schemes, the rebuilding of the neglected irrigation systems that frequently caused such terrible devastation and starvation in China. In China most of the land was owned by rich landowners or rich peasants. Mao wished to change all this and impose on China his own communist economic system.

Social problems and solutions

Because of the backward economy there were still immense social problems to be solved.

- Most of the peasants were in a state of severe poverty and need. Ninety percent of the population owned less than one third of the land and the average farm was very tiny indeed, not enough to support a family.
- Disease and malnutrition were common throughout China. Tuberculosis, cholera, typhoid and other epidemic diseases were frequent visitors. One child in every five died within a few months of birth.
- Eighty per cent of the Chinese population were illiterate. China lacked trained scientists, engineers, teachers and other professions.
- The position of women in China badly needed reform. They were regarded as the slaves of their husbands or fathers.
- All these problems were worsened by the immense growth of the population. The more the population grew, the harder it was for the

economy to catch up with it. This problem however was not fully realised or dealt with until later.

All of these problems Mao intended to deal with in a communist way.

Since 1949 Mao and the Communist Party have striven hard to deal with all these problems. You will be able to judge how successful they have been at various stages of their history. Communist rule in China has not been in one single, unchanged direction. Several main stages have been identified:

1949–1952 Post-war reconstruction
1952–1957 The First Five Year Plan
1958–1961 The Great Leap Forward
1961–1965 Revisionism
1965–1970s The Cultural Revolution
1970s Onwards. The Reappearance of Revisionism.

In order to make any sense out of Chinese history, it is important to understand the main features of each stage and the sudden changes that often took place. In following through these stages, you will begin to understand that Mao and the other Communist Party leaders often had extreme disagreements about how to deal with China's problems. The different stages showed the different methods of dealing with these problems that Mao and the others attempted.

Q

1 Which of the many problems mentioned above would be the most difficult to deal with and why?
2 To which problems do you think Mao would give priority, and why?

3 To which country do you think China would turn for advice, and why?
4 In which ways do you think the communists would be better able to cope than the KMT?

1949–1952 Post-war reconstruction

During this short period a start was made on dealing with the very basic problems of China.

Political developments

China immediately became a one-party state with Mao Zedong as chairman. All other political parties were stamped out, especially any remaining Kuomintang officials. Lawlessness was severely put down.

A start was made in imposing communist ideas on people.

As a one-party state China, like Hitler's Germany and Stalin's Russia, used similar methods . . .

1 Terror

This was carried out largely by the People's Liberation Army which took an active part in keeping the country in order. Estimates of the killings of opponents, such as landowners vary between half a million and three million, although some go much higher. Many were also punished by being sent to remote villages and

made to confess their former 'crimes' in 'People's courts'. One such incident is shown in the photograph.

2 Propaganda

The government controlled all newspapers, radio and the arts, although most of the population

A people's court condemns a former landlord to death

were not reached by these. Travelling actors adapted traditional plays to put across communist ideas. Posters and cartoons were extensively used. However, the majority of the population was hardly affected at all by this propaganda.

3 Communist Party organisation

The government sent *cadres* all over China. These were groups of party members and PLA soldiers, usually very young. Their task was to run local affairs and convince the peasants of the rightness of communism.

Economic developments

Industry

All large scale industries like coal, steel, engineering and railways were nationalised and improved. By 1952 the previous levels of the 1930s, the last years of peace, were reached. Small industries remained in private ownership.

Agriculture

Vast numbers of people were put to work repairing flood control systems, terraces and irrigation. By 1952 famine had been removed, although agriculture remained very backwards, and was likely to remain so as it was owned by the peasants.

Social developments

Poverty and the position of the peasants

The worst poverty and deprivation was dealt with by the strict rationing of all goods, especially food. In 1950 the Land Reform Act was passed, taking away land from the landowners and the richer peasants and distributing it equally among all peasant families.

Health

Huge propaganda campaigns were organised to educate the people in cleanliness. More doctors began to be trained, especially 'bare foot doctors', people with six months' training in carrying out vaccination against major diseases and dealing with minor ailments. The health of the people really began to improve by these simple methods.

Posters showing the peasants how they have benefitted from the communist takeover: land distribution

Education

The main policy was to combat illiteracy and to begin to provide primary education for all children, although this was difficult as there were not yet enough teachers. Universities and secondary schools expanded fast.

Women's emancipation

'Women hold up half the sky,' said Mao, desiring to break the age-old oppression of women. Many laws were passed to improve women's conditions, such as the 1950 Marriage Reform Act, the abolition of child and arranged marriages, of the killing of unwanted girl babies and of polygamy (having more than one wife). Equal rights were proclaimed in every area of life. Women's Committees were set up to put these new laws into practice and to break down old attitudes and ideas about women.

Q

1 What sort of strong emotions and arguments do you think the peasant has in the photograph?
2 *The posters.*
a What message is each poster trying to get across?

b Do you understand everything that is going on in the posters? What gets in the way of your understanding?
3 Which of the above changes do you think was the most successful? Give your reasons for thinking so.

1952–1957 The first Five Year Plan

It was only to be expected that China, as a communist state, would follow the example of Russia. Soviet advisers and money were pouring into China, encouraging the government to go ahead with similar policies to those that Stalin had followed in the 1930s. Thus the First Five Year Plan was announced in 1952. It brought with it important political, economic and social developments.

Political developments

The *cadres* continued to organise the whole of China, but it was becoming clear that most of the people, as in Russia, were still clinging to their traditional beliefs, rather than being converted to communism.

Economic developments

Industry

The whole of industry was now nationalised, including even small workshops and the remaining foreign companies still in China. The whole economy was controlled from Beijing and no local interests were allowed. Virtually all investment went into heavy industry. Coal, steel, oil-refining and other important, basic industries all doubled or even trebled in these five years. New electric power stations were developed using hydro-electric power. New engineering industries were set up, producing China's first lorries, planes and oil tankers. Vast bridges, canals and dams were constructed, like the Yangtse Bridge in the photograph. All this industrial development took place on a huge scale in immense factories concentrated in the cities.

Agriculture

Much less money was invested in agriculture, but here too the Russian pattern was followed. At first, in 1952, 'mutual aid' teams were set up. These were small groups of six to eight peasant farms working together. Soon, in 1955, collective farms were introduced. They contained one hundred to three hundred small peasant farms, and no private ownership of land was allowed except for a small plot for each family.

Agricultural production did increase by about 25% during these years, causing large scale famine to disappear for the first time in Chinese history. The main difference from Russia was that in China, collectivisation was carried out by persuasion rather than by force.

Social developments

The living standards of China's thousands of millions of peasants certainly improved during this period, but China also experienced the growth of new classes. Because so much industrial development was taking place, a new working class began to grow, soon reaching thirty million. In the Russian style, industrial workers were favoured over peasants, receiving higher wages and incentive bonuses dependent on the amount they produced. Another social class also began to grow in China, a middle class of engineers, managers, scientists, lecturers and teachers, even more highly paid than the workers.

In health there were tremendous advances, causing epidemics to diminish and the infant death-rate to fall to only 28 in every thousand children. In education too, the illiteracy rate dropped to 40%, and the number of university places quadrupled. Growing numbers of women benefitted from their emancipation and began to take advantage of new opportunities, especially in the cities.

During the Five Year Plan China had taken great strides, but remained under-developed

Building the first bridge across the Yangtse at Wuhan

industrially, producing only one twentieth of America's levels of production. Agriculture still remained very old-fashioned in its methods. Another worrying problem was that the Chinese government took a population census and was astonished to find out that the population was nearer 600 million than the estimated 450 million, and growing very, very fast indeed. This threatened a return to famine and, even if China became more successful economically, the growing population would drag her down.

Mao Zedong was greatly dissatisfied with China's progress. He had always thought that the Chinese would achieve true communism more easily and more quickly than Russia ever could. He was determined to prevent China from becoming like Stalin's Russia. However he could not always have his own way. He was certainly China's main leader, but not its sole leader. By 1957 a serious split had developed in the Communist Party between the right and left wings.

Q

1 What propaganda advantages would the Yangtse bridge, pictured above, have for the communists?
2 Which of the above changes was the most outstanding? Give your reasons.

3 Which was the most serious problem facing China in your opinion? In Mao's opinion?

The split in the Communist Party

The split in the Communist Party is difficult to understand, but you will understand it better if you remind yourself what communism was all about. Read through Marx's views as described in Chapter 3.

The table on the next page will help you to compare the aims and ideas of the two groups. The main differences are summarised in the diagram opposite.

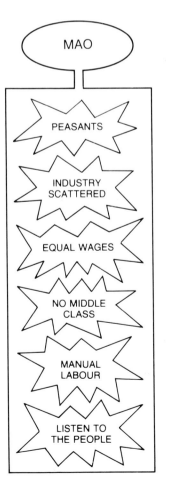

MAO

PEASANTS

INDUSTRY SCATTERED

EQUAL WAGES

NO MIDDLE CLASS

MANUAL LABOUR

LISTEN TO THE PEOPLE

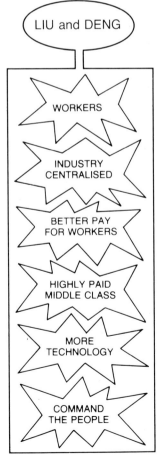

LIU and DENG

WORKERS

INDUSTRY CENTRALISED

BETTER PAY FOR WORKERS

HIGHLY PAID MIDDLE CLASS

MORE TECHNOLOGY

COMMAND THE PEOPLE

Maoists and Revisionists ▶

The left wing—Maoism

The right wing—Revisionism

The left wing—Maoism	The right wing—Revisionism
Mao Zedong led the left wing of the party. He wanted China to develop in its own way. Mao had been developing his ideas ever since the years when the communists had been under attack by the Kuomintang . . .	Revisionism was the name given to this wing of the party which wanted to follow Russia's example. Its main leaders were Liu Shaoqi and Deng Xiaoping. Their ideas were different from Mao's . . .
The peasants can become the basis of true communism. Mao had used the peasants to bring revolution to China and still believed in them.	China can only become communist if its people become industrial workers first.
Industry must develop, but must do so in small units scattered throughout the countryside of China, so that the peasants could also be workers.	In order to create a large working class, industry must grow very quickly in huge, centralised industrial areas. Peasants must move to these areas and become workers.
Wages must be equal between all classes, as higher wages are unfair and are against the belief in equality of true communism. The peasants must share in the greater wealth of the economy.	Wages must be higher for workers to encourage them to produce more industrial goods. Peasants can be paid less.
No middle class of specialist workers such as managers, engineers and intellectuals should develop because this is unequal and it is against communism. Mental work makes people vain and feel superior to the peasants.	A specialist middle class must develop to lead China to the industrial future. They need to be highly paid to encourage them.
The main method of increasing China's production of agricultural and industrial goods must be not highly advanced technological machinery, but China's vast force of manual labour. Manual labour is good for people.	More and more advanced machinery must be used in both industry and agriculture to increase production quickly.
It is the duty of the Communist Party to convert people to communism by persuasion, and to listen to the criticism coming from the masses. This is known as the 'mass line'. People's whole outlook, their values and beliefs must be changed, so that human nature can be transformed from being competitive and aggressive into being equal, co-operative and peaceful.	Until China becomes truly communist at some time in the future the people must be forced to obey the government. Criticism must be stamped out and change should be imposed.

— Q —

1 Which of the above wings of the party was
a the most practical?
b the most idealistic?
2 Do you agree with Mao's last point about changing human nature? Explain why or why not?

3 Using your knowledge of Maoism, list those points of the first Five Year Plan that Mao would disapprove of.

1958–1961 The Great Leap Forward

During the first Five Year Plan, Mao Zedong and his left wing won the power-struggle against the revisionists in the party. In 1958 they introduced the Great Leap Forward, the first attempt to put Maoism into practice. Mao said he wanted to turn every Chinese person into

> a new communist, who would accept iron discipline and give up independent thinking, family ties, friendship, leisure and material well-being.

Political developments

At the top of the power structures lay the Communist Party, now under Mao's control and making all important decisions. Yet Mao's main method of trying to make his ideas work was not by increasing the size and control of the Communist Party but by introducing the People's Communes into China. Mao thought that if everyone lived in a commune it would be easy to convert China into a communist society. The government supported the effort with a huge propaganda campaign encouraging the Chinese to work harder, not for themselves, but for Mao, for a strong China and for world revolution.

People's communes

Communes were quickly set up throughout China in both town and countryside. Each one contained ten thousand people or more, and soon there were 26,000 communes throughout China.

Running each commune was a *cadre* of young communists, chosen for their political enthusiasm rather than for their professional and technical knowledge. They not only provided the

government for the commune, but ran its economy as well and provided its social services. The commune itself organised large projects like factories, irrigation programmes, flood control and hydro-electric power (HEP) schemes. Each commune was divided into several Production Brigades, each containing several villages, which ran smaller factories like flour mills and built schools and hospitals. Below these were Production Teams, usually comprising a whole village and running village affairs. At the bottom came the Work Team of one or two families responsible for its own affairs.

Thus it was hoped that the whole of the Chinese people, led by politically enthusiastic *cadres*, would cease to live for their own interests and would live and work for the good of all. The communes would take power from the central planners and politicians, and would genuinely spread power around. They would prevent the growth of a small and dominant ruling class at the top, which Mao so hated. The communes would also prevent the growing difference between highly paid industrial workers and lowly paid peasants. Mao always looked after the interests of the peasants, whom he regarded as the future of communism.

Economic developments

Industry

The government continued with the industrial developments which had already been started, but few new projects were begun and the central planning of the economy fell into disuse. The government regarded its task as the provision of power, raw materials, oil and basic equipment and machinery, such as tractors and electric motors, needed by the commune. The communes in the cities ran the smaller factories.

A workshop in a basket factory

'Blue ants', clad in boilersuits at work on a canal

However, as Mao's main purpose was to bring industry to the whole of China, the countryside communes introduced industries as well. Each commune would set up small factories, processing food, making products such as baskets, as shown in the photograph, (above left) or even opening small coal mines and quarries. The communes also built roads, bridges and canals. During this period an astonishing 40 million people were occupied in digging canals. Manual labour was always used, as you can see in the photograph (above right). The most famous examples of this countryside industry were the 'backyard furnaces' for making steel. Soon there were 600,000 of these throughout the communes of China.

Agriculture

At the top, the commune created irrigation and flood prevention schemes to improve agriculture, while lower down, the peasants not only tilled the land but cleared new land, planted forests and terraced hillsides. All private plots were abolished, and the peasants worked in teams on commune land, not as families on their own land.

Social developments

Mao was determined to make all people more socially minded and more like the peasants. Millions of workers were sent away from the cities to work in agricultural communes, as were many intellectuals and managers. Health and education improved as the communes built more hospitals, schools and old people's homes. In many communes the *cadres* tried to create a communist society in miniature by making

people change their traditional way of life, by living in dormitories instead of in family homes, by paying them in food and clothing instead of in money. Many of the intellectual and professional classes were demoted and replaced by inexperienced *cadres* and peasants.

The consequences of the Great Leap Forward — was it a success or a failure?

Political consequences

Between 1959 and 1961 it seemed that the Great Leap Forward was a disaster. It officially ended in 1961 and many of its ideas were overturned. The right wing of the Party, the Revisionists, used the failings of the Great Leap Forward to demote Mao Zedong from his position as the Chairman of the Peoples' Republic of China, although he remained the Chairman of the Communist Party.

The people had not become true communists in these two to three years. There were signs that they were turning against Mao's attempts to make them give up their own ways, and were even beginning to resist. Discontent amongst intellectuals, managers and other professional people was rising.

Economic consequences: Industry

At first the government claimed huge successes, producing twelve million tons of steel in 1959, three million of which came from the 'backyard furnaces'. However, after 1959 industrial production slumped by 75% and many products made in the new commune factories were of such poor quality that they could not be used. But, although most of the backyard furnaces were closed down, many of the other factories remained and, under more expert management, developed rapidly after 1961.

Economic consequences: Agriculture

After the increases in wheat production in 1959, agricultural production also dipped so sharply that the government had to import food. Some foreign observers said that famine returned to

China on a large scale, aided by natural drought and floods. However, the communes were not ended, and many of their projects continued. Thirty billion trees had been planted during the Great Leap Forward, and one hundred million acres of land irrigated and millions more cleared. All helped to increase production later on.

Social consequences

Many of the *cadres'* experiments in trying to change people's traditional ways of life were resented and resisted, although the improvements in health, housing and education were welcomed.

Q

1 Why would Mao strongly approve of the photographs in this section?
2 Which parts of the Great Leap Forward would the Russians disagree with and why? Make a list.

3 List **a)** the short-term consequences of the Great Leap Forward. **b)** The long-term consequences.
4 Was the Great Leap Forward, in your opinion, a success or a failure in bringing changes to China? Give your reasons.

1961–1965 Revisionism

Now Liu Shaoqi was the Chairman of Communist China and Deng Xiaoping was the Vice-Chairman. These men were much less concerned than Mao in making the Chinese people communist in all their ways and attitudes. Their policies were a mixture of

methods. Some were taken from Russia, some from China, some from the capitalist West. Liu and Deng were practical men who wanted practical results, especially in the economy.

Political developments

The authority of the Central Communist Party was reimposed on the whole of China, especially on the *cadres*. Mao's 'mass-line' idea of listening to the people was discouraged. There was a deliberate slowing down in all the experiments to make China more communist. The communes remained, mainly in the country areas, but were much less important and were not run by *cadres*.

The government made it clear that it favoured a specialist class of professional people, managers and scientists, who were given higher salaries and special privileges. The workers came next and lowest of all were the peasants.

Economic developments

Industry

The government once again started some

Government delegation on the way to Moscow to improve relations with Russia

Part of the huge workforce of a coking plant in Beijing

massive industrial enterprises, one of which is shown in the photograph. It also kept on and encouraged the growth of small and medium enterprises set up by the communes, even in rural areas, but it ran them more efficiently.

The pay of industrial workers was increased to a much higher level than that of the peasants, and incentive payments were introduced to get people to work harder.

Industrial production increased rapidly in all industries.

Agriculture

The government was determined to avoid any possibility of famine. The agricultural communes remained, but the peasants were paid incentive bonuses for the work that they did on the land. No longer were the *cadres* in control. Instead agricultural experts and managers were employed.

The peasants were once again given their own privately owned plots, some quite large, and were encouraged to produce as much as they could for as high a price as they could get on the open market. The result was a great increase in food production, most of it coming from the private plots. A class of rich peasants began to emerge, owning land, employing other peasants as labourers and spending their money on better housing. This class came to dominate the communes.

Social developments

Improvements continued in all areas of life. Particular attention was now paid to education, as the government wished to increase the number of technical experts, engineers, scientists and managers. Primary education was made compulsory for the first time, and the illiteracy rate dropped to below 20% by 1965. More and more children went on to secondary schools. In these secondary schools and in the universities much less attention was given to communist ideas and more time was spent on academic and technical excellence.

Watching all this was Mao Zedong, increasingly worried that his ideal of a perfect Communist China would be lost for ever. In 1965 he made one more bid to achieve it.

Q

1 What aspects of the photograph would Mao find objectionable?

2 Of which achievements of this period would the Revisionists be proud? Make a list.

1965–1970s The Cultural Revolution

The Great Proletarian Cultural Revolution is one of the most dramatic attempts ever made in history to change the way people think and behave as well as the way they live and work. Mao had tried and failed to do this in the Great Leap Forward. Even though Mao had been overruled in the early 1960s, his personal influence was still high and he built up the left wing of the Communist Party in opposition to the Revisionists. Supporting Mao in this was Lin Biao, the leader of the Peoples' Liberation Army, and Mao's wife Jiang Qing. In 1965 they unleashed the Cultural Revolution.

The reasons for the Cultural Revolution

Historians and observers disagree about the possible reasons for the Cultural Revolution. There are several suggestions.

The word cultural in this sense has little to do with art and literature, those things we usually regard as cultural. The word 'culture' can also be used to mean a way of life, a set of values, attitudes and beliefs.

1 Mao's purpose was to change the culture of China, its way of life, its values and beliefs, from what it actually was to what he wanted it to be. He was trying to create perfect communism in China. To Mao this meant real equality, and co-operation in the interests of the community. It also meant the removal of all other ideas that stood in its way—religious beliefs, old customs and habits, even human emotions like vanity, pride and personal incentive. Mao had worked hard at his ideas during his period of powerlessness in the early 1960s. Now he was determined to deal much more ruthlessly with those people, ideas and beliefs which stood in his way. This meant removing or transforming not only Revisionist leaders like Liu and Deng, but also whole groups of people. The specialist class of managers, scientists, intellectuals and engineers would have to go. So would the rich peasants. So would the workers with their high incentives. In this way the peasants would become the foundation of true communism.

2 Mao, out of power during the Revisionist period, was using the Cultural Revolution simply to get back the power that he had lost. It has even been said that he had become power-mad to the extent of wanting to become the Emperor of China. At least he wanted to ensure that he was not passed over again.

3 A combination of the two reasons above.

Political developments

First of all Mao made sure of the support of the PLA. A shortened version of Mao's thoughts, entitled *The Little Red Book of Chairman Mao*, especially written for the army, was used to win over young peasant recruits. In July 1966 Mao issued a call to the young of China to 'Bombard the Headquarters' of the Communist Party itself and to attack the Revisionists who were still in power there. In August Mao won over the party's Central Committee, which made all important decisions, by a single vote. He and the Committee then called for an attack on the Revisionists.

The people who carried out the attack were the Red Guards, organised by the left wing. They were university and secondary school students, mostly of working class and peasant origin rather than professional people. For the next two years the Red Guards, helped by the PLA, carried out their revolutionary activities. The Red Guards roamed the streets and forced their way into colleges, schools, factories and even into

Cultural Revolution poster: Red Guards protest against anti-Maoist authors

Party Headquarters. Their targets were the teachers, lecturers, writers, scientists, managers, even the Revisionist leaders including Chairman Liu himself. All this was done in the name of Mao and of communism. Many people were deliberately humiliated by their inferiors, forced to criticise their former behaviour and to confess their crimes of vanity and greed. They were forced to ask Mao for pardon. Some were legally executed or simply killed outright, probably in their thousands, and others were imprisoned. The most common punishment was to be sent to remote villages for 're-education'.

Temples and churches were wrecked and burned, and archaeological sites destroyed. Schools, universities and even factories were closed down for several years. Traditions and customs were ridiculed. Pride in one's personal appearance was criticised as vanity. Boiler suits were worn by everyone as a sign of equality and simplicity.

In 1967 and 1968 Mao had most of the

Peasants recruited into the Red Guards, brought to Canton for a demonstration

Revisionist leaders dismissed. Liu was disgraced and sent to his village where he died. Deng was exiled to a remote commune for his re-education. Mao, Lin Biao and the Left were in full control of the country.

In 1968 the Red Guards were disbanded. Some historians think that they had caused law and order to break down so badly that it had to be restored by the PLA who used bombs and tanks against the Red Guards. Revolutionary Committees replaced the Red Guards in charge of communes, towns, and factories. They contained Maoist party members, soldiers and local people.

Mao remained in control until his death. In his later years he came more and more under the influence of his wife Jiang Qing and three of her colleagues, known as the Gang of Four.

In 1971 Lin Biao disappeared. It was officially claimed that he had tried to seize power from Mao and that his plane had crashed escaping to Russia. Others say that Mao feared Lin Biao so much that he accused him of plotting and then had him shot down.

By 1973 most of the Revisionist leaders had been returned to power. Liu had died, leaving Deng as the main upholder of Revisionism. The Gang of Four opposed this, causing a power struggle to develop during the last years of Mao's life.

Throughout this period propaganda became dominated by the cult of Mao himself. He was built up into a god-like hero. All China's successes were attributed to him. His 'Little Red Book' sold 740 million copies.

Economic developments

Industry

At first the Cultural Revolution hit industry badly, and production fell as managers and engineers were sent away to the countryside. However, after a year or two, industry recovered and grew at an annual rate of eight per cent. Large enterprises were shared out throughout China, even in remote country areas. Railways were built everywhere and vast hydro electric power schemes were set up to bring electricity to remote provinces. There was also a big increase in the smaller factories owned by the people's communes. Many peasants became workers and vice versa. Industrial workers were not paid more than peasants and were not paid bonus incentives.

Agriculture

As in industry, there was a fall in the first part of the Cultural Revolution. Private plots and incentives were banned once again. More attention was paid to agriculture, and more money was invested in modern equipment. Even so, agricultural production increased only moderately in these years.

Social developments

Education was badly hit by the Cultural Revolution. Most schools and universities closed down for at least a year, hitting the education of many young people, particularly the Red Guards themselves. When schools re-opened, much of the day was spent in political instruction and in manual labour for all. The peasants and workers were allowed to go to university as long as they had done two years manual work.

At last the growth in population was recognised as a major problem as it approached one thousand million people. Birth control was introduced and huge propaganda campaigns gradually began to slow down the population increase.

Harvesting the grain under the gaze of Mao ▶

Q

1 Which of the three reasons given for the Cultural Revolution, do you favour? Why does it appeal to you?
2 What sorts of people would be offended by the cover design? Why?

3 How could the Red Guards in the photograph be easily used by those who favoured the Cultural Revolution?
4 What do you think is the purpose of Mao's picture in the piles of grain in the photograph?

Extension

Understanding the Cultural Revolution

The following evidence from the Cultural Revolution should help you to understand it more clearly.

A Red Guard recalled . . .

In our village we knocked down statues of gods. The main aim was to educate people and to burn religious objects. Some people refused. Then the Guards would put a board on their shoulders and parade them through the streets. We were made to attack our old leaders. We all had loyalty to Chairman Mao. We felt he was the saviour.

John Gittings, a journalist who is an expert on Chinese affairs, commented on the Cultural Revolution . . .

There are two impressions of China, one positive and one negative. On the positive side is an impression of a confidence in the future based not just on individual ability but on one's part in a group. The expression 'we are all in one family' really means something to the student in the countryside or the manager at the workbench. For the negative impression, we must return to what Mao said in 1966, something about the masses paying attention to political matters. Ten years later the orders are still being given from Peking. There is a problem here and it still has to be solved.

Jin Chunming, a Communist Party Official Researcher, who studied the Cultural Revolution for many years, wrote in 1986 . . .

At the time we were constantly told that Revisionists had infiltrated the party, the government and the army. It was in this atmosphere of deep suspicion that Mao Zedong made mistaken decisions and was determined to

launch the Cultural Revolution. Such things are unthinkable today, but at that time many believed them. This is why at the beginning of the Cultural Revolution millions upon millions plunged themselves into it.

Statement of the Communist Party Central Committee in 1981 . . .

Mao Zedong was the principal person to be held responsible for the Cultural Revolution.

B. Wootton, a British psychologist, wrote . . .

On the whole people do what is expected of them by the society they live in. If they are taught from the age of three to 'serve the people', then who knows? It may become a habit.

W. Churchill, a British MP, said . . .

Mao is trying to change human nature but I'm afraid that even he cannot do that.

Q

1 Write down how each of the sources of evidence helps (or not) to improve your understanding of the Cultural Revolution. Bear in mind who said it, as well as what is said.

2 How much of a failure was the Cultural Revolution in bringing about political, social and economic change?

1970s to 1985—Revisionism returns

Even before Mao died, a power struggle was going on in the Communist Party. The Gang of Four wanted to continue with the Cultural Revolution, but the Revisionists led by Deng Xiaoping, who returned to office in 1973, were equally determined to stop it. After Mao's death there was a period of confusion in the leadership. Hua Guofeng, the new Chairman, arrested and imprisoned the Gang of Four in 1979, but was himself removed in 1980.

Throughout this period the main decision maker was undoubtedly Deng.

Political developments

Deng and the Revisionists called off the Cultural Revolution and then denounced Mao in the 1980s. Deng abolished all the Revolutionary Committees and took power away from the commenced in local government, giving it back to. party officials. Deng built up the positions of the specialist class of managers and professional people, and re-introduced higher wages and incentives.

Economic developments

Industry

Deng was determined to make China into a fully industrialised country. Large industrial enterprises were moved back to the coastal areas and to the main cities instead of being situated in the poorer interior. All industries were increasingly put under the control of managers and professionals, rather than *cadres* and workers. Making a profit was the main purpose of the new industrial enterprises.

Small private businesses were allowed to set up with loans, not from the State, but from the Bank of China. Some large factories sold shares to their employees. Factories were encouraged to compete with one another to make a profit. Deng was very keen to import high technology from the West, and set up Special Zones, such as the Shanghai Economic Zone, where American, Japanese and EEC money was invested in enterprises run partly by foreigners and partly by Chinese. By the late 1980s industry earned 80% of China's income and occupied 25% of its workforce.

Agriculture

The communes continued to exist, but were now ruled by professional managers and had to make a profit. Private plots were allowed, and incentives were paid for hard work. Deng introduced the Responsibility System which allowed individual families to own quite large tracts of land and to keep the profits. This led to the growth in the countryside of a class of rich peasants, which often controlled rural industries like food processing and timber production. One of the slogans used by the government to encourage people like this was 'To get rich is glorious'.

The production of grain increased quickly up to 1985 and then began to fall behind as the rich peasants preferred to grow luxury crops for which they could get a better price. Because so much emphasis was placed on profit, expensive schemes like flood control, irrigation and soil protection received less and less attention, creating potential dangers.

Poster for the four modernisations—agriculture, industry, science and defence

Social developments

Population control became of crucial importance as the government saw the dangers of all its achievements being held back by a continuous population explosion. Government policy was to allow one child per family but it was not really successful outside the cities. However the population was not growing quite as fast as it had been previously.

In education, competitive examinations were introduced for entry into secondary schools and universities, and even special selective schools were set up for very bright children. There was a much greater chance of secondary education in towns, because in the countryside the communes could no longer afford to build new schools other than very basic primary schools.

In health, there was still great reliance on barefoot doctors, of which there were two million, mostly in rural areas. The number of hospitals increased but they were situated mainly in the cities.

What next?

Mao always said that there would have to be a number of cultural revolutions before true communism could be reached. There have already been two attempts at this—The Great Leap Forward and the Cultural Revolution. Will there be a third? China has not had a stable, straight line of development in this century. Will it continue to vary in the future between one extreme and another?

1 Identify the three features of this period which Mao would find the most objectionable. Why? Use the photograph on page 191 to help you.

An assessment of Mao Zedong

There is no doubt that Mao Zedong was one of the major leaders of the twentieth century. You can come to your own assessments of his achievement by building up a balance sheet, with one side in his favour and the other side critical of him. Allocate points from the list below to one side or the other.

Mao as the ruler of China

Mao emerged as the main leader during the Communist Party's hardest period, the Long March. He led it to victory during the Civil War. He was a very charismatic leader, able to appeal to the masses, especially to young people and to the peasants. He was always the ultimate leader, even though sometimes his policies were not always followed by other leaders, as in the First Five Year Plan and the Revisionist period.

In his treatment of rivals, Mao did not behave as Stalin did. His rivals were not killed, although they were badly treated during the Cultural Revolution. The use of terror under Mao was never as extensive as it was under Stalin. There was considerable loss of life in the early years, especially against landowners, and during the Cultural Revolution. However terror was never used against the peasants, as it had been in Russia during the collectivisation of farms. Mao managed to do this without terror. Mao's basic aims were very idealistic. He seemed to believe that true communism would be attained in China, and made two attempts to attain it—The Great Leap Forward and the Cultural Revolution. Was this too hopeful? Or was it worth attempting? Mao was determined to avoid communism in China ending up as it had in Russia; unidealistic and unequal.

Mao's two major attempts to achieve his aims failed. The Great Leap Forward and the Cultural Revolution did not work as he wished, and brought much suffering, even famine, to China.

The social improvements brought about under communist rule were immense. In the areas of health, education, general standards of living and the position of women, much had been achieved. In economic developments, agriculture was much more effective, and produced enough food even for a much larger population. Industry too had grown so that by the end of Mao's life China was becoming a first-rate industrial power.

In his use of propaganda, Mao was very effective and inspiring. Towards the end of his life the cult of his own personality emerged, especially during and after the Cultural Revolution.

The commune was Mao's main method of actually bringing change to China. Was it a good idea? Did it work as a means of mixing agriculture and industry and spreading the benefits of industry throughout China? Did it work as an attempt to bring co-operation and equality to China? The commune remained in some form or another through most of China's changes during the communist period.

Extension

Was Mao power-mad?

Read the three pieces of evidence . . .

Edgar Snow, an American journalist who knew Mao well and who first visited him at the end of the Long March in 1936, wrote . . .

I met Mao soon after my arrival. My impression was of an intellectual face of great shrewdness. There would never be any one saviour of China, yet undeniably one felt a certain force of destiny in Mao. One felt that whatever there was extraordinary in this man grew out of the uncanny degree to which he sympathised with and expressed the urgent demands of millions of Chinese and especially the peasants. Yet, while everyone knew and respected him, there was as yet no hero-worship built up around him. He appeared to be quite free from symptoms of power-madness but he had a deep sense of personal dignity and something about him suggested a power of ruthless decision when he thought it necessary.

A foreign journal published in Hong Kong in 1985, put forward the following views . . .

> Mao was never a revolutionary, but always intended to set up his 'dynasty' [family], to rule China as Emperor.

Professor Jin Chunming, a Communist Party Official Researcher, stated in 1986 . . .

> Although Mao was, in his later life, dictatorial in his behaviour and in his selection of his successor, there is no evidence that he wanted to establish his own dynasty.

Q

1 Use the three sources of evidence and your own knowledge to decide whether Mao was power-mad or not. Be critical of the evidence.

Discussion topics

1 Do you think that Maoism could really work in China? Is it worth trying again? Could it work elsewhere, such as in Britain?
2 What sort of phase—left or right wing—is China going through now?

Essays

1 How successful was Chiang Kaishek in dealing with China's problems? Why did he lose the Civil War?
2 Outline the main developments in China between 1949 and the death of Mao Zedong.
3 Describe the causes and features of the Cultural Revolution. What developments have occurred in China since then?

INTERNATIONAL ORGANISATIONS

The need for international organisations

How disputes are solved WITHIN a nation

Your country is made up of millions of people like yourself and your neighbours. Imagine that you and your neighbour have a dispute about a small strip of ground between your two gardens. You have several choices of action . . .

- You can take the case to court for a judge to decide who legally owns the land. The court's decision is final.
- You can fight with your neighbour to see who can take possession of the land. You could even find friends to help you and arm yourselves in order to fight better.
- You could come to an agreement between yourselves.

One of these three alternatives, fighting, is not acceptable in a civilised country. If you try to do it the police and the government will stop you. They will then try to sort out the problem between you.

How disputes are solved BETWEEN nations

The world is made up of nations like your own and other peoples'. Imagine that your nation and another nation has a dispute over a strip of territory. You have several courses of action . . .

- You can take the case to an international court, where a judge will make a decision about the legality of the dispute. However, you do not have to accept the court's decision if you do not wish to.
- You can go to war if you want to. You can seek out allies and arm yourself with weapons. No-one can stop you.
- You can come to an agreement with the nation with which you have the dispute.

All these ways of solving disputes are possible *between* nations. They all happen all the time and always have done. Which of these methods of solving disputes is unacceptable? Is there a need for international organisations to try to deal with this problem?

Before the Great War, an international organisation would have been impossible. All countries were so nationalistic that they all believed that they could do as they wished and that an international organisation was quite wrong and unnecessary. Two World Wars taught many people differently.

After the First World War, the League of Nations was set up. After the Second World War, it became the United Nations organisation.

---

1 What are the differences in the way problems are dealt with *within* a nation and *between* nations?

2 Do you agree that there is a need for an international organisation to deal with disputes between nations?

The League of Nations

The League of Nations was set up in 1919 as a result of the horrors of the First World War. People really thought that the League would be successful.

The aims of the League of Nations

1 Peace

The main aim of the League was to keep the peace and to prevent war. It had three main ways of doing this.

Peace through collective security

This meant that all nations would gain a sense of security by joining the League. Other nations too would be members of the League, and all would feel so safe that they would no longer need to make their own separate alliances. After the war alliances were regarded as very dangerous, because it was thought that they made countries feel stronger than they really were, and encouraged the outbreak of war.

Peace through disarmament

It was believed that nations only built up their arms to dangerous levels because they were afraid. Therefore, if all countries were to disarm under the control of the League of Nations, there would be a greater sense of security. Countries would simply not have the arms to make war.

Peace through arbitration

Any major disputes between nations should be put before the League, which would then arbitrate (decide) between them. Special peace-keeping 'machinery' was set up to achieve this. If aggression were to be involved, the aggressor would face the rest of the League of Nations, and would be disciplined by the League.

2 Social and economic progress

Another aim of the League of Nations was to bring about social and economic progress throughout the world. This was to be done by setting up special organisations or agencies to deal with specific problems.

The organisation of the League of Nations

How the League worked

There were three main bodies within the League of Nations' Headquarters in Geneva . . .

The Council	The Assembly	The Permanent Court of International Justice
The Council consisted of four permanent members—Britain, France, Italy and Japan— and four others, elected by the Assembly. Only the Council could deal with major disputes between nations. Its decisions had to be unanimous, so any single country could veto (forbid) any action by the League.	The Assembly consisted of all the members of the League. In the Assembly each nation was equal, having one vote each. The Assembly dealt with general issues, but had no real power to solve any disputes between its members.	This court dealt only with *legal* disputes between nations. Nations were not bound to obey its decisions.

Under the control of the Assembly were the following . . .

The Commissions and Agencies
The most important ones were the Disarmament Commission, which was expected to bring about disarmament through negotiations, and the Mandates Commission, which was in charge of the colonies taken from Germany and Turkey. There were several others dealing with particular social and economic problems.

The Secretariat
This was the civil service of the League of Nations, under the Secretary-General Sir Eric Drummond. The Secretariat carried out the orders of the Assembly and the Council, but had no real power of its own.

Membership

There were only 42 member-states at the beginning. At first Germany and the other defeated nations were not admitted. Nor was Russia because it was communist. However, they all joined later on. America, which most strongly supported the setting up of the League of Nations and was the most powerful country in the world, never joined the League. At that time most parts of the world were part of the huge European empires like the British and French Empires, therefore they were not independent nations. At most the League had only 56 members.

Methods of solving disputes

If the Council decided to act against an aggressor, the following disciplinary actions were put into operation:
1 **Economic sanctions,** when all members would refuse to buy or sell goods to an aggressor.
2 **Military sanctions,** when League of Nations armed forces would act against an aggressor.
3 **Expulsion** from the League of Nations.

The United Nations Organisation

The UN was set up in 1945. The League of Nations was now discredited by its failure to stop aggression, but a world organisation was still needed. Even so, people did not have very high hopes for it.

The aims of the United Nations

1 Peace

The main aim of the United Nations was to keep the peace and to prevent war. This time very little attention was paid to collective security or to disarmament. However there was some peace-keeping machinery under which the United Nations could deal with problems of aggression and disputes between nations.

2 Social and economic progress

Another aim was to increase and to extend the social and economic work already carried out by the League of Nations. In this area, much greater emphasis was laid on the extension of human rights, such as freedom of speech, freedom of religion and equal rights.

The organisation of the United Nations

How the United Nations works

There are three main bodies at the United Nations headquarters in New York . . .

The Security Council

The Security Council consists of five permanent members—America, Russia, Britain, France and China—and ten members elected by the General Assembly to represent less important nations. It has the authority to deal with major disputes between nations but any one of the permanent members can veto any action by the United Nations.

The General Assembly

The General Assembly consists of all member states, each of which has one vote each. Decisions do not have to be unanimous. If it has a two thirds majority, it can overrule the Security Council, if it thinks the Security Council is not dealing with a dispute properly, or if one of the permanent members is vetoing action. The General Assembly does not normally overrule the Security Council, but it has done on two important occasions—the Korean War and the Suez Crisis.

The International Court of Justice

This court, as under the League of Nations, deals only with *legal* disputes between nations and its judgements are only binding if all the nations agree.

Under the control of the General Assembly are the following . . .

The Economic and Social Council

This Council is in control of all the old League of Nations Commissions and Agencies which were continued under the United Nations. Many new ones were also set up with special interests and with much more power.

The Secretariat

The Secretary-General has much more power than the League of Nations Secretary-General. He can take important decisions when the Security Council and the General Assembly are not in session, and can act on his own initiative to help the cause of peace.

Membership

At first the defeated nations of the Second World War were not allowed to join, nor was Communist China. Gradually, however, all the nations of the world have joined the United Nations, and new nations are welcome. Most of the member-states are small countries formerly ruled by Britain and France as part of their empires. In 1945 there were 51 members. By the 1980s there were over 150 members.

Methods of solving disputes

If the Security Council decides to take action against an aggressor *or* if the General Assembly decides by a two thirds majority to overrule the Security Council and act against an aggressor, the following actions can be taken:

1 **Economic sanctions**—all members would refuse to buy or sell goods to an aggressor.
2 **Military sanctions** — United Nations armed forces would act against an aggressor.

Another way of solving disputes is if a member state *invites* the United Nations to help it with its problem. However the United Nations may not send troops without such an invitation.

Q

---

1 How the two organisations worked.
a What was the difference, if any, between the two organisations in
—The Council and Security Council?
—The Assembly and General Assembly?
—The Courts?
—Social and economic work?

—The Secretary-General?
—Methods of solving disputes?
b Which organisation had the most power at its disposal?
2 Which organisation had the advantage over the other in membership? Why?

The League of Nations in practice: keeping the peace

Many problems were dealt with by the League of Nations. Read through the following list of disputes and issues. Some were solved successfully, others not.

Problem

Action taken

1921 Sweden and Finland

Both claimed the Aaland Islands and there was a danger of war.

The Council decided that Finland had the rightful claim. Sweden objected, but accepted the decision.

1921 Poland and Lithuania

Both claimed the town of Vilna, which Poland actually occupied and refused to leave, even though the League ordered it to do so.

The Council failed to stop occasional fighting between Poland and Lithuania for several years. However, in 1927 Poland was allowed to retain Vilna, although Lithuania was very dissatisfied.

1922 Austria

Austria seemed about to collapse as a result of terrible economic and political problems. She appealed to the League of Nations to save her.

The Council arranged a huge loan to Austria. This helped to solve Austria's economic problems and to save the country.

Problem

1922 Germany and Poland

Both nations claimed Silesia, which had been handed over to Poland by the Treaty of Versailles. The referendum by the people of Silesia showed that they wanted to stay in Germany.

1923 All nations

The Treaty of Mutual Assistance was arranged, which would strengthen the collective security of the League. All countries would sign it and promise to come to the aid of any country which was attacked. They promised to do this with the economic and military sanctions decided by the Council.

1923 Italy and Greece

After the unsolved murder of three Italian officers in Greece, war seemed likely. The new Italian government of Mussolini was in an aggressive mood. The Italian navy bombarded the Greek island of Corfu, demanding large compensation.

1925 All nations

The Geneva Protocol. A suggestion was put forward by the British Labour Government for all countries never to use force until the League's sanctions had been tried. This would certainly have strengthened the League of Nations.

1925 Greece and Bulgaria

Greece invaded Bulgaria after several incidents of fighting on the border.

1931 Japan and China

Japan, a major League power and a permanent member of the Council, invaded and seized Manchuria, a huge province of China. China appealed for help to the League of Nations to turn Japan out of Manchuria.

Action taken

The Council split Upper Silesia into two, with most of it going to Germany. Neither nation was really satisfied, but the arrangement worked for several years.

Several nations, led by Britain, opposed the Treaty because they did not wish to go to war in another nation's interests. The Treaty was dropped.

The Council, after much hesitation, forced Greece to pay compensation. Italy was one of the four leading League of Nations powers and was a permanent member of the Council, which Greece was not.

A General Election in Britain brought a conservative government to power in place of the labour government. This new government vetoed the Geneva Protocol in the Council.

The Council forced Greece to withdraw and to pay compensation.

The Council ordered Japan to withdraw, but Japan refused. The Council then sent a special Commission, under Lord Lytton, to Manchuria to investigate the situation. This Commission tried to get round the problem by proposing that the League itself should rule Manchuria. Japan rejected this. The Council did not consider any sanctions against Japan because Britain and France did not want to risk war. Nothing at all was done.

In this German cartoon, the League of Nations fires a note of warning which Japan ignores in seizing Manchuria

Problem

Action taken

1932–1933 All nations

The World Disarmament Conference met, attended by sixty countries, but France and Germany quarrelled over the level of armaments. After Hitler came to power in 1933, he withdrew from the Conference and, shortly afterwards from the League itself.

The League could do nothing to prevent the Conference from failing or to stop Germany from leaving the League.

1935 Italy and Abyssinia

Italy invaded Abyssinia with immense force. The Italian army occupied Abyssinia and made it an Italian colony. The Emperor of Abyssinia, Haille Selassie, appeared in Geneva personally to appeal to the League for action against Italy.

The Council and Assembly condemned Italy and imposed sanctions on her. Britain and France however did not wish to offend Italy and would not impose coal, oil and steel sanctions. They even allowed Italy to use the Suez Canal to transport its troops to Abyssinia. Even so, Italy left the League.

The late 1930s

Several aggressive incidents took place throughout the world. The worst were the Japanese invasion of China and the German seizure of Austria, Czechoslovakia and Poland.

No action was taken. No-one listened to the League any longer.

Q

1 List:
a The successes of the League.
b The failures of the League, in order of importance.
2 Which sanctions did the League never use, and which did it only use half-heartedly?

3a Which countries were mainly responsible for the League's failure?
b Why could the League do nothing about them?
4 What does the cartoon suggest about the opinions of the paper in which it was published? Is it, in your opinion, a fair assessment?

The United Nations in practice: keeping the peace

Since 1945 the United Nations has dealt with several disputes and problems. Some were successes, some were failures . . .

Problem

1948 onwards: The Middle East

The first Arab–Israeli war, 1948. The UN was officially in charge of Palestine, although Britain held the mandate to rule the country. In 1948 Britain pulled out of Palestine because it was unable to control the civil war between Arabs and Jews. Britain handed its responsibility back to the United Nations. When a full scale war broke out between the Jews, who had set up the state of Israel, and the Arab nations, the Jews were victorious.

The second Arab–Israeli war, also known as the Suez Crisis, 1956. When Egypt seized the Suez Canal from its owners Britain and France, they joined with Israel to invade Egypt.

The third and fourth Arab–Israeli wars. In 1967 and 1974 two more wars broke out between Israel and the Arab nations. Both were won by Israel, which seized more land from the Arabs against the instructions of the UN.

The Lebanon civil war, 1970s and 1980s. Lebanon, invaded by both Israel and Syria, appealed for UN support.

The Iran–Iraq war. Throughout the 1980s this war took a toll of over one million lives and almost brought both countries to ruin.

UN action

At first the UN divided Palestine into separate Arab and Jewish territories. This was ignored by both sides, who each claimed the whole of Palestine for themselves.

In the Security Council Britain and France, both permanent members, vetoed any action to solve the problem. However, the General Assembly used its new powers to overrule the Security Council. They called on Britain and France to leave Egypt. As America and Russia were against them as well as the whole of the United Nations, Britain and France did depart. UN troops were called in to patrol between Egypt and Israel.

The UN, on several occasions, called on Israel to restore Arab land. Israel always refused, and the Arab nations refused to recognise Israel.

The Security Council sent troops to Lebanon but they were not allowed to take action between the various warring groups.

The UN tried, and failed to bring the two sides together. Only when Iran was exhausted, in 1988, did it use the Secretary-General to negotiate an armistice.

Problem

UN action

1950–1953: Korea, China and America

The Korean War. In 1950 the communist North Koreans invaded South Korea. Through the UN, America became deeply involved. China too entered the war when America threatened its territory. The war went on for three years with over one million dead. (See Chapter 7.)

Russia was absent from the Security Council when the Korean dispute arose. Therefore, backed up by the General Assembly, the Security Council imposed military sanctions upon Korea. America would have sent an army to South Korea anyway, but let its troops become the main part of the UN army. The UN army won back South Korea. Fifteen other nations sent smaller contingents to join the UN army against North Korea and China. The Secretary-General, Trygve Lie, pursued the war forcefully. Although the country remained divided, as it had been in the beginning, the Korean War showed that the United Nations could act effectively and strongly.

A Soviet cartoon showing the UN Secretary-General bringing germ warfare to Korea

1956 and 1968: Russia, Hungary and Czechoslovakia

When the Hungarian and Czech people rose up against their own communist governments, the Russian army was sent in to crush the rebellions.

Security Council action was always vetoed by Russia.

1960–1961: Congo

When Belgium granted independence to the Congo and left the country in poverty and disorder, a civil war soon broke out. The country seemed about to enter a state of permanent civil war and several parts threatened to break away. The Congolese Government appealed to the UN for help.

The Security Council sent in a large army of over twenty thousand troops, which soon restored order. The UN Secretary-General, Dag Hammarskjold, then used this army against Katanga province, which wished to break away from the Congo. This was exceeding his authority, because UN troops should not have been used so directly to help one side. However, the Congo was kept together as a single nation and much worse violence was prevented.

Problem

UN action

The Secretary-General and the UN also sent the social and economic agencies into the Congo and poured in vast amounts of money and help. This effort was of great service to the Congo before the UN left in 1964.

1964: Cyprus, Turkey and Greece

When Britain granted independence to Cyprus, war soon broke out between the Greek Cypriots, who made up 80% of the population, and the Turkish Cypriots, who comprised 20%. The bloodshed continued on and off for several years until 1974, when Turkey invaded the island to help its people there, and seized the northern part of the island, expelling all Greeks.

The Secretary-General sent troops to Cyprus in 1964 to keep the peace between the two sides, but could not prevent Turkey from invading in 1974. UN troops patrol the border across the island but no proper solution has been found.

1970: All nations

In order to strengthen the UN, its Secretary-General, U Thant, proposed to set up a permanent UN army to enforce all the decisions of the Security Council and the General Assembly.

No action was taken. Most countries, particularly the major powers, do not wish to give up total control of their own actions.

1971: Russia and Afghanistan

Russia invaded Afghanistan.

The General Assembly called on Russia to leave Afghanistan, but it ignored the call until 1988.

1982: Britain and Argentina

The Falklands War. Argentina seized the Falklands by force and a British Task Force was sent to regain the islands.

The Security Council called on Argentina to give up the islands, but she refused. The Security Council wished to recall the British Task Force, but Britain vetoed this action. No solution was found to the problem of the Falklands.

1945 to the present: All nations

The arms race. Not only did the major powers possess and increase their supplies of nuclear weapons, but frequent testing of atomic weapons continued. The arms race was one of the gravest threats to mankind.

The UN continually tried to encourage disarmament by arranging talks at its Disarmament Commission in Geneva. It had very little success. The UN arranged treaties to ban the testing of atomic weapons, but France and China refused to sign. The Strategic Arms Limitation Talks (SALT) held in the 1970s, and the agreement to limit intermediate missiles by Russia and America in 1988 did not really involve the UN.

Q

1 List
a The successes of the UN.
b The failures of the UN.
2 What does the cartoon tell you about Russian attitudes to the UN? Is it a fair assessment, in your opinion?

3a What *sort* of countries has the UN been successful with? Name them.
b What *sort* of countries has the UN not been successful with? Name them.
4 Which sanctions has the UN used successfully, compared with the League?
5 Is the UN on the whole, a success or a failure at peace-keeping? Explain your views.

Economic and social work of the international organisations

The League of Nations

One of the aims of the League of Nations was to bring about social and economic progress throughout the world. The League set up several new organisations and increased the work of others. One of the most successful of these was the International Labour Organisation under its French director Albert Thomas. It helped to improve working conditions, wages, unemployment and sickness benefits in many nations. The Refugee Organisation helped to deal with those who fled from their homes, such as Greeks who fled from Turkey and refugees from Nazi Germany. The Health Organisation spent a great deal of money and effort on helping to get rid of infectious diseases, especially typhus. Other organisations helped to deal with drugs, slavery and the traffic in women and children. So successful was the League in these areas that in 1939, just as the League was closing down in failure for other reasons, a report suggested the setting up of an Economic and Social Council to increase its social and economic work.

The United Nations

Like the League, the UN aimed to bring about social and economic progress. Right at the beginning of the United Nations the Economic and Social Council was set up. This part of the United Nations' work is much more extensive than that of the League. The world since 1945 has been much more conscious of economic and social problems than it was before. This is particularly true in the poorer countries of the world, who formerly belonged to the European empires.

There are many more organisations and agencies in this part of the United Nations' work, and each one spends much more than the League of Nations ever did. Unfortunately the problems too are far greater, especially those caused by population increase, refugees and drought.

The World Health Organisation, illustrated in the poster on this page, has as its motto 'health

A WHO publicity poster

for all by the year 2000'. It finances huge education programmes on hygiene, family planning and basic health care. It trains 'bare-foot doctors', health workers who can deal with common diseases, vaccination and minor injuries in the world's poorer nations. It has tried, not very successfully, to stamp out the world's worst killer diseases, such as malaria, bilharzi and dysentery. However, one remarkable success has been the complete elimination of smallpox, by vaccination. In the 1980s the WHO spent fifteen billion pounds on providing drinking water and drainage to areas without such facilities. This will save more people than all the vaccinations and medicines put together because it prevents many diseases.

The Food and Agriculture Organisation not only arranged food aid as a temporary solution for famine, but promoted the development of all sorts of agricultural improvements and the use of high-yield grains. UNICEF has the responsibility for helping the world's children through all sorts of food and health programmes, while UNESCO concentrates mainly on education. The International Refugee Organisation cares for the world's refugees, who are unfortunately increasing rather than decreasing in numbers. The ILO continues to improve working conditions, especially in poorer nations.

In economic matters the International Monetary Fund helps to solve immediate financial crises and helps countries out of short term difficulties. On the other hand, the World Bank provides very large long-term loans for large projects in the poorer nations. The United Nations Conference on Trade and Development tries, not very successfully, to get better prices for goods that the poorer nations sell to the richer ones.

Q

1 How successful were the League and the UN in their social and economic work?
2 Why has this aspect of the UN's work been so much more extensive than it was of the League's?
3 How effective is the WHO poster in getting across its purpose?

Case study

Comparing the League and the United Nations

The League of Nations was clearly a failure. After 1935, only sixteen years after it had been set up, it was ignored. The UN has not suffered the same fate, although it is clearly not very successful in some parts of its work. Look back over this chapter and compare the two organisations under the following headings to see why the one was more successful than the other. Your answer to each question will be either 'the League of Nations' or 'the United Nations' or 'the same'.

Aims

Which organisation set itself the more ambitious and difficult aims?

Organisation

Which international organisation had the greater and stronger ability to take action under the following headings?
1 The Assembly.
2 The Council.
3 The Secretary-General.

Membership

Which international organisation had more major world powers as members?
Which had the larger membership?

Peace keeping

Which international organisation had to cope with the greater problems caused by major nations deliberately flouting and opposing it? Which international organisation was the most successful in dealing with disputes and incidents of aggression?

Social and economic work

Which international organisation had more success in social and economic progress?

Differing views of the international organisations

These may help you to your own conclusions about the organisations.

Philip Noel-Baker was a strongly idealistic believer in the League of Nations. He was a leading member of the League Secretariat in the inter-war period. In 1945 he wrote . . .

> We know now that we who stood for the collective security system were always right and that our opponents, who ridiculed us, were wrong. We know that we could easily have stopped Mussolini [invading Abyssinia] if we had taken the sanctions that were obviously required.

A typical reaction from Israelis when asked about the UN . . .

UN? United Who? United Nobodies!

A historian, having studied the United Nations, wrote in 1974 . . .

It is at the service of world peace, and development, but it will succeed only if its members are prepared to use it. The UN will give out to its members as much as they put in to it.

Strengthening the United Nations

You have realised by now that the United Nations has no power of its own. It may only take action if the nations of the world wish it to do so. They often do not wish this, usually because it is not in their own interests. Several ways have been suggested to strengthen the UN, but all would involve each nation giving up a little of its power. The UN might then act against the interests of the nation concerned.

1 Should the UN be allowed to enter a country or to deal with a dispute without being invited? For example, a troubled area of the world such as the Middle East? Or perhaps to deal with a problem in *your* country?
2 Should the veto of the permanent members of the Security Council be abolished? This might mean that the UN might take action against the

Indian troops were part of the UN forces patrolling the Middle East in 1957. Since the Korean War the UN has not used troops of the major powers for peace-keeping

interests of the world's greatest powers, which could be dangerous.
3 Should a permanent UN army be set up to enforce the will of the UN whenever it decides to take action? Up to now different nations send contingents when they are invited to do so by the UN, on those occasions when it does send peace-keeping forces, as shown in the photograph.

Q

1 Using your answers in the case study, write a comparison of the two organisations.
2 *Comparing the League and the UN.* Differing views of the International Organisations.
a Briefly explain the three views expressed about the International Organisations. Why did these people have such views, in your opinion?
b Which of the three views is the nearest to your own? Why?
3 *Strengthening the UN.* Do you agree with any of the above suggestions? Why or why not?

Discussion topics

Make a list of world problems that could be helped by UN action. Consider why such action is not being taken. Should it be?

Essays

1 Describe the aims and organisation of the League of Nations *or* the UN. How successful was it in keeping the peace?
2 Describe the differences between the League of Nations and the UN under the following headings:
Organisation   Keeping the Peace

THE EUROPEAN COMMUNITY

Why a European community?

Europe is the world's smallest continent but one, yet it has always been split into many nations and peoples, usually fighting one another.

In theory there were many reasons why the Europeans should unite together to become a single European Community.

Two views of the European Community

There tend to be two different views of the European Community. One is known as the federalist view and the other is the realist view. These views do not of course oppose one another, but they do look at the European Community from different angles.

The federalists

The federalists believe very strongly in a federal or united Europe. Their arguments run as follows:

1 Europeans belong to a single European culture. This means that there are many similarities in language, history, religion, ideas, tastes and behaviour. In reality their similarities are much greater than their differences. Therefore they should belong to the same community, rather than to separate, warring nations.
2 Twice in this century Europe has torn itself apart in two World Wars, weakening its power and causing dreadful suffering. To prevent this the European nations, even former enemies, should band together to prevent such another terrible experience.

Europe—EC members and Soviet bloc

3 Since the Second World War Europe has been much less important in the world than before. By 1945 the super-powers had emerged. One super-power, America, was outside Europe altogether. The other, Russia, was almost a continent in itself. The European powers lost their imperial possessions in other continents, greatly diminishing their importance. Unification therefore, would give Europe much more importance than separate European nations could ever possess. Europe could be a power for good in the world.
4 Democracy started in Europe. The Second World War had been viewed as a fight for democracy against dictatorship. The democracies of Europe, therefore, must band together in a

A prize-winning design for a poster showing European co-operation, after the war

community of democracies to help one another. This would be a protection for Europe against communism and fascism.

Many Europeans since the Second World War have held these arguments very strongly. They feel genuinely European. They do not object to merging their separate identities into a European Community.

The realists

Realists feel that theoretical reasons for making a European Community are not enough. If a country joins a community of nations, there have to be strong, self-interested, realistic reasons for

doing so. The line of arguments of the realists is based on the idea that each nation must benefit as the result of joining together with others, as in the following ways:

1 **Economic reasons.** A nation's economy would improve and increase more quickly inside the community than outside it. Industry would expand if there was a common, planned industrial policy, especially in big industries. Agriculture would expand if there was a common agricultural policy, modernising and improving farms. Trade would be made easier if there was a common market for a country's goods. Each nation would be able to sell its goods to a population of over two hundred million, instead of merely to its own people.
2 **Status and respect.** A country would be more highly thought of as a member of a successful community than as an individual nation, especially if it were a leading member. Even if it were a small member of a community, a country's influence could be less easily ignored.
3 **Security.** A country would feel more secure as a member of a community than finding its own security in arms and alliances. After the Second World War all Western European nations regarded their main enemy as the Soviet Union, which, they thought, was getting ready to move into Western Europe. After all it had just moved into Eastern Europe. The European nations were also still very wary of one another too. France, for instance, was afraid of Germany growing again, even though Germany had just been defeated. Germany too would serve its own interests by rising within a community, thus gaining in security, instead of being feared and despised on its own.

Some of the federalists are very idealistic indeed, and believe in the European Community even if it does not benefit their nation. On the other hand some realists have no interest at all in the theory of the Community and only support it because it benefits them. In between are those who have both sets of reasons. When self-interest can join up with idealism, it is a very powerful combination.

Extension

Now read below some quotations from the leaders of Europe whom you will come across in this chapter. You should be able to tell from what they said whether they were federalists or realists or both . . .

Winston Churchill:

> If Europe were once united in the sharing of its common heritage, there would be no limit to the happiness, prosperity and the glory that its three hundred or four hundred million people would enjoy. Yet it is in Europe that has sprung up that series of nationalistic quarrels which we have seen wreck the peace and mar the prosperity of all mankind. We must build a United States of Europe.

Ernest Bevin, the British Labour Foreign Secretary:

> Creating a European State might appeal to idealists. But in the world of politics one is bound to proceed step by step. It is necessary to be realistic and practical.

General de Gaulle of France:

> Since 1940, my every word and act has been dedicated to establishing a political, economic and defence bloc, and to establish this organisation as one of the three world powers, and, if it becomes necessary, as the balance between the two super-powers.

Konrad Adenauer of Germany:

> It is in the real interests not only of Germany but also of Britain and France to unite Europe under their leadership. We would be much closer to the ultimate goal of a Union of the States of Western Europe.

Jean Monnet of France:

> The heart of the European enterprise is equality between all countries, the need to abandon purely national ways, the search for the common interest and the setting up of a common political organisation.

Margaret Thatcher of Britain:

> We must make Europe work for us.

> To talk of a United States of Europe is a fairy tale.

Edward Heath of Britain:

> We shall always work with our friends in Europe for the true strength and unity of the continent.

Harold Wilson of Britain:

> There is a long term potential for Europe, and therefore for Britain, in the creation of a single market of three hundred million people, with the scope that this will provide for British industry.

Harold Macmillan of Britain, in 1961:

> If joining the Common Market is to upset the long standing and historic ties with the Commonwealth, the loss would be greater than the gain.

Harold Macmillan in 1967:

> The European Community is not just about fixing the price for prunes and a method of marketing bananas. It is about whether Europe, having made a great contribution for two thousand years, is finished or whether it can be revived with a great rebirth.

1 Identify the statesmen mentioned above, from their quotations, as federalists or realists or both. Pay particular attention to Harold Macmillan. Can you be certain of your identification? Why or why not? Explain your answer.

2 What arguments would opponents of the community have against the federalists' beliefs?

3 What arguments would opponents have against the realists' beliefs?

4 Looking at the map, which countries would feel most threatened by Russia? Which countries would feel least threatened? Why?

5 To accompany the poster on page 208, write a brief propaganda pamphlet from a French *or* German point of view to show why you should join the Community.

The Community in action

How the Community works

The European Community works on the idea that each member nation gives up some of its powers to the Community which then makes the policies for the whole of Europe. It is important to understand what organisations there are in the Community and how they work in practice. The organisations in the diagram below have existed ever since the Community was first thought of. They are essential to the smooth working of any community of nations which has power over its members.

The Council of Ministers

This Council makes *all* important decisions. Its membership varies. Sometimes it contains all the prime ministers of the Community, at other times the industry ministers or the agriculture ministers and so on. In this Council each country's representative can veto (forbid) a policy by only one vote if it feels strongly enough. This right to veto policies protects the interests of each nation.

The European Court

This is under no-one's control. It makes judgments about legal matters and rights, which all member nations have to accept.

The Parliament

This consists of MEPs (Members of the European Parliament), elected by voters in their own countries. The Parliament has very little power. The Council of Ministers has to consult it but does not have to obey it. Many federalists feel that it should have more power because it is democratically elected and therefore should make the major decisions.

The Commission

This is the civil service of the Community under the control of the European Commissioner. The Commission takes its orders from the Council of Ministers, but it does have its own views and often succeeds in putting them into operation.

Matters dealt with by the European Community

In theory all matters are capable of being controlled by the European Community. Since the 1940s, more and more of these affairs have been given up by the member states to the Community. Some, however, still remain firmly under the control of the member nations.

1 Economic matters

A **Industry.** Should all industry be under Community control, or only particular industries such as coal, steel or atomic power?
B **Agriculture.** Should all agricultural products be under Community control, or only particular products such as wheat, lamb or vegetables?
C **Trade.** Should there be any trade barriers— import and export duties—between member states? Should there be barriers around the Community against goods coming from outside states?
D **Labour.** Should there be a free movement of labour between member states?

2 Social matters and human rights

Should the Community decide on working conditions, housing, health, education, social security? Should these be the same throughout the Community?

3 Defence and foreign policy

Should the European Community have a single defence policy against its enemies? Should it have a common army instead of national armies? Should the Community have a common foreign policy towards outside matters, such as super-power rivalry or the Arab–Israeli problem?

4 Political matters

Should the European Community take over the actual government of member states? In fact, should there be a European government instead of national governments? If so the European Parliament would become much more important. The Council of Ministers would become much less important, as would national governments, such as the British government in London. Should we set up a United States of Europe?

Within all these matters there is much scope for disagreement and conflict. During the rest of this chapter you will see how some of these matters have gradually come under the control of the European Community, while others have remained outside its power.

Q

1 Which of the two organisations – Council of Ministers and European Parliament – would a) the federalists and b) the realists prefer to be supreme? Why?

2 List the issues above, beginning with the easiest for the Community to deal with and ending with the most difficult. Explain the last on your list.

The early development of the Community up to 1957

In 1957 'the Six' signed the Treaty of Rome, which set up the European Economic Community. These six were the original members, France, Germany, Italy, Belgium, the Netherlands and Luxembourg. Britain, the main European power outside the Six, refused to participate at that time.

Up to 1957 several important developments took place which showed the Six that closer unity could be successful.

The Marshall Plan and the OEEC 1948–1952

In 1947 the American Secretary of State, General Marshall, announced that vast amounts of money would be made available to European governments *if* they would co-operate in economic matters. Most governments in Western Europe agreed to participate, and the

Organisation for European Economic Co-operation (OEEC) was set up to organise the spending of the money. America did not impose any conditions on the money and let the OEEC members themselves decide how to spend it. During the four years of the plan over thirteen and a half billion dollars were given or lent to European nations. Britain had the largest share of over three billion, followed by France, Italy and West Germany. America wanted a European community to develop.

Why should America help Europe?

1 President Truman and General Marshall genuinely believed in helping Europe over the effects of war. In 1947 the European economies had not recovered from the war and were in serious trouble.

2 The Marshall Plan would help the American economy to recover, since Europe would buy American goods as it became more prosperous with Marshall Plan investment.

In this Soviet cartoon, the waiter serves War with a menu of economic growth, cooked by America

3 The Marshall Plan would help Europe to develop into an important power bloc against Russia and would prevent a Russian takeover of Europe.

Winston Churchill called the Marshall Plan the 'most unsordid act in history'.

The results of the Marshall Plan

Europe did recover extremely well with American money. America also benefitted economically because most of Europe's goods were bought from America. Russia was certainly upset by European co-operation. However a stronger European community did not develop because of British opposition.

The Council of Europe 1949

In most European countries there was a strong demand for a United States of Europe. Many politicians too, like Churchill, Adenauer and Schumann, the Foreign Minister of France, were interested. They met in 1948 at a Congress of Europe, where they agreed to set up the Council of Europe in Strasbourg, which democratic European nations could join. Its members had to be members of the separate national parliaments. It dealt with social problems and human rights, but had no real power at all because several nations, especially Britain, were against giving it any power over its members.

Unsere
BUNDESWEHR
stellt Freiwillige ein

A West German recruitment poster from the early 1950s

The European Coal and Steel Community 1951

Most French people were afraid of a growth of West German power after the Second World War, yet they realised that national hostility should not grow up again. Two French leaders in particular realised this. One was Robert Schumann, the Foreign Minister, and the other was Jean Monnet, a top civil servant. The new Chancellor of West Germany, Konrad Adenauer, also shared their view.

Following the success of working together under the Marshall Plan, France and Germany suggested merging their coal and steel industries under a common industrial plan. Both would gain economically from such co-operation. France would also gain in security as it would be better to keep Germany closely bound to France by economic ties rather than drifting apart. Germany would also gain in status, instead of being regarded as an outcast.

Other nations also decided to join—Italy, Belgium, the Netherlands and Luxembourg—but Britain refused, not wanting to give up control of its own coal and steel industries to a European body which would have power over Britain. In 1951 the first real European Community came into existence. It was the Coal and Steel Community and it contained all the organisations necessary to run such a community and could easily be expanded.

The Council of Ministers

The Council made the important decisions.

The Assembly

This was a kind of parliament.

The Court of Justice

This dealt with disputes of member nations.

The civil service of the Coal and Steel Community, known as the High Authority. Jean Monnet was in charge of this.

The European Coal and Steel Community was a tremendous success, keeping prices low yet causing the production of coal and steel to rise and to become more modernised. The community even provided new jobs in new industries in the run-down coal and steel areas.

The European Defence Community and German rearmament 1952

It was obvious that the West needed German armed forces against the Soviet threat. After all, Germany was next door to the Soviet Bloc. A proposal for a European Defence Community was put forward, to include its own parliament and other organisations, based on the Coal and Steel Community. The European Defence Community would also have a common army instead of national armies. The German government keenly supported this idea, realising that in this way Germany would be allowed to re-arm more easily. The French too agreed to join, hoping to have more control over a German army if it were part of a European army than if it were independent. A treaty was actually signed by the Six. However, when it became clear that Britain would not join the EDC, thinking that NATO was strong enough, the French withdrew. They felt too insecure without Britain. The EDC never came into being. Instead Germany was allowed to re-arm, but all its troops were placed under NATO control. This was a sad blow for the federalists, who wanted the growing community to have control over more and more issues.

The European Economic Community 1957

The Treaty of Rome

The success of the ECSC led the Six to begin discussing a common policy on other matters such as transport, atomic power and trade. The main workers behind the scenes were Jean Monnet of France and the Belgian Foreign Minister Paul-Henri Spaak. Meeting at the Messina Conference in 1955 the Six agreed to expand the ECSC to include other matters: They drew up the Treaty of Rome, which they signed in 1957. They invited Britain to participate but once again Britain refused. The new community was named the European Economic Community and its organisations grew out of the already existing bodies of the ECSC . . .

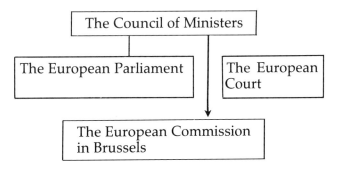

As well as coal and steel, the new community controlled the following matters:

1 Trade

There were to be no customs duties between the Six. All countries outside the Six would pay customs duty on sending their goods into the Common Market.

2 Labour

Workers were allowed to move freely from any part of the Community to any other part to find jobs.

3 Atomic power

Under a separate treaty called the Euratom Treaty, the Six agreed on a common policy of planning and investment in atomic power for peaceful purposes.

All these matters were economic matters. However, for the future, the European Economic Community agreed to bring the following matters under its control.

1 Agriculture

The Six agreed to work out a common agricultural policy.

2 Social policy

The Six agreed to work towards a common social policy in future.

The really difficult issue of closer political ties was left open. It would depend on how successfully the existing economic co-operation worked.

Q

1 Use the reasons given for the Marshall Plan to say whether you agree with Churchill's verdict on p. 212.
2 In what ways is the Russian cartoon biased? What does it reveal about Russia?
3a Why did France support the ECSC and not the EDC?
b Why did Germany support both?

4 Why did the Six agree to co-operate on some matters in 1957, and to delay others?
5 In what ways is the German recruitment poster different from what a similar Nazi poster would have been? What impression does it seek to create?
6 Would the federalists or the realists have been most pleased by the Treaty of Rome? Why?

Britain out ... then in ...

Up to 1957 there seemed to be several powerful arguments to prevent Britain from joining the European Community.

1 The absence of 'European feeling'

Many British people and leaders objected to giving up some of the British government's power to a body outside the British Parliament. They wanted total control over what happened in this country.

European idealism was not strong in Britain. Britain had just won the Second World War, and had not suffered as much as many other European nations had through invasion.

The British Empire and Commonwealth was still in existence in the 1950s and 1960s. This was something for Britain to be proud of, much more so, it appeared, than a European Community.

2 Economic reasons

Only 25% of Britain's trade was with Europe in the 1940s. Most of it was with the Commonwealth, which produced food and raw materials for Britain. New Zealand, for instance, produced butter and lamb, the West Indies produced sugar. The Empire could not be brought into the Common Market along with Britain. It was not European. Britain also wished to modernise its own industry independently.

3 Defence reasons

Britain preferred not to be involved in European affairs, especially in helping France against Germany. Britain relied heavily on what it called its 'special relationship' with America and felt that the NATO alliance was enough.

A British demonstration from the 1960s

What happened after 1957 to make Britain change its mind?

1 Economic affairs

In 1959 Britain took the lead in setting up the European Free Trade Association (EFTA), along with other European nations not included in the EEC. They were known as 'the Seven', Denmark, Norway, Sweden, Switzerland, Austria and Portugal, as well as Britain. Later Finland and Iceland joined also. These countries abolished tariffs between one another but that was as far as they went. There was to be no other common policy. The combined population of EFTA, without Britain, was only 38 million, while the EEC was about 200 million.

Between 1958 and 1964 the total income of EEC members increased by 68% and Britain's by 36%. European industry increased in size by 49%, and Britain's by 31%. The average income of each person increased in Europe by 51% and in Britain by 23%. During these years Britain's trade with the Commonwealth increased by 1.6% and with the Community by 98%.

2 European feeling

By the late 1950s and early 1960s Britain had lost most of its Empire. Although most of its former colonies remained in the Commonwealth, the idea of the Commonwealth was not as popular or appealing as the idea of the Empire had been. It was no longer so powerful an alternative to the European Community. However, there is little evidence that British public opinion as a whole was becoming more committed to Europe, although some politicians like Edward Heath were influencing people towards a more European outlook.

'We don't want fatty Commonwealth' says De Gaulle in this French cartoon

3 Defence matters

Britain still preferred her closer ties with America rather than with Europe. In 1962 the British Prime Minister, Harold Macmillan, accepted the American offer, granted only to Britain, to buy Polaris missiles. Britain deliberately chose this instead of closer military co-operation with France.

British entry

In 1961 the British Conservative government applied to join the EEC, and put Edward Heath in charge of negotiations. Five out of the Six, especially West Germany, were delighted to accept Britain's late entry. However, General de Gaulle used the French veto to prevent Britain from joining. He said that Britain was too closely tied to America and was not really European enough to join the European Community. Britain could do little about this.

De Gaulle prevents the second British attempt to join the EEC

In 1967 the Labour government of Harold Wilson once again applied to join. This time General de Gaulle said the British were not quite ready.

In 1971 Britain applied again. By this time de Gaulle was no longer the President of France, and the British application was accepted. In 1973 Edward Heath signed Britain's acceptance of the Treaty of Rome. At the same time, Ireland, Denmark and Norway joined the Community.

1 Write down in order of importance what changes occurred to make Britain change her mind about entering the Community?
2 Explain the objections of the British demonstrator in the photograph on page 215.

3 Were Britain's reasons for joining federalist or realist in your opinion?
4 What objections did Europeans have to the Commonwealth? Use the cartoon to help you.

Developments in the European Community since 1957

The original six members of 1957 expanded into 12 members almost 30 years later. Although Norway left the Community, Greece joined it in 1981 and Spain and Portugal became members in 1985. In 1967 its name changed to the simpler European Community. How has the EC dealt with the matters that the member nations handed over to it? Have they been successful? How will they develop in the future? You must try to assess these questions yourselves.

Economic developments

Trade. After 1957 the way was open to vastly increased trade. There were customs barriers against outside nations, but no customs barriers between members. There were still some restrictions on quality and safety regulations, to be removed in 1992. It was a genuine 'common market', the largest single market in the world. The wages and spending power of Europeans rose and rose. Trade between all members increased rapidly to 35% of total world trade. The member nations became more and more dependent on one another. Britain, for instance, increased its trade with Europe from seven billion pounds in 1973 to forty billion pounds in 1980. Trade was the most important part of the Community because it encouraged all other parts of the economy to develop with it.

Industry. Apart from the original coal and steel policy, there never was a common industrial policy. There has been very little joint planning in most industries. The growth of industry was left to the separate governments of the Community. Most industries certainly did take advantage of the huge demand available through the Common Market. Between 1957 and 1970 the industry of the Community actually doubled, a higher growth rate than any other nation.

Member nations co-operated on vast industrial projects, as Britain and France did on the Concorde project. Such investment would have been beyond their separate means. Europe became so competitive that it attracted other nations, such as Japan and America, to invest in its factories and even to build their own in Europe. Over 1,000 American and Japanese factories were set up. The European Investment Bank and the Community's Regional Fund were set up to invest money in new industries in the old declining areas of Europe. Between 1958 and 1981 these organisations invested £10 billion in depressed areas like Southern Italy.

Unfortunately, when Britain entered the Community in 1973, the world entered a serious economic recession. Industry grew much more slowly, if at all. The Community did not have a common policy to deal with this, and left it to individual countries to solve their industrial problems. Some did this better than others.

One industry that did have a planned programme was the nuclear power industry which was organised by Euratom after 1958. However, the British and French governments preferred to develop their own nuclear programmes rather than co-operate in the common Western European system which the other countries joined.

Agriculture. Although industry could take care of itself through the opening up of trade, agriculture could not do this. It has always been the Community's largest single problem.

The problem with agriculture was that in many countries, particularly in France and Italy, it was very inefficiently organised. In those countries the size of the average farm was very small indeed, and individual farmers could not afford the expensive equipment needed to modernise their old fashioned farms, as seen in the photograph overleaf. This made their agricultural produce very expensive, compared with the cheaper agricultural goods produced in the more modern farms of Britain, Holland and parts of Germany. In addition a large proportion,

A typical French farm of the 1960s

about fifteen per cent, of the voters of France and Italy—and less so in Germany—were peasant farmers. Their governments, therefore, had to pay great attention to their demands. The French peasants in particular often resorted to serious disruption and violence to get their own way. French governments always seemed unable or unwilling to deal with this very basic problem.

A **Common Agricultural Policy** (CAP) was not properly worked out until 1969, mainly because of France. What France wanted—and got—was the Farm Fund. This was an organisation which got its huge income from VAT and from taxes on foreign food and goods entering the Community. The price for agricultural goods, for example wheat, was then set—but not in competition with cheaper foreign wheat. Instead the price was set specifically to provide Europe's less efficient farmers with a good living. If a farmer produced too much of a product, the Fund would buy it from him at the artificially high rate. This encouraged farmers to produce too much of goods that were not needed so that huge surpluses were created. These became the famous 'butter mountains' and 'wine lakes' of the CAP.

Another unfair feature was that countries that imported large amounts of goods, especially Britain, paid the most to the Farm Fund, even though British agriculture was efficient. Thus Britain became the largest contributor to the European Community. As three quarters of the total Community budget was spent on agriculture, this seemed unfair to the British. In the 1980s, Margaret Thatcher, the Prime Minister, managed after very persistent negotiations to get a reduction in the British contribution, but she could not get the other members of the Community to modernise their agriculture.

Results of the Common Agricultural Policy

The CAP made all European nations, especially Britain, more self-sufficient in food by encouraging more efficient agricultural production among the better-off farmers. However it still encouraged inefficiency in poorer farms because prices were guaranteed. It meant that France, Italy and Germany never really got to grips with their basic agricultural inefficiency. Another result was that all Europeans, as consumers of food, had to pay increasingly high prices.

Social developments

In various ways the European Community tried to raise the living and working conditions of most of its people. The Community Social Fund was set up to contribute to job creation schemes in depressed areas such as southern Italy, northern France and parts of Britain. Britain, Italy and France took one quarter each of this fund while Germany received only 3% because its people were much better off. The Social Fund takes only 5% of the Community's budget and is not large compared with the vast amounts of money spent by individual governments.

There is no common social policy, but governments are encouraged to improve their national laws in health, safety, equal opportunity and equal pay. Individual people are also encouraged to sue their governments in the European Court to enforce EC decisions relating to human rights. In this way, the British government has been forced to improve Social Security payments for handicapped people and to phase out corporal punishment in schools.

Defence and foreign policy developments

No real progress was made towards a common European defence policy. Although most members of the Community were also members of Nato, there were no further suggestions for a revival of the European Defence Community. Europe needs America too much to be separate. Also France is not a member of NATO and prefers to look after its own defence interests.

There was also little co-operation in foreign policy. In the Falklands war, for instance, the Community supported Britain in the first stages, then the members adopted different policies based on their own interests in Argentina. However, they did co-operate on a common treatment of Middle-Eastern problems, being more even-handed between Arab and Israel than America was.

Always standing in the way of co-operation in foreign and defence matters are the separate national interests of the member nations.

Political developments

The federalists always wanted closer political links between nations. They looked forward to a United States of Europe with a single European government dealing with major issues. National governments would deal with less important matters and would have much less power and influence. In this vision of Europe the European Parliament has much more power and the Council of Ministers has much less.

The Parliament developed to a very small extent. Its only real power was to approve the Community's spending budget each year. On several occasions it delayed approval but never dared not, finally, to approve the budget, as this would have caused a major crisis. However, the European Parliament did gain in status as Europeans became more used to it, especially after 1979 when its MPs were first elected directly by the people. However most people always looked to their own governments and parliaments for the solution to their problems, not to the European Parliament.

The Council of Ministers did not decline in importance. Most European governments, all of whom send members to the Council of Ministers, were reluctant to give up their national powers to the Community. In the Council of Ministers any individual government could veto any change, and many did so. General de Gaulle was very nationalistic in his outlook and stood out against the others in the 1960s, as did the British government of Mrs Thatcher in the 1980s. There was a proposal in the 1980s that decisions, even important ones, should be made by a majority rather than a unanimous vote. This, however, was difficult to bring about. There was no general demand for it to happen. Most people in all countries were realists rather than federalists.

1a The community helps industry and agriculture in different ways. What is the difference?
b What have been the main changes in each of the above areas since 1957?
c Were they, in your opinion, successful?
2 Explain the Farm Fund . . .
a from a British point of view.
b from a French farmer's point of view.
3 Do you want to see more changes in the following? If so what?
—Economics, especially in agriculture.
—Defence and foreign policy.
—Closer political links, leading to a United States of Europe.

4 Are you a federalist, a realist or an opponent of the Community? Give your reasons.

Discussion topics

What recent developments are taking place in the European Community? What is your attitude to them?

Essays

Describe the developments that took place between 1948 and 1957 and led to the formation of the European Community.
What has been Britain's attitude to the Community between 1948 and the present?

LINKS

Making sense of history

International communities

No international organisations are fully successful. We live in a world of nation-states, not of full-scale international co-operation. Nevertheless some international organisations are more successful than others. The European Community is generally regarded by its members as a success; so much so that it continually increases its membership. The United Nations, although not a failure like its predecessor the League of Nations, has serious limitations.

Answering the following questions should enable you to work out why the European Community is more successful than the United Nations.

Size

Which of the international organisations has more than 150 members and which has 12?

Which has members scattered all over the world and which contains neighbouring members from the same continent?
Do these facts help to make one more successful than the other?

Power

To which organisation are its members prepared to give up some of their powers in their own interests?
To which organisation are its members not prepared to give up any of their powers for fear that it might threaten their own interests?

Reasons for being a member

Which organisation best serves the national self-interest of its members in the following ways
—economic prosperity and development?
—a greater sense of security in numbers?
—a sense of status in being a member?
Which of these interests are served best of all?

Q

1a Did any pattern emerge in answering the questions above? Did any one organisation have, in your opinion, any qualities that made it more successful than the other?

b If so, list the reasons for success in order of importance. Give reasons for your views.

## 12

RACIALISM

Race

What is a race?

The word race is often used in describing the physical differences between various groups of human beings. *All* human beings come from a common ancestor, not from several ancestors of different race. In fact, whereas man has been on earth for possibly up to eight million years, the races have only been separate for about 100,000 years. Although there are several types of racial groups, such as the Caucasian – usually known as whites – and the Negroid – usually known as blacks – there are also many subgroups and many mixed groups. It is impossible to define race in terms of behaviour, beliefs, and values as these things are mostly caused by the environment in which people live.

Extension

The word *racialism* is a general, all-purpose word to describe negative or hostile feelings about people considered to be of a different race.

Other words too are in constant use, such as 'racial discrimination' and 'racial segregation'. To help you make sense of these terms, read the extracts and look at the photographs on these pages.

Trevor Huddleston, a British parish priest in an African township in South Africa, wrote in 1956 . . .

On Easter Saturday morning I was not too pleased when there strode into my office the manager of the local milkfarm. He was an ex-serviceman, a European working in an African township. 'Its Jacob . . .' he began . . . 'Father, I'm damn' well going to do something about this. It's a bloody shame. Father, you've got to help me.'

On the previous Thursday, Jacob Ledwaba had been arrested for being out after the curfew and without his pass. On Saturday morning he came home. He told his wife he had been kicked in the stomach in the cells and that he was in such pain that he could not go to work. Would she go and tell the boss, and explain?

All I want to say is this. Jacob was taken to hospital and died of a bladder injury, leaving a widow and a month old baby. We brought a case against the police, and in evidence produced statements concerning the injury from the two doctors who had attended Jacob. We also had the services of an eminent lawyer. The verdict was that he had died of VD. The magistrate added that the police had been shamefully accused in this case, and that there was no evidence whatsoever against them.

To me Jacob is Jacob Lebwaba, husband, head of a family and worshipper in my church. To the ordinary South African citizens, he is a native 'boy' (and he would still be a 'boy' if he lived to 70) who had not got a pass and was probably cheeky to the police when they arrested him. A pity he died, but we must have *control*.

Prime Minister Malan of South Africa said . . .

> Why did the Creator make the mistake of creating countries, nations and languages? He should not have done so, and in addition the Creator also proceeded to create different colours. I say that opposition to apartheid is opposition to Creation and to the Creator.

An expression commonly heard in South Africa . . .

> Come here, boy.

More sayings . . .

> I think the Chinese are inscrutable. You can never tell what they think.

> I'm not a racialist, but I don't think that races should mix.

> I'm afraid I couldn't give him a job in my factory. You see, he's of a different race from all the other workers, and would upset them.

A black South African shows his passbook stating the places where he has the right to live, work and even be present at certain times of the day

A white man hits a black beggar in South Africa

Railway stairs

> I'm not against them as a race, but I don't like their religion. You never know what goes on in their ceremonies. And I don't like their food. It smells horrible.

The above extracts and photographs should help to identify the meanings of the words mentioned earlier. Which of the following definitions most accurately describe these terms—*racial discrimination, racial prejudice, racial segregation?*
● The deliberate separation of whole races from one another. This is usually legally enforced by a dominant race upon other races. Apartheid is an example of this on a grand scale. It literally means apartness, being completely separate and it entails different treatment in every way.
● An emotion or a belief about race held by a person or by a group of people. It is usually negative, but it does not mean that the people concerned do anything about it. It is usually based on ignorance and on fear and is therefore very difficult to deal with.
● An action taken against people considered to be of a different race. This is not necessarily illegal, although the action is usually harmful. It usually involves treating people as inferior in some way or denying them equal treatment. It might lead to intimidation or violence.

Q

1 Identify the terms given above and give examples of each term from the extracts and photographs on this page.

2 Why is racialism such a difficult idea to define?

South Africa

Basic facts

Black Africans: Fifteen million, divided into several tribes, each with its own traditions and often with its own language. The Zulus are the largest tribe. However, tribes are not so important in the cities.
Coloureds: Two million people of mixed race.
Indians: One million, descended from Indians brought to South Africa by Britain in the late nineteenth century. The majority live in Natal province.
Whites/Europeans: Four million, of whom over two million are Afrikaners, or Boers, descended from the original Dutch settlers. Most of the Afrikaners are to be found in agriculture, in the lower-level professions and in the poorer white classes. The other one and three quarter million whites are mostly of British origin and tend to be more important in business and commerce.

South Africa

The racial situation after the Second World War

South Africa, as part of the British Empire, operated racial discrimination on a large scale. However in 1948 a new political party, the National Party, won the General Election. It was a very racialist party, comprising mostly Afrikaners, and was influenced by a secret Afrikaner society called the *Broederbond*—the band of brothers. It believed that racial segregation had been ordained by God. Now, for the first time, it gained a majority over the British whites and more moderate Afrikaners. During the next few years, under its Prime Ministers D. P. Malan, J. G. Streijdom and H. F. Verwoerd, it set up the system of apartheid.

The Constitution

The Constitution contains no list of individual rights for blacks which can be upheld in court. Blacks do not have the right to vote. Nor do they have the right to strike, although their unions are not illegal. Under a special law called the 'Supression of Communism Act' the Government can ban any meeting, organisation or public gathering, even a social gathering. It can do this on the grounds that the banned meeting or organisation would further communism. Individual people can also be put under a banning order and forbidden to have any communication with others or to leave their houses.

Racial segregation

The terms apartheid or 'separate development' are often given to the policy of deliberately separating the various races on a large scale. Special tribal homelands and Bantustans were set up in 1959, such as Transkei, Kwazulu and Bophutatswana. They are widely scattered and are usually found in barren areas, where their inhabitants live in very poor conditions. They comprise only 13% of the whole of South Africa.

They are ruled by black leaders and are supposed to be independent. In theory all black Africans are citizens of these 'countries', but cannot live there because they are needed to work in 'white' South Africa.

Only about seven million black South Africans live in these homelands and Bantustans. The rest live in white South Africa as workers and servants. They are termed 'migrants' and can be sent back to their homelands if they cause trouble.

Under a law called the Group Areas Act, different areas are marked off for residence for different racial groups within white South Africa. Cities like Johannesburg are usually white only, but are surrounded by immense black townships such as Soweto with its one million people. The blacks travel to work in the white cities but have to be out of the white areas by 9.00 pm.

The Population Registration Act

All South African citizens have to be classified by race according to colour and the shape of their head or nose and so on. Their classification is written down in a special book known as a passbook. Borderline cases are decided by special boards and many who lose their case see their family split up, lose their jobs and lose the right to reside in particular areas. All non-whites not carrying their passbooks can be arrested and detained under the Pass Laws.

Classification proves very difficult sometimes. Japanese are classified as whites, Arabs are classified as white or coloured depending on whether they are Christian or Muslim. Black citizens from other countries have the rights of whites while they are in South Africa.

A black school

Living conditions in a black homeland

Separate amenities

A wide range of separate amenities was set up for different racial groups after 1948. Cinemas, buses, restaurants, toilets, beaches are all racially divided. Amenities do not have to be of an equal standard. Under the **Bantu Education Act** schools have different facilities, each white child having the equivalent of 16 black children. There are different subjects taught, to different levels, with different ages of leaving school. As the Minister of Native Affairs said . . .

> there is no place for Bantu [black] in the racial community above the level of certain forms of labour. What is the use of teaching the Bantu mathematics, when it cannot be used in practice? That is quite absurd. Education must train people in accordance with their opportunities in life, according to the sphere in which they live.

Racial discrimination

Discrimination was part of most whites' way of thinking. The Afrikaners in particular believed that God created people unequal. They preached this in their churches. Feelings of superiority and command were the right of whites, inferiority and obedience were the lot of blacks. Blacks had been trained to accept the superiority of white civilisation since their conquest by white men. They accepted low pay, low standards in everything. Blacks tended to live in rural areas where conditions were poorer anyway. The average wage of the white was five times more than the black. Discrimination is part and parcel of everyday life in South Africa, quite apart from the apartheid laws.

America

Basic facts

In 1945 blacks made up approximately 15% of the American population. Most of the blacks were descendents of slaves brought from Africa in the eighteenth century. Most of the traces of African traditions have been lost, and most blacks are of mixed race. In 1945 three quarters of the blacks lived in the southern states, where slavery had been common and where they made up about a quarter of the population.

The racial situation after the Second World War

The blacks had been freed from slavery in 1861 but had made little progress since then. Up to the 1940s neither the Republican nor the Democratic parties were interested in black problems.

The Constitution

The American Constitution upholds the rights of all individual Americans of whatever colour. Every American can take his case to the Supreme Court which has the power to order the

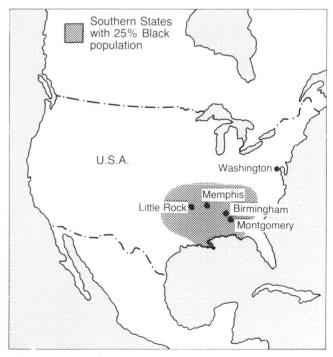

USA

Government to uphold his or her rights. All blacks received these rights when they were liberated from slavery in 1861. For instance, blacks had the right to vote, but had to register as a voter. In most states, especially in the south, registration was made impossible by having to pass a reading test or having to pay a tax or, at worst, by violence or threats. Virtually no blacks used their right to vote.

Racial segregation

As in South Africa, a system of segregation was operated in America, mainly in the southern states, although some segregated laws were national. The army, for instance, was legally segregated on racial lines, with completely separate units, camps and training for blacks and whites. Legally there were no separate areas set aside for blacks in America, although they did tend to live in separate black 'ghettos', sections of towns which they were afraid to leave.

Separate amenities

The law said that amenities could be separate, although they had to be equal. Most schools throughout America were segregated, although black schools were certainly not the equals of white ones. It was in the south that most segregation was operated. There there were laws separating blacks and whites in restaurants, cinemas, park benches and buses. For instance, if buses were full, whites could sit in black sections and blacks had to stand.

Racial discrimination

Blacks were simply not treated in the same way as whites in jobs, wages and in residential areas. They were regarded as inferior by most whites. In fact most blacks too accepted their inferiority. They had very low expectations and took their low status for granted.

As blacks moved to northern towns after the Second World War, discrimination against them grew amongst northern whites. They got the poorest-paid jobs, if they got one at all. They could only afford the worst housing, and whites

A white lynching mob

moved out of neighbourhoods, which quickly became 'black' neighbourhoods. In these neighbourhoods, schools and other facilities deteriorated and the next generation remained the poorest and most deprived. The black ghettos became depressed inner-city areas with high crime rates, high unemployment, heavy drug problems and widespread mental and physical illness.

Discrimination took place in court against the blacks, especially in the south. More convictions were gained against blacks, and penalties for blacks were always heavier than for similar offences committed by whites. Worse of all was discrimination that took the form of violence. This was frequently used against blacks who used white amenities or strayed into white areas. The Ku Klux Klan (KKK), a secret society, was the most notorious exponent of such racial violence, often even lynching or burning blacks. The police did little to prevent this.

Q

Comparing America and South Africa

1 In which country is racialism stronger?

2 In which country are the non-whites in a majority? In what ways do you think this would increase the racialism of the white minority?

3 In which country are the non-whites in a minority? In what ways, and why, might this affect the racialism of the white majority?

4 How do the South African and American constitutions differ in their attitudes to non-whites?

5 Which nation took racial segregation to the furthest extent? In what ways?

6 What is the difference between a South African black township and a black ghetto in an American city?

7 What would be, in your opinion, the reaction of a kind, caring, religious believer in apartheid towards the two pictures of South Africa on page 224?

8 What is so horrifying about the faces of the onlookers in the American burning pictured above? Explain what is in their minds.

South Africa

Protest begins, 1950–mid 1960s

Protest from non-whites

1952 The Defiance Campaign

Ever since 1911 a small organisation called the African National Congress (ANC) had worked against racialism through peaceful methods. Now its leader, Chief Herbert Luthuli, organised a Defiance Campaign against the new apartheid laws. Africans broke the separate amenity laws by visiting restaurants or beaches. When the campaign failed after the brutal crushing of the protest and the arrest of many members, ANC membership rose from seven thousand to one hundred thousand.

1955 The Freedom Charter

This was issued by a Congress of the People, which contained members of all races and groups such as the ANC. Its main points were:

> 1 South Africa belongs to all who live in it, both black and white, and no government can claim authority unless it is based on the will of the people. Every man and woman should have the right to vote.
> 2 There should be equal status in all official organisations for all groups and races. Racial discrimination should be a punishable crime.
> 3 The national wealth of the country is the heritage of all South Africans, and should be given back to the people. The mineral wealth, banks and monopoly industries should be transferred to the ownership of the people as a whole. All the land should be redistributed to those who work on it.

1956 The Treason Trials

A hundred and fifty six people of all races were tried for treason for issuing the Freedom Charter, including Nelson Mandela and Oliver Tambo of the ANC. When the trial ended in 1961, none of the defendants were found guilty. However, protest in South Africa became much stronger as a result of the trials.

1957 The Pan African Congress

The Pan African Congress was founded by Robert Subukwe, a breakaway group from the ANC. It began to organise demonstrations and protests against the Pass Laws.

1960 The Sharpville Massacre

The black township of Sharpville had never been known for protest, but in 1960, 500 families were evicted there from other areas. The Pan African Congress organised a protest, and a crowd of 5,000 gathered outside the police station. When the crowd surged forward, young constables panicked and fired without orders. The crowd fled but the firing continued. 19 blacks were killed and 180 wounded, mostly in the back. Protest increased dramatically. Luthuli and the ANC organised the first nationwide black protest, including a stay-at-home strike.

The Sharpville Massacre, 1960

1961–1964, Umkonto we sizwe (Spear of the nation)

In 1964, Oliver Tambo left South Africa to raise funds abroad. Nelson Mandela stayed behind to organise the movement in South Africa. It was decided to commit acts of sabotage against Government property, but on no account to injure or kill people. Inevitably some policemen and informers were killed. By 1964 the movement had been crushed through police torture and informers. Mandela was imprisoned in 1963 and stayed there for 27 years until his release in 1990.

Protest from whites

Almost all Afrikaners supported the National Party and, increasingly, so did British whites. Although they were not so committed to apartheid, they wanted to keep up their high standard of living, and to do this it was necessary to keep black standards down. As black protest grew stronger and became increasingly violent, they became more and more afraid and more determined to react against protest.

However, some whites participated in some of the black protest movements from the beginning, such as Patrick Duncan, the son of a former Governor-General, who joined the Defiance Campaign. There were 21 whites among the 156 defendants in the Treason Trials. The Liberal Party, led by Mrs Helen Suzman, stood for Parliament on a policy of opposing apartheid, but it gained only a tiny minority of white support. A white women's organisation called Black Sash supported the black right to vote and stood in silent protest on important occasions, but it had little effect.

Protest from abroad

From 1948—United Nations protests

In the UN, India, acting for the South African Indians, took a lead in denouncing South Africa and calling for economic sanctions against her. The UN Security Council always vetoed such attempts because Britain and America were opposed to economic sanctions as they would hurt their own interests.

1960—The 'Winds of change'

The British Prime Minister, Macmillan, made a live radio speech on a visit to South Africa. In it he criticised apartheid and warned of the 'winds of change' blowing through Africa. This was the first protest from a leading 'white' nation and it shocked many whites.

1960s—Increasing isolation

Several world organisations expelled South Africa from membership. The Commonwealth did this in 1960 and the Organisation of African Unity in 1963. The Olympic Games refused to accept South Africa, even though South Africa offered to send a multi-racial team. South Africa was forced out of the International Labour Organisation and the United Nations Educational, Scientific and Cultural Organisation.

The Government's response to protest

All three African Prime Ministers in the 1950s and 1960s had a simple response to opposition. They crushed it. The police and the army were often used, not only against actual riots, but also to frighten the blacks even before trouble developed. The police were allowed to detain people without charge for 12 days. In 1965 this became 180 days and was frequently used. The Government simply did not listen to white and foreign protest. The most severe of these Prime Ministers was Doctor Verwoerd. Typical of his response to protest was his reply to Macmillan's radio 'Winds of change' speech. He simply said that South Africa would give up accepted standards of behaviour if necessary.

Q

1 Why would many whites be frightened by the Freedom Charter? Examine it in detail.
2 Write a brief account to go with the Sharpville picture from the standpoint of
a an Afrikaner

b a black African
c a supporter of the British government.
3 Why did Macmillan's speech shock many white South Africans?

Protest, 1960s to the present

Black protest

The later 1960s

Gradually, many blacks became more politically aware. A movement called Black Consciousness spread among the city blacks, especially among the young. It was influenced by the American Black Power movement and its leading spokesman was a medical student named Steve Biko. Otherwise the forces of repression were so strong that black protest was simply not effective.

1975 Soweto riots

When the Government decided that black pupils should be taught in Afrikaans (Dutch) rather than their tribal language or English, the situation deteriorated. Riots, demonstrations and school strikes broke out, worsened by police violence. A nationwide strike took place and rioting quickly spread, most of all in Soweto, the largest black township. When Steve Biko 'died' in detention, violence erupted again. Gradually the unrest was put down, but the black townships were seething with discontent.

How did Steve Biko die?

By 1975, 45 black detainees had died in police custody, allegedly by suicide or by accidents such as slipping on soap or falling out of windows. In 1977, Biko and his friend were arrested in a routine roadblock near Port Elizabeth and were taken to the police station. The police tried to find out the links between Biko and the ANC, of which he was never a member. The statements made about his death vary.

Biko's friend, arrested with him, said later . . .

> He was killed by the henchmen of the apartheid system, who wanted to kill the Black Consciousness Movement.

The Coroner, who investigated the death shortly afterwards reported . . .

> Biko died as a result of severe blows to the head.

(The Coroner stated nothing about how the blows occurred, and named no-one responsible.)

The Minister of Justice, Kruger, said a few months later, in an excited speech to a large Afrikaner audience . . .

> Biko died after a hunger strike.

1980s — Violence increases

In the mid-1980s violence flared up. In 1985, 20 blacks were killed in Langa township on the anniversary of the Sharpville Massacre, as well as several in Sharpville itself. A new development at this time was the hostility and tension between non-white groups, especially between blacks and Indians. Within the black townships, law and order virtually broke down and crime and murder became commonplace. Violence between black groups developed, particularly between different black tribes. The most dominant tribe was the Zulus, who often terrified other tribes. There was also hostility and violence between young blacks known as 'comrades', who tended to be more extreme and older, more moderate 'elders'.

Three main black protest groupings developed.

1 The ANC

The banned ANC, the most extreme group, turned increasingly to guerrilla tactics, training terrorist or freedom fighters outside South Africa for action within the country. More and more raids took place inside South Africa. Oliver Tambo remained the leader of the ANC, and Mandela remained its main inspiration, although he was in prison. The ANC had a very large black following inside South Africa.

2 The United Democratic Front (UDF)

The United Democratic Front was formed in 1983 by a black Methodist minister Dr Allan Boesak. It had no clear organisation, and tended to work through the unions, which the Government did not ban and which grew greatly in importance. Because of its informal organisation, the UDF proved difficult to combat. It supported peaceful protest and grew more and more in popularity. Boesak was an outspoken critic of apartheid and was himself put under house arrest. Another vigorous critic was Archbishop Desmond Tutu, the leader of the Anglican Church in South Africa, but he had no organisation of his own.

3 The Inkatha Movement

The Inkatha Movement emerged as a purely Zulu movement led by Chief Buthelezi. The Chief was a member of the Zulu royal family and the Prime Minister of Kwazulu, the Zulu homeland. He wanted to maintain the power of the traditional chiefs of South Africa. Inkatha was the least extreme protest movement.

White protest

White protest continued to be very limited, especially as the National Party gained more and more support in elections from both the Afrikaner and British communities. However increasing numbers of white students and intellectuals, as well as members of the Anglican and Catholic churches, made a vocal minority. Perhaps more effective than these was the increasing number of white businessmen, especially of British descent, who feared that the economy would be ruined by continuing unrest and who pressed for changes in apartheid.

One of these slogans at a white demonstration might make a supporter of apartheid think twice

Protest from abroad

For several years the British and Americans vetoed economic sanctions against South Africa in the United Nations, but boycotts and isolation increased. The pressure from many countries grew to expel South Africa from the UN, but Britain and America always vetoed this too, thinking that South Africa was better dealt with inside the organisation than outside it. The Gleneagles Agreement to blacklist sportsmen and entertainers who visited South Africa increased South Africa's sense of isolation, as they were a very sporting people.

South Africa's closest neighbours became hostile, with the coming to power of black governments in Mozambique in 1974 and Zimbabwe in 1980. These countries were a haven for ANC guerrillas and were often raided by South African bombers or commandos, but basically these 'front-line' states depended upon the South African economy and dared not go too far in case their own economies collapsed.

In 1985, however, foreign pressure began to be effective when the world's major banks refused to renew huge loans to South Africa unless changes took place in the system of apartheid. Foreign companies and new investors became less interested in lending money to South Africa, and even began to withdraw it.

1a Assess the reliability of the three pieces of evidence about Steve Biko's death.
b How do you think Steve Biko died? Give your reasons.
2 Which of the slogans pictured in the South African demonstration might make some sense to supporters of apartheid? Why? Why would the others not?
3 If you were a white South African supporter of apartheid, which of the three black protest movements would you prefer to deal with? Why? Why not the others?

Government response

There were two Prime Ministers during this period. B. J. Forster (1966–1978) increased repression by setting up BOSS—the Bureau of State Security—and detaining thousands of blacks without trial. P. J. Botha, Prime Minister from 1978 to 1989, faced a terrible dilemma as to how to deal with the deteriorating situation of the mid 1980s. Either he would remove apartheid—as slowly as possible—or face increasing black violence and hostile world opinion that might lead to economic sanctions against South Africa.

'We must adjust, otherwise we shall die,' he said. 'The moment you start oppressing people they fight back. Apartheid is a recipe for permanent conflict.' Many Nationalists, known as the *verligte* (enlightened) wing of the National Party agreed with him. If he did make any reforms, the *verkrampte* (hard line) wing of the Party threatened to oppose him. The Party was in danger of splitting in to two. On the repressive side, Botha was as harsh as any in putting down disorder by force, as at the Langa riots in 1985. It did not seem to work as effectively as in the past. The repression continued on a large scale, but so did the discontent and the protest.

On the other hand Botha created a separate House of Parliament for coloureds and Indians, although they had very little power. He announced that the Pass Laws would be lifted, but progress was very, very slow.

America

Protest begins, 1950–mid 1960s

Protest from blacks

Ever since the ending of slavery up to 1958, a tiny minority of blacks had achieved respect and status, mostly in the professions of teacher, minister or doctor. These people were the driving force behind black protest in the 1940s and 1950s. They formed a willing audience, especially after the war. Many blacks had fought for America and for democracy, and were not prepared to put up any longer with oppression. Two organisations emerged—the National Association for the Advancement of Coloured People (NAACP) and the Congress of Racial Equality (CORE)—but they had little popularity among blacks, who accepted their inferior status.

The Civil Rights Movement, 1955 onwards

From 1955 a series of incidents sparked off a wave of protest among blacks. Leading the way were the NAACP and CORE, but the Civil Rights Movement was more of a mass movement than a tightly organised group. Soon its acknowledged leader was the black preacher, Martin Luther King. Following the example of Mahatma Gandhi in India, the Civil Rights Movement insisted only on *peaceful* protest. It also believed in deliberate direct action to force the Government to make changes in the law. This direct action often provoked a violent reaction from the authorities and from many racialist whites. A very important method of forcing change was to take cases of discrimination to the Supreme Court. This meant that the Constitution could be used to protect and extend the rights of blacks.

Transport

The first incident came in 1955. Mrs Rosa Parks of Montgomery, Alabama, a black member of the NAACP, refused to give up her seat in the black section of a bus to a white passenger. She was immediately arrested as a communist agitator. Martin Luther King took up her case and organised the Montgomery bus boycott, and was also sent to prison. However, the case was taken to the Supreme Court, which decided that segregation in buses was illegal. The southern states all ignored the Court's ruling. In 1961 James Farme of CORE organised the Freedom Rides in integrated buses across the southern states, ignoring separate facilities in bus stations. The ride was abandoned when violent white youths and KKK men in Alabama used terrible brutality against the riders. However, other rides soon followed. In November 1961 the Supreme Court ruled that segregated waiting rooms were also illegal.

Education

In 1954 a black family in Topeka, Arizona, named Brown, appealed to the Supreme Court, stating that segregated schools were unjust and illegal. The Topeka Education Authority claimed the freedom to set up separate schools. The Chief Justice of America in the Supreme Court upheld the blacks' case and in the following year, realising that nothing had been done, instructed the states of America to integrate schools. Very slowly they began to obey, but the real test did not come until 1957.

Elizabeth Eckford, being interviewed after her attempt to enter Little Rock High School

Government troops escort a black student into school

In that year nine black 15 year-old boys and girls tried to enter the white high school at Little Rock, Arkansas. Governor Faubus used the local volunteer soldiers, known as the National Guard, to stop them. A huge crowd of hostile whites swore and spat at them. President Eisenhower, a Republican, was reluctantly forced to send in regular army troops to clear a way for the first black student Elizabeth Eckford to enter the building. However, the integration of schools only went on at a very slow pace. The whole affair was followed with the most intense publicity and public interest throughout all the media.

The photographs and the following extract show something of the emotions and feelings raised by the children's entry to the school.

A man who had been very prominent among local racialists expressed himself in these terms . . .

> Gentlemen you've just observed how a Communist dictatorship works. There is a tear in my eye because of the loss of freedom in the United States.

The same protection had to be given to a black student James Meredith, when he tried to register at Mississippi University. At first Governor Wallace actually stood in his way but President Kennedy had to send in regular soldiers.

One important result of the Civil Rights Movement was the frightening violence from whites who supported segregation, against Civil Rights supporters. This resulted in murder, bombings and the burning of homes, and usually went unpunished. In Birmingham, Alabama, the Council and the Police brutally turned police dogs and hosepipes onto Civil Rights demonstrators. Still Martin Luther King and the Civil Rights Movement stuck to their peaceful direct action. In August 1965 they organised a huge march on Washington, one of the biggest demonstrations ever held. Its purpose was to give support to President Kennedy's Civil Rights Bill. The song sung by Joan Baez at this march became the symbol of protest—'We shall overcome'. Shortly afterwards a bomb exploded in a Birmingham black church and four black girls were killed. By this time some blacks were beginning to feel that a peaceful protest was not enough.

White schoolboys hang the model of a black boy

White protest

There was always a minority of whites who supported the black rights movement, but they were mainly in the northern middle classes. Many young people, especially students, supported President Kennedy's election campaign in 1960 because they thought that he would bring more changes. With so much publicity, more whites began to feel sympathy for the black cause, especially as they regarded America as a democratic country. They were sickened by the brutality used against protests at Birmingham, Alabama and other places. This brutality they saw in detail on their television screens. Many whites joined in the Civil Rights protests and demanded more laws to protect black civil rights. About one quarter of the crowd in the march on Washington was white.

Government response

The American Government only began to make changes when the need for change became essential. But what caused this need for change?

President Truman

President Truman wanted to pass several laws to end discrimination in his 'Fair Deal' of 1945. Unfortunately Congress (the American parliament), refused to do this as there was a majority of opponents of change there. Only one law was passed in 1948 to de-segregate the armed forces and to allow blacks to hold government office.

President Eisenhower

President Eisenhower's programme between 1952 and 1960 was called 'Movement Forward', but it contained little for blacks. As a Republican, Eisenhower did not wish to change the existing situation, and only reluctantly sent in regular troops to integrate the Little Rock school in 1957. If he had not done this, Eisenhower would not have been upholding the law. Two laws were passed in 1957 and in 1960 to protect the blacks' right to vote, but Eisenhower did nothing to force the southern states to keep the new laws.

President Kennedy (1961–1963)

President Kennedy had won the election partly on the votes of white Liberals and northern blacks. They hoped for more civil rights reforms from his 'New Frontier' programme. However, Kennedy was unable to get any laws through Congress, because Congress was Republican and he was a Democrat. Kennedy was also very reluctant to use the power that he possessed as President to deal with the increasing white violence, and to enforce the existing laws in the south. Only after his assassination in 1963 did Congress pass the Civil Rights Act of 1964, put forward by Kennedy's successor President Lyndon B. Johnson. This Act made segregation in all public places illegal.

There were several reasons why the Civil Rights Act was passed in 1964, but historians disagree about their importance. They were . . .

• The Civil Rights Movement's increasing use of peaceful direct action, such as the march on Washington and its organised breaking of the law.
• The violent white reaction.
• The wave of sympathy after President Kennedy's assassination for the law that he had failed to pass.
• The growing fear of black violence.

Q

1 Use the pictures and extract on page 232 to explain the views of white racialists in the Little Rock case.
2 Why was the Supreme Court so valuable in de-segregating America? Give examples.
3 List the various types of protest – from blacks and

from whites – in order of their importance. Give the reasons for your choice.
4 Write a paragraph explaining convincingly why the Civil Rights Act of 1964 was passed. Make clear the relative importance of the various reasons.

Black protest turns to violence

When Martin Luther King was given the Nobel Peace Prize in 1964, Malcolm X, the black extremist, said . . .

> He got the prize, we got the problem. I don't want a white man giving me medals. If I'm following a General, and he's leading me into battle and the enemy tends to give him rewards, or awards, I get suspicious. Especially if he gets a peace award before the war is over.

Black extremists and militants, who did not believe at all in peaceful action but in violence, spread their influence mainly in the huge black ghettos of the northern and Californian cities. Martin Luther King had little control over these groups. The Black Muslims were one of these, rejecting the integration of blacks and whites and demanding separate development. They chose Islam, an African religion, as their creed, and attacked the American system instead of trying to fit into it. Malcolm X was one of those who gave up his 'slave' surname of Little and formed a breakaway group before his own assassination in 1967.

Black Power developed in the 1960s under the influence of blacks like Stokey Carmichael who aimed to convince blacks that 'black is beautiful',

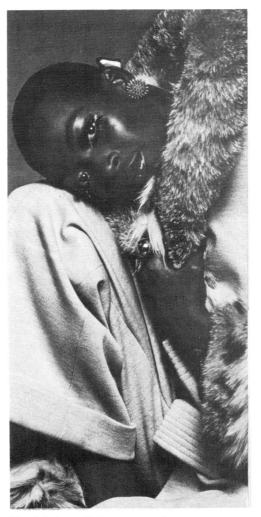

'Black is beautiful' — a magazine extract

to set up their own businesses and to run their own communities with a greater sense of pride. He also encouraged blacks to take the law into their own hands and to use violence if necessary. The ideas of Black Power were shown at the 1968 Olympics when black-gloved black athletes gave the clenched-fist salute during the American national anthem. The incident caused jubilation on one side and outraged antagonism on the other.

The Black Panthers were the most violent underground group, which had several bloody battles with the police in the late 1960s, when most of their leaders were killed or imprisoned.

The mood of violence quickly spread among the black communities and erupted into community violence when sparked off by an incident. The killing of a black youth in 1964 started rioting in New York. More seriously, the black suburb of Watts in Los Angeles in 1968 was the scene of widespread, days-long rioting in which 80 people were killed. 'Copy-cat' riots spread to other cities, especially when Martin Luther King was assassinated in 1968 and riots were touched off throughout America.

After 1968, when new civil rights laws were passed, much of the racial violence died down. In the 1970s and 1980s many black people made a success in various professions and businesses. Many prospered and employed other blacks. Several black members were elected to Congress, and many towns and cities elected black mayors. The integration of schools was, by this time, virtually complete, and more and more blacks were going to university too.

However most blacks did not do well. The vast

The clenched fist salute at the 1968 Olympics

majority still lived in the black ghettos of the north and California. They were usually the poorest sector of any city. Discrimination against them was immense, and the problems of deprivation and poverty with all their terrible consequences — drugs, prostitution, exploitation and unemployment — certainly did not improve but deteriorated. Protest, however, did die down.

Q

1 What was Malcolm X's view of Martin Luther King and peaceful protest?
2 In what ways does the photograph of the model illustrate the saying 'Black is beautiful'.

3 Explain the two opposing reactions that occurred when the picture of the black athletes was shown.

Government response

President Johnson did more for the blacks than any president. In 1964 he was elected on a programme known as the 'Great Society', which promised racial equality as well as other reforms.

Following the 1964 Civil Rights Act came the Voting Rights Act of 1965, which at last ensured that blacks could register to vote. A few black

Congressmen and town councillors were elected, but in the southern states the law was difficult to enforce and blacks still tended not to vote.

Then, in 1968, came another Civil Rights Act, perhaps the most important of all. This Act took on the immense task of attacking racial discrimination, wherever it existed, and making it illegal. It outlawed discrimination in jobs, government service and the law, and set up an organisation to ensure that the Act worked. It is put into operation whenever discrimination can be proved. Many blacks have benefitted by it, as has the whole black community in general. Legally, blacks became the equals of whites. Unfortunately, however, laws cannot stop racial prejudice, even though they outlaw the discrimination that arises out of prejudice.

Although legal segregation has gone in America, and although discrimination is less than it was, much still remains. Much prejudice remains too. In many senses the blacks remain second-class citizens. Most of the blacks of America are in the poorest third of American society. The cycle of deprivation, poverty and discrimination against blacks continues to be America's number one problem.

An assessment

Comparing progress in South Africa and America

The strength of the racialist system

Write a paragraph about this, dealing with the following questions in each country . . .
What was the proportion of blacks to whites in the population?
Did the whites NEED to keep the blacks down? Why?
How powerful were the racialist attitudes of whites towards non-whites?
How full, strong and thorough were the laws against non-whites?

Factors leading to progress

Write a paragraph about this, dealing with the following questions in each country . . .
Did the Constitution help or hinder blacks?

Were the courts favourable or unfavourable to supporting the blacks?
Did protest from whites help the black cause?
Did protest from abroad help the black cause?
Did peaceful protest from blacks help the black cause?
Did violent protest from blacks help the black cause?
Which of the above factors most helped the black cause in America?
Which of the above factors has helped or will help the black cause in South Africa?

The future

1 Do you think that apartheid in South Africa will:
a Remain as it is for the forseeable future?
b Be gradually removed, under pressure, by the government?
c Be removed by a black upheaval and seizure of power?
Give your reasons.
2 Do you think that blacks will really become the equals of whites in America? If so, when? Do you think black protest will revive again in America? Why?

Q

Discussion topics

1 How strong is racialism in Britain today? What examples are there of it in operation? Are the laws against it strong enough?

Essays

1 Briefly define *apartheid*. Describe the opposition to it since 1950.
2 Describe *four* of the following and assess their importance in the Civil Rights Movement:
Transport integration in the south; educational integration; The Civil Rights Act of 1964; Black Power; The Civil Rights Act of 1968.

## 13

DECOLONISATION

Imperialism, empire and commonwealth

The period between the two world wars was the highest point of European imperialism. Vast areas of the world outside Europe, particularly in Asia and Africa, were within the empires of a few European nations. Britain had the largest empire of all, with over fifty colonies, followed by France and then by the Netherlands, Portugal and Belgium.

The reason for possessing such large empires was because they brought benefits to the 'mother' countries. Some possessions were almost empty lands for European settlers to colonise, others provided economic benefits such as raw materials and food for the mother country and a place to sell exports and to invest in railways, mines or factories. Colonies also brought great status to their possessors; they were glittering prizes to be spoken of with immense pride. The possession of important military and naval sites, too, were reasons to seize foreign lands such as Malta, Singapore and Cyprus.

Yet within twenty years these empires had virtually disappeared. Colonies had been given — or had taken — their independence. The old empires were replaced by freer, more equal organisations. Within the British Empire there had always been the *Commonwealth*, consisting of 'white' colonies to which Britain had willingly given independence previously. As the non-white colonies became independent most of them joined the Commonwealth. The 'Empire' gradually disappeared. Similarly the French Empire became the 'French Community' in 1958.

The changeover from Empire to Commonwealth was not easily achieved. The imperial powers did not lightly hand over their possessions, which they felt were necessary, valuable and beneficial to them. Some of the larger and more distant possessions such as India and Pakistan could simply not be prevented from becoming independent. Others, such as Algeria or Kenya, where there was a large proportion of dominant white settlers, were not given up without a fight. Nor were colonies of military value like Cyprus. In some places decolonisation was almost a routine and good natured hand-over of power; in others it was horrifyingly painful.

Why did decolonisation take place?

The colonial peoples

Nationalism was perhaps the strongest emotion and belief that inspired most colonies to gain their independence. The shock of being defeated, occupied and ruled often took a long time to get over, but in the end nations did do so. This was certainly happening in many of the colonies in the 1930s and 1940s. Nationalism was an immensely powerful force in the imperial possessions. Most of them had long histories and long-established civilisations and religions, often older than those of their European rulers. They had strong social structures and strong traditions of independence and nationhood. The only reason they had fallen to the imperial powers in the first place was that they lacked modern military technology and modern industry. Now some of them were beginning to possess these features. Some of the imperial powers had modernised their colonies with modern communications and investment. By the 1940s many colonies had achieved once again the national self-confidence to assert themselves against their masters. No longer could they be regarded as 'backward' nations who would take hundreds of years to catch up.

Some of the imperial countries, particularly the British, believed strongly in democracy. Indeed they had fought a Second World War for democracy and for their *own* independence. They had taught their ideals to their subject peoples in the colonies. Freedom and the desire for self-rule certainly inspired the colonial peoples in their demands for independence. The British envisaged a very gradual sharing of power with their subject peoples. This was too slow. Many of the independence movements demanded a more democratic future—and at once.

Many of the colonies produced leaders of outstanding ability and vision, who were able to use the rising feelings of nationalism and independence against their rulers. Some were brilliant guerrilla leaders, others were clever negotiators skilled in using the situation against the imperial powers. Gandhi and Nehru of India, Jinnah of Pakistan, Nkrumah of Ghana, Ben Bella of Algeria, and Nyerere of Tanzania all possessed undoubted powers of leadership.

The imperial rulers

As the tide of nationalism arose in their empires, the European powers found themselves at one of the lowest points in their history. In the Second World War most of them had been defeated. Britain alone had been victorious but was completely exhausted. The European powers were in no position to hold on to their colonies, especially those in Asia, from which they had been chased by the Japanese during the war. Sometimes they tried, and had to learn the hard way.

Julius Nyerere at Tanzania's independence celebrations

European nations were no longer the most important countries in the world. America and Russia were now super-powers in the way that no European power could ever be, and both of the super-powers were opposed to European imperialism. America hated it and would never help its European allies to keep their colonies. Russia wanted to use the growing independence movements for her own purposes.

The war had broken the white man's sense of absolute superiority. Twice Europe had battered itself and shown that it was not superior to other races and nations. The colonial peoples saw this clearly enough and were determined to be treated as inferiors no longer.

Q

1 Why do you think the imperial powers wanted to hold on to their colonies? What particular reasons would cause them to hold on more strongly?

2 Write a paragraph to go with the photograph above to be printed in:
a A British newspaper of your choice.
b A Tanzanian newspaper.

Extension

Different views of empire

Read the following quotations about imperialism. They should give you an insight in to what different people thought about it.

Kwame Nkrumah of Ghana demanded independence in the following terms in 1953 . . .

> Long before England had gained any importance, our ancestors had attained a great empire, which lasted until the eleventh century. That empire stretched across West Africa. Lawyers and scholars were much respected and the inhabitants of Ghana wore garments of wool, cotton, silk and velvet. There was trade in copper, gold, textiles and jewels.
>
> Thus we may take pride in the name of Ghana not out of pride in our history, but as an inspiration for the future. It is right and proper that we should know about our past. What our ancestors achieved in their society gives us confidence that we can create, out of that past, a glorious future, not in terms of war and military pomp but in terms of social progress and peace.

Lord Lugard, a British colonial Governor, wrote in 1922 . . .

> As Roman imperialism laid the foundations of modern civilisation and led the wild barbarians of Britain along the path to progress, so in Africa today we are repaying the debt, and bringing to the dark places of the earth, the home of barbarism and cruelty, the torch of progress, while helping the economic needs of our own civilisation.

Nehru of India wrote in 1936 . . .

> Railways, telegraphs, telephones, wireless and such like were no proof of the goodness and goodwill of British rule. They were welcome and necessary, and, because the British happened to be the people who brought them first, we should be grateful to them. But even these beginnings of modern industry came to us mainly for the strengthening of British rule.

Sir James Robertson, a former Governor-General of Nigeria, wrote in 1979 . . .

> I think a great deal is now spoken by people who do not know much about our rule in Africa. When we took over these countries there was very little government, there was very little civilisation, there was a great deal of tribal warfare. Our policy in Africa was to impose the ways of peace and that is what we did.
>
> One thing our critics forget is that we had no money. The British Government gave us nothing for many years. When we came to Africa there were no railways, telegraphs, schools, hospitals, no proper government at all. People had all manner of barbaric practices. When we left there were railways, there was a system of roads, there was a police force, there was an army, there were hospitals, schools and even universities. All this was done in about fifty years. We had set up a civilisation which had not existed before.

Q

Each of the quotations above is biased. Think about each one:

a What is its bias? What does it leave out? What does it emphasise?

b Why does it have such a bias?

Decolonisation . . . from colony to independence

The first example of decolonisation took place in 1947, when India and Pakistan became independent of Britain. By the mid-1960s most of the imperial possessions had ceased to be colonies. Only a tiny few remained, like Hong Kong and Gibraltar, mostly because they depended so much on the mother country.

However, the newly-independent nations did not all gain their independence in the same way. Some had to fight for it bitterly over a period of years. Others were granted it easily and immediately.

Because every case was different, it becomes difficult to make sense of decolonisation. The rest of this chapter attempts to deal systematically with each case. Only a small selection from the vast number of examples of decolonisation has been chosen. In each case, the problem will be looked at from the standpoint of both the imperial rulers and the colonial peoples. This will enable you to see clearly the important issues and, afterwards, to understand the whole question of decolonisation by comparing the cases that you have studied.

India

Independence and partition

In 1947 the British left their Indian Empire. As they left, the old India was replaced by two new nations, India and Pakistan. Independence and partition took place at the same time and were very closely linked. However there were different reasons for them.

Independence

The imperial rulers

The British had ruled India ever since the eighteenth century. India was known as the 'jewel in the imperial crown', and the King of Great Britain was also the Emperor of India. British India, known as the Raj (rule), consisted of about two thirds of the sub-continent, including what is now Pakistan and Bangladesh, as you can see on the map. The remaining one third comprised over three hundred states ruled not by the British, but by their own princes— Rajahs, Maharajas, Nizams and so on. The largest of these princely states were Kashmir and Hyderabad.

The British kept very firm control over India. The British government in London made all important decisions, and its orders were carried out by the Viceroy in Delhi, the Indian capital. The Indian Army, the Indian Police and the Indian Civil Service were run by thousands of British officers and officials, although the less important positions were taken by Indians.

The British had two ways of maintaining their authority. One was to grant power very gradually and in tiny amounts to the Indians. The other was to use force when necessary. Before the Second World War, the British had introduced many reforms in the way India was ruled. In 1935 they set up an Indian Parliament in Delhi and in the provinces of India there were provincial parliaments. However, these were not very democratic. Most Indians did not have the vote, and the British never gave any real power away. The system did not work very successfully and many Indians refused to co-operate with it.

If gradually giving up power would not prevent trouble, then the British had force on their side. The most important example of this was the massacre at Amritsar in 1919 when almost 400 Indians were shot dead by the Indian Army under General Dyer.

The British were determined to keep India within the British Empire. Then came the Second World War. Winston Churchill said in 1940, 'I did not become the King's Prime Minister to preside over the disintegration of the British Empire.' By 1942, even he realised that Britain had no choice but to leave India. The war had shown that British power could simply not be maintained. All Britain could do was to withdraw as gracefully as possible. In 1942, the British promised India its independence as soon as the war was over.

In 1945 when a Labour government was elected in Britain, one of its first decisions was to declare its willingness to grant independence to India. A special Cabinet Committee was sent to make arrangements, and Lord Mountbatten was sent as Viceroy in 1947. Unfortunately, it was not possible to withdraw from India in as peaceful a way as desired, but this was due to disagreements on the Indian side. On 1 August 1947, the British finally withdrew from India.

The colonial people

Up to 1919 the call for independence was not very strong and was limited to better-off Indians. However, the Amritsar massacre of 1919 outraged Indian public opinion so that the demand for independence became a mass movement. Congress was by far the most important party leading the Indian demand for independence. Another was the Muslim League. The inspiration of India's independence was Mahatma Gandhi, the leader of Congress. Gandhi was an unusual kind of leader. He was a passionate Indian nationalist and wanted to get the British out of his country, yet he did not believe in violence as a means of doing this. Instead he used 'passive resistance'. This meant deliberate disobedience and non-co-operation with British rule to force the British out. Gandhi was also unusual in that he was not interested in attaining power for himself. He often left the leadership of Congress to other politicians in order to spend more time in quiet contemplation in his remote village.

The most important of Congress's leaders after Gandhi was Nehru. Nehru was a great believer in democracy and was a very clever politician and negotiator. Together he and Gandhi forced the British to make more and more changes, even granting a Parliament in 1935. However the pace was much too slow for Congress and it refused to co-operate with the British. By and large Gandhi and Nehru kept control of the independence movement, but often rioting and violence broke out. Whenever this happened the British repressed it.

During the Second World War, Congress refused to co-operate with the British war effort and most of its leaders were imprisoned. When the British announced in 1942 that they would give independence after the war, Congress started its 'Quit India now' campaign. They felt that, if they held back, Britain would never leave. After the war it was the Congress leaders who negotiated independence with the British Government.

British troops quell a riot of Indians demanding ▲ independence, 1940

Lord and Lady Mountbatten with Indian children, 1947 ▶

Partition

Unfortunately the movement towards independence was not simple. When the British withdrew in 1947 they left not one nation but two; India and Pakistan. Up to the beginning of the Second World War no-one thought in terms of India being partitioned when it became independent. There were many causes of partition . . .

Religious division and hostility

Almost two thirds of Indians were Hindus. The remaining third were mostly Muslims, belonging to the religion of Islam. Both religions were convinced of their own rightness. For centuries they had been hostile to one another. Up to the war the British were always able to keep order between the two religions. Most Hindus became increasingly intolerant of Islam, and were reluctant to grant equal rights to Muslims in the new independent India. In response, the Muslims became more and more afraid that they would be discriminated against, or even persecuted, in the new India. In some areas the Muslims had a majority, but in most parts of India they were in the minority and feared for their lives. At first Congress represented both Hindus and Muslims, but during the later 1930s most Muslims left Congress and joined the Muslim League.

The Congress leadership

This was divided. Gandhi was strongly opposed to partition, although he was not intolerant of Muslims and wanted all religions to live together in a united India. Most of the other Congress leaders, Hindus, refused to give any rights or power to Muslims who were not in the Congress party. Nehru, an atheist, could not understand how deeply most of his fellow Indians felt about religion. He thought, wrongly, that the religious divisions were being exaggerated, and that they would diminish as India became independent. The Congress leadership refused to consider partition, thinking that the British would grant independence to a united country. Only in 1946 did Nehru and the other leaders accept partition, although Gandhi was always against it.

The Muslim League leadership

The Muslim League was under the control of Mohammed Ali Jinnah. Although Jinnah was originally a member of Congress and a firm supporter of a united India, he became convinced in the late 1930s that the Hindu leaders could not be trusted. From 1940, he and the Muslim League became determined that partition was the only way to protect their religion and their interests. Once they had made up their minds, they never really were prepared to compromise.

British leadership

The British Government tried hard to keep India as a single nation by suggesting that there should be separate governments in Muslim and Hindu areas. They proposed that the Indian central government should be weak, so that it would not over-rule the Muslim areas. Congress rejected this as they wanted a stronger central government. The Muslim League was also opposed to this idea because by this time it was determined on partition.

Violence: the threat of civil war

In August 1946 violence broke out on a large scale in many parts of India. Muslims and Hindus began to massacre one another. The situation was made much worse in some areas, such as the Punjab, where Sikhs, adherents of a

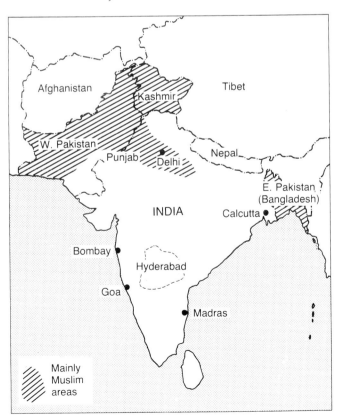

India

minority religion, and the Muslims slaughtered one another. Violence increased rapidly and quickly became out of control. The British Government and the new Viceroy, Lord Mountbatten, simply could not cope with such a level of violence. The Indian Army itself was divided along religious lines and could do nothing to control the violence. Realising this, the British Government and Lord Mountbatten

knew that partition had to take place. It seemed the only alternative to a bloody civil war. By this time the Congress leaders too, apart from Gandhi, had accepted the need for partition.

In August 1947 India was divided into two nations, as you can see from the map. Pakistan itself was split into East and West Pakistan on either side of India. It was a sad beginning for both new nations.

Q

1 Why did the British policy of maintaining their presence by the use of force *and* the gradual granting of reforms fail?
2 Both photographs on page 241 illustrate British power in India. Explain how they do this in different ways.

3a Which of the various causes, mentioned above, which led to partition, might have been different?
b Arrange the causes of partition in order of importance. Give your reasons for your views.

Gold Coast/Ghana

The imperial rulers

The British had ruled most of West Africa, including the Gold Coast, for a hundred years. There were very few British settlers and only a tiny British ruling group of colonial officials and businessmen. The main British interest in the Gold Coast was tropical agricultural products, especially cocoa. The British did allow some Africans, mostly tribal chiefs and wealthy African businessmen, a small share in the government, but hardly any Africans were allowed to vote for the Parliament.

The colonial people

The various tribes of the Gold Coast had traditionally ruled themselves before the British came, and felt insulted that their British rulers considered them incapable of ruling themselves. A small black middle-class of businessmen, cocoa farmers and professional people wanted more power for themselves. Among the African masses there was a fast-growing sense of nationalism, inspired by the success of India in gaining independence from British rule in 1947.

Kwame Nkrumah came from a blacksmith's family and got a scholarship to school and university in America and Britain. Returning to the Gold Coast, he feared that the British and the wealthy and powerful Africans would share power between them. He preferred to give

power to the whole people. In 1949 he founded the Convention People's Party, and soon became a very popular leader. In 1951 the British Governor imprisoned Nkrumah for organising a general strike against British rule. Even while he was in prison he was elected to Parliament.

Independence

The British Government realised that it had no alternative but to release Nkrumah and let him become Prime Minister. Even so, the Gold Coast was not given its independence. In the next few

Kwame Nkrumah speaks on Independence Day, Ghana, 1957

years the new black government prepared for independence by building schools and factories and setting up a good communications and transport system. The British could do little but accept this. Their own economic needs were not hurt at all, therefore they bowed out gracefully, keeping close economic links with the Gold Coast. In 1957 the Gold Coast became independent, as you can see in the photograph on p. 243, and took the name of Ghana. It was the first black African colony to be freed.

Nkrumah's speech at the independence celebrations, which are shown in the photograph, included the following . . .

> At long last the battle has ended. Ghana our beloved country is free forever. From now on, today, we must change our attitudes, our minds. We must realise that from now on we are no more a colonial but a free and independent people.

However, after independence, Nkrumah became a dictator and had to be overthrown in 1966.

— Q —

1 Why did Britain not decide to hold on to the Gold Coast at all costs?

2 In what ways, in Nkrumah's speech and in the photograph, is pride being shown in Ghana's new nationhood?

Algeria

Of all the European powers, the one that was hardest hit by the independence of its colonies was France. In the case of Algeria, the very stability of France was at stake.

At first France tried hard to prevent decolonisation. It fought a terrible war in its Asian colony, Vietnam. There France was badly and decisively beaten. France lost 95,000 soldiers and failed utterly to prevent Vietnamese independence. In 1954 France was compelled to give in. Immediately afterwards, France's North African colonies, Algeria, Tunisia and Morocco, demanded their independence. Tunisia and Morocco were granted independence easily. But what would happen in Algeria?

Colonies dealt with in this chapter with the dates of their independence

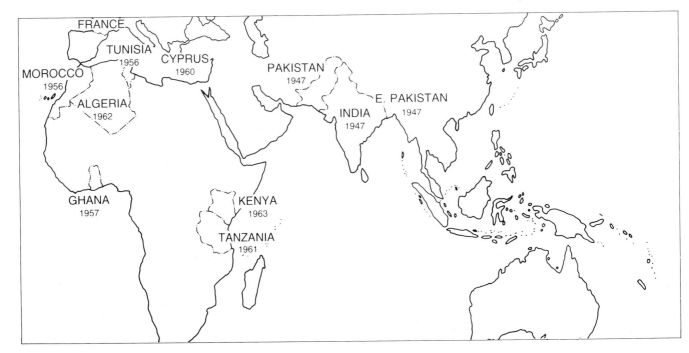

The imperial rulers

Algérie Française

Algeria was France's most important colony, situated directly opposite France across the Mediterranean. Algeria had a population of about nine million. Eight million of these were Muslim Arabs, who had no political rights. The other million were French *colons* (colonists). The *colons* consisted of a small group of very rich capitalists and landowners, who owned most of the wealth of Algeria, and a large number of ordinary French middle and working class people who had been settled in Algeria for up to one hundred years. All the *colons* had the right to vote for the French Parliament in Paris itself. In theory Algeria was actually part of France. The French Army too was very strong in Algeria and the officers in particular were determined to keep Algeria French. *Algérie Française* was the slogan of French Algerians.

In France itself, the French Government was in a terrible state of indecision. Ever since the Second World War France had been ruled by the Fourth Republic, but it was a weak, unstable and unpopular government. Its prime ministers and cabinets lasted usually for a very short time and often there was no government at all. In these circumstances France could hardly pursue a very strong policy in Algeria. Algeria soon became France's most serious problem. It threatened the safety of France herself. Up to 1958 French policy was to keep Algeria French by force, but the French people were growing sick of war, and expected the Government to find a better solution.

The colonial people

Algeria's eight million Muslim Arabs, very much second-class citizens, were in a mood of rising nationalism. They had seen French rule destroyed in Vietnam and given up in Morocco and Tunisia. They now wanted the same. In 1954 the FLN, the Algerian independence movement led by Ben Bella, began guerrilla warfare in the countryside and deserts of Algeria and bombing campaigns in the cities. By 1957 the French had poured one third of a million troops into Algeria. The FLN had the support of most Muslim Algerians, as the French Army used ruthless tactics, including widespread torture, against the population. During these years up to half a million Arab Algerians were killed.

In this Soviet cartoon, General Massu has tried but failed to remove the bloody word 'Algeria' from his uniform

The crisis in France

It seemed that the Fourth Republic was on its last legs. The Algerian problem was simply beyond its ability to solve. French governments came and went quickly without any authority, certainly without the authority to deal with Algeria. France itself seemed about to collapse.

Waiting in the background was General Charles de Gaulle, the wartime leader, a military man of fairly right-wing views. He had ruled France for a short time after the Second World War, but had retired in 1947 when French politicians refused to set up a strong system of ruling France with himself as President. De Gaulle had set himself the task of saving and strengthening France. Algeria came second to this.

In May 1958 a new French government was formed that seemed ready to start negotiations with the FLN. Immediately the French Army in Algeria, under the leadership of Generals Massu and Salan and the most important *colons*, seized power in Algeria. They were hoping that this would help General de Gaulle to come to power in France. In this they were right. They also thought that, because he was right-wing and traditional, he could be trusted to hold on to *Algérie Française*. In this they were wrong.

General de Gaulle was given power in France and, with the support of 80% of the French people, set up the Fifth Republic with himself as President. His own power and that of France itself was considerably increased and strengthened.

On the matter of Algeria, de Gaulle said very little. He kept his intentions deliberately unclear. Everyone—the French Army, the *colons*, the FLN, and the French and Algerian peoples—waited to see what he would do. For four years de Gaulle delayed.

It gradually became obvious that *Algérie Française* was not to be. Negotiations began with the FLN and de Gaulle announced that he would get the best deal he could for France. In frustration the generals once again seized power in Algeria in 1961, but this time they had little support. Most of even the ordinary French national service soldiers did not want to keep Algeria French. The French people had now completely changed their minds. The army collapsed. In 1962 an agreement was made with the FLN at Evian, granting full independence to Algeria, but still protecting French oil interests. Most of the *colons* returned to live in France.

Q

1 Examine the Russian cartoon. What sort of people in France and Algeria would object strongly to the Russian viewpoint? Explain your answer.

2 Why do you think France decided to hold on to Algeria so tightly?

3 Why do you think de Gaulle delayed doing anything about Algeria for so long?

Extension

What did General de Gaulle really think?

De Gaulle actually said very little, especially at the time. He deliberately kept his intentions so well hidden that not even his closest advisers knew what he thought. However there are some clues to his attitudes. Here are some of his statements and writings in chronological order.

De Gaulle, speaking privately to a friend in 1955 . . .

> There is a wave carrying all the peoples towards independence. There are fools who will not understand it; it's not worth talking to them about it.

De Gaulle speaking to a Socialist minister in 1957 . . .

> The only solution is independence.

De Gaulle to a crowd of cheering French *colons* demanding *Algérie Française* in Algiers on his first visit after taking power, June 1958 . . .

> I have understood you.

and later in the same day to another crowd of cheering *colons* . . .

> Long live *Algérie Française*

(This was the only time he used this phrase.)

De Gaulle to a group of French officers in an Officers' Mess in Algeria, while he was on a tour in 1960 . . .

> France must not depart. She has the right to remain in Algeria. She will stay there.

De Gaulle, writing his memoirs in 1970 after his retirement from politics . . .

> Whatever may have been dreamed previously or might be regretted today, whatever I myself may have hoped at other periods, there was no longer any way out in my eyes, except Algeria's right to decide for itself.
>
> It can be imagined that I would not do it easily. For a man of my age and my type it was really cruel to become, on my own intitiative, the man who brought about such a change.

Q

1a Answer the following question about each one of de Gaulle's statements: *What do you think it means?* Take into account the circumstances in which it was made and the people to whom it was made.

b Which of the statements do you think is the most reliable in revealing de Gaulle's real views? Give your reasons.

Kenya

The imperial rulers

Britain had ruled Kenya since the beginning of the twentieth century. After the Second World War, Kenya became a popular country for white migration, and about 60,000 British settled there. Many of these were ex-officers and upper-class landowners, with large plantations and estates. They had great influence on the British Government of Kenya and on the Conservative Government of Britain during the 1950s. Britain was determined to prevent Kenya from gaining its independence or, at least, determined to protect the interests of the white settlers. Large numbers of British troops were sent to Kenya and a large black Home Guard with British officers was raised to prevent independence.

The colonial people

Kenya contained several tribes, the largest of which was the Kikuyu, with over one and a quarter million members. It was mainly Kikuyu land which the British Government had granted to white settlers. By the 1940s a strong sense of nationalism was growing throughout Africa and a determination in Kenya to get independence. The leader of this movement was Jomo Kenyatta, who set up the Kenya African Union in 1944. This was mainly a Kikuyu organisation, and, under the cover of the Union, a secret society called Mau Mau emerged. Only Kikuyus could belong to Mau Mau and its purpose was to restore the lost lands and to get rid of white settlers.

A Kikuyu Home Guard points out a Mau Mau suspect

In 1952 Mau Mau became increasingly violent, although its many victims were mostly non-Mau Mau Kikuyu, members of other tribes and very few white settlers. Mau Mau raised intense hostility among the British settlers and the British public. Over ten thousand Mau Mau were killed, mostly through the efforts of ex-Mau Mau informers, as you can see in the photograph on p. 247. Kenyatta was imprisoned in 1953 for 'managing' Mau Mau. In 1960 the Government had defeated Mau Mau, but African feeling had not been crushed.

The gaining of independence

By 1960 the British Government had changed its mind. It had come to realise that it could not select which colonies it could keep and which it could let go. The Conservative Minister in charge of colonies was Iain Macleod, who believed in colonial independence. In 1960 the Prime Minister, Harold Macmillan visited Africa and made the famous speech in which he spoke of 'the winds of change blowing through Africa'. He realised that the Kenyan claim for independence had not died and that the white settlers should not have so much power and influence. In the end, he believed black nationalism would be too much for Britain, therefore Britain should get out gracefully.

In 1963 Kenya became independent and Kenyatta became its first Prime Minister. Many British settlers left Kenya and moved to parts of Africa such as Rhodesia and South Africa, where whites were still dominant.

Tanganyika/Tanzania

The imperial rulers

Britain only took over Tanganyika from Germany in 1919, and ruled it as a mandate for the League of Nations, and afterwards for the United Nations. The UN regularly asked Africans for their opinion of British rule, therefore Britain was more limited than usual in what it could do. Britain did very little to help the Tanganyikan economy, which was mainly agricultural, and it was one of the poorest states in Africa. In the 1940s the Government tried to take land for white settlers, but failed.

The colonial people

As early as the 1920s the Tanganyikan African Association had been founded by black teachers and civil servants. It gained much popular support in the 1940s after the British had tried to seize land for white settlers. In 1953 Julius Nyerere became its leader. Nyerere was the son of a chief of one of Tanganyika's many tribes, and had been educated at a British university. In 1954 he turned the TAA into the Tanganyikan African National Union. It represented most of Tanganyikan public opinion, and began to demand independence inspired by the independence movements elsewhere in Africa.

The gaining of independence

In 1961 Tanganyika—re-named Tanzania— became completely independent as Britain realised that it could not stop the independence movements in Africa. It was a very easy transfer of power.

Cyprus

The imperial rulers

Britain seized Cyprus from Turkey in 1878 for military reasons—to protect the Suez Canal. Cyprus was a vital military, naval and air base on the route eastwards to the rest of the empire. Britain's economic interests were very limited in Cyprus and there was virtually no British settlement. The British government of Sir Anthony Eden announced in 1955 that Cyprus would remain permanently British and would *never* become independent.

The colonial people

Unlike most imperial possessions Cyprus was a European island. 80% of its people were Greeks. The remainder were Turks. In Cyprus the people did not want independence. The Greeks, under their leader Archbishop Makarios, wanted simply to unite with Greece herself. The Turks, fearing the Greeks, wanted to stay within the British Empire. However the Greeks were absolutely determined to break away from Britain, especially after Britain said 'never'. Violence erupted in 1955. One group of terrorist freedom fighters, known as EOKA, began to sabotage British bases and to kill British troops. There was also growing violence between Turks and Greeks on the island.

The gaining of independence

British policy became very unclear, varying from one view to another. In 1956 Britain said that it would grant more self-rule but not independence. Then, fearing that Archbishop Makarios, a brilliant negotiator, would outwit them they deported him to a remote island in the Indian Ocean. This situation deteriorated as the British public became more and more outraged by the murder of British soldiers and civilians. In turn the Greek population of Cyprus was incensed by the execution of captured murderers. Violence on the island became so intense that a civil war almost broke out between Turks and Greeks, with the British in between. Greece and Turkey themselves also became increasingly involved. At last Archbishop Makarios realised that the Turks, backed up by Turkey itself, would never approve of union with Greece. In 1956 he announced that he would be content with independence instead of union with Greece. The British Government too accepted that they must give in. They

A British soldier guards Greek Cypriots imprisoned in a detention centre

announced that they were prepared to grant independence to Cyprus as long as Britain was allowed to keep its military bases on the island.

Independence was granted in 1960. No-one was satisfied and the island soon became ungovernable. Civil war broke out, the Turkish army invaded and Cyprus was divided into two.

A historian has written . . .

No doubt a more generous and far-sighted policy by Great Britain in the early 1950s would have made possible a just and practicable solution and one more advantageous to Britain. The story of Cyprus is one of the most dismal pages in the history of the Empire.

Q

1 Why did Britain decide to hold on to Kenya up to 1960? Deal with the more important reasons first.
2 Why did Britain not hold on so strongly to Tanganyika?
3 Why did Britain grant independence to both Kenya and Tanganyika in the early 1960s?
4 What does the photograph of the black informer show about British power in Kenya?
5 Why was Britain determined to hold on to Cyprus at all costs?

6 What do you think would be the reaction of
a A member of the British public
b A Turkish Cypriot
c A Greek citizen
to the photograph of the British detention camp on Cyprus?
7 Do you agree with the historian that 'a more generous and far-sighted policy by Great Britain in the early 1950s' was a real possibility, or did Britain have to be forced into granting independence? Explain your answer.

An assessment

Making sense of decolonisation

What were the main reasons for decolonisation? Why was the actual granting of independence so different from one place to another? Answer the following questions briefly about each of the following nations—India, Ghana, Algeria, Kenya, Tanzania, Cyprus. You can do this in a form of a table with the names of the countries across the top and the questions down the side.

- What was the date of independence?
- Did the imperial power have any interests to protect (e.g. economic interests, white settlers, military interests)? How important were these interests?
- Did the imperial power have the determination and will to hold on to the colony?
- Did the imperial power have the ability to hold on to the colony?
- How strongly did the colonial peoples feel about independence?

- What lengths were they prepared to go to get their independence?
- What were the main factors in the situation that contributed to independence?

When you have answered these questions about each nation, write down any important similarities, differences or facts that you have noticed about decolonisation.

Discussion topic

1 How strongly do British people feel about the Commonwealth today?

Essays

1 Why did the European powers withdraw from their empires? Briefly describe how two colonies gained their independence.

2 How and why did Britain withdraw from India in 1947? Describe how partition took place and why it caused such problems.

ACKNOWLEDGEMENTS

The publishers would like to thank the following for permission to reproduce material in this volume: Beijing Review for the extracts from *Beijing Review* 29 September, 1986; Century Hutchinson for the extract from *Twenty Letters to a Friend* by Svetlana Alliluyeva, Penguin (1968); Chatto and Windus and The Hogarth Press for 'Disabled' from Jon Stallworthy (ed) *The Poems of Wilfred Owen*; China Now for the extract by John Gittings from *China Now No 119*, 1986; William Collins Sons and Co Ltd for the extract from *Hope Against Hope* by N Mandelstam (1971); Columbia University Press New York for the extract from *The Germans and their Modern History* by Frita Ernest (1966); Faber and Faber Ltd for the extract from *Memoirs of an Infantry Officer* by Siegfried Sassoon; The Financial Times for the extract by J Monnet, *Financial Times* 20 July, 1972; Hamish Hamilton for the extracts from *Remember Russia Volume 2 1915–1925* by E Fon; Harrap Publishing Group Ltd for the extract from *Nyerere and Nkrumah* (1974); Her Majesty's Stationery Office for the extract by Ernest Bevin, Hansard 4 May, 1948, the extract by E Heath, Hansard 2 May 1967 and the extract by Wilson, Hansard 31 July, 1961; Michael Joseph Ltd for the extract from *Bomber Command* by Max Hastings, copyright by Romadata 1979, 1987; The Listener for the extract by Harold Macmillan, 2 June, 1972; Macdonald for the extracts from *Purnell's History of the Twentieth Century*; Macmillan London and Basingstoke for the extracts from *The 20th Century* by J Hamer (1980); Nigel Nicolson for the extract from *Peace Making 1919* by Harold Nicolson, Constable (1933); Oxford University Press for the extract from *Journey Through Obscurity Vol 13: War* by H Owen (1965) and the extract from *Stalin* by Isaac Deutsher (1949); Peters Fraser and Dunlop Group Ltd for the extract from *Douglas Haig, The Educated Soldier* by John Terraine, Hutchinson Publishing Group Ltd (1963); Prentice-Hall for the extract from *Contemporary Europe: A History* by H S Hughes (1976); The Estate of E M Remarque for the extract from *All Quiet on the Western Front* by E M Remarque, published by The Bodley Head; Routledge for the extract from *Gaullism* by A Hartley (1972); Lois Wheeler Snow for the extract from *The Red Star Over China* by E Snow; Studs Terkel for the extract from *Hard Times*, copyright 1970 by Studs Terkel; Thorsons Publishing Group Ltd for the extracts from *The Hell They Called High Wood* by Terry Norman (1983); The University of Michigan Press for Khrushchev's Speech by N Khrushchev from T P Whitney (ed) *Khrushchev Speaks* (1963); Virago Press for the extracts from *Testament of Youth* by Vera Brittain, copyright 1970 by the Literary Executors of Vera Brittain; George Weidenfeld & Nicolson Ltd for the extract from *Inside The Third Reich* by A Speer (1979); Wheaten Books for the extracts from *A Coursebook In Modern World History* by P F Speed (1982).

The author and publishers thank the following for permission to reproduce copyright illustrations: Bettman Archive Pictures, p 72; British-Israeli Public Affairs Committee, pp 157, 163; Bundesarchive pp 91L, 98L; Camera Press, pp 184R, 185, 222TL, 230; Communist Party Library, p 141; Edimedia; John Gittings, p 191; Sally and Richard Greenhill, p 184L; John Hillelson Agency Ltd, pp 65T, 94L, 186; The Hulton-Deutsch Collection, pp 123, 153, 218, 227, 232 (both), 233, 235, 238, 241; IDAF, p 223R; Imperial War Museum, pp 12 (both), 95R, 115 (both), 117, 120, 124 (all), 127 (all); Keystone Collection, pp 21, 247; Landesbildstelle Berlin, p 30; David Low/Daily Mirror Centre for the Study of Cartoons and Caricature, University of Kent at Canterbury, p 113; Magnum, pp 128, 222R, 224L; Mansell Collection, p 48; Moro Roma, p 32L; Novosti Press Agency, pp 38, 58TR, 122; Popperfoto, pp 58L, 95L, 101, 243; Punch, p 24; School of Slavonic Studies, pp 202, 245; Society for Cultural Relations with USSR, pp 39, 54T, 58BR; Topham Picture Library, p 44BL; Ullstein Bilderdienst, pp 29B, 94R, 96, 100, 120, 130T; The Wiener Library, pp 98R, 102; Western Mail, pp 20, 27, 29T, 21.

INDEX